WITHDRAWN

smart investing
@ your library®

A partnership between American Library Association
and FINRA Investor Education Foundation

American
Library
Association

Investor Education
FOUNDATION

FINRA is proud to support the American Library Association

KIDS, WEALTH,
AND
CONSEQUENCES

Also available from

Bloomberg Press

Family Wealth Transition Planning:
Advising Families with Small Businesses
by Bonnie Brown Hartley and Gwendolyn Griffith

Family: The Compact Among Generations
by James E. Hughes Jr.

Family Wealth—Keeping It in the Family
by James E. Hughes Jr.

The Dilemmas of Family Wealth:
Insights on Succession, Cohesion, and Legacy
by Judy Martel

Money Well Spent:
A Strategic Plan for Smart Philanthropy
by Paul Brest and Hal Harvey

———————

A complete list of our titles is available at

www.bloomberg.com/books

KIDS, WEALTH,
AND
CONSEQUENCES

Ensuring a Responsible
Financial Future
for the Next Generation

RICHARD A. MORRIS
and JAYNE A. PEARL

FOREWORD BY James E. Hughes Jr.

BLOOMBERG PRESS
NEW YORK

BLOOMBERG, BLOOMBERG ANYWHERE, BLOOMBERG.COM, BLOOMBERG MARKET ESSENTIALS, *Bloomberg Markets*, BLOOMBERG NEWS, BLOOMBERG PRESS, BLOOMBERG PROFESSIONAL, BLOOMBERG RADIO, BLOOMBERG TELEVISION, and BLOOMBERG TRADEBOOK are trademarks and service marks of Bloomberg Finance L.P. ("BFLP"), a Delaware limited partnership, or its subsidiaries. The BLOOMBERG PROFESSIONAL service (the "BPS") is owned and distributed locally by BFLP and its subsidiaries in all jurisdictions other than Argentina, Bermuda, China, India, Japan, and Korea (the "BLP Countries"). BFLP is a wholly-owned subsidiary of Bloomberg L.P. ("BLP"). BLP provides BFLP with all global marketing and operational support and service ·for these products and distributes the BPS either directly or through a non-BFLP subsidiary in the BLP Countries. All rights reserved.

This publication contains the authors' opinions and is designed to provide accurate and authoritative information. It is sold with the understanding that the authors, publisher, and Bloomberg L.P. are not engaged in rendering legal, accounting, investment-planning, or other professional advice. The reader should seek the services of a qualified professional for such advice; the authors, publisher, and Bloomberg L.P. cannot be held responsible for any loss incurred as a result of specific investments or planning decisions made by the reader.

First edition published 2010

1 3 5 7 9 10 8 6 4 2

Library of Congress Cataloging-in-Publication Data

Morris, Richard A.

Kids, wealth, and consequences : ensuring a responsible financial future for the next generation / Richard A. Morris and Jayne A. Pearl ; foreword by James E. Hughes Jr.—1st ed.

p. cm.

Includes bibliographical references and index.

Summary: "High-net-worth individuals learn how to pass on financial, intellectual, and emotional capital to their children, leaving them responsible, well-adjusted stewards of that wealth. This book enlightens high-net-worth parents about unique issues they must explore. It addresses "hard" financial issues such as investing and estate planning and "soft" emotional issues such as values, family, and communication"—Provided by publisher.

ISBN 978-1-57660-348-2 (alk. paper)

1. Children of the rich—Finance, Personal. 2. Estate planning. 3. Wealth—Management. I. Pearl, Jayne A., 1954- II. Title.

HG179.M6627 2010

332.0240083—dc22   2009048896

Mixed Sources
Product group from well-managed forests, controlled sources and recycled wood or fiber
www.fsc.org Cert no. SW-COC-000952
© 1996 Forest Stewardship Council
FSC

*To Ryan Hommel, whose wealth of love, humor,
and music nourish the soul
and
To Linda Morris, the inspiration in Rich's life,
who has provided valuable insights
and support throughout the researching
and writing of this book.*

Contents

Foreword

Richard Morris and Jayne Pearl have taken on a large task. They start with some key questions. How can parents raise their children so that they can successfully integrate into their lives the financial wealth their parents, or an earlier generation, created? How can the children of these parents learn to bring their own dreams to life, rather than be drained of dreams by stewarding the dreams of others? How can these children become self-confident and balanced, with appropriate humility? How will these children learn to distinguish between inheritances that cause entropy and lack of wellness and those that can enhance their happiness?

Morris and Pearl offer us, as parents and grandparents of children and grandchildren who will inherit financial wealth, the questions we seek in the hope that our heirs' lives will be enhanced, not depreciated, by their inheritance. Their questions to us are frank, yet their meanings can be subtle. I found, as I pondered these questions, that the longer I thought about them, the more valuable my answers became. But I also found that in reviewing my answers hours later, after absorbing Morris and Pearl's wisdom and compassion about human behavior, my answers often were very different. Please know you are likely to be quite surprised by the courage you will need to answer these questions with the whole truth about your views and actions. As you uncover that second set of answers, you may also feel somewhat diminished by how you've handled some of these questions in the past.

As we know, the examined life—a life open to questions—is the life worth living. Living with answers too quickly formed all too often leads to poor results. Morris and Pearl's iterative process, chapter by chapter, leads parents to deeper and deeper questions—and more profound answers—and they never leave us unaccompanied. Since so many of us find ourselves in Dante's "dark wood" as we try to help our children avoid lives of inutility, pain, Lethe, and anomie, it is comforting to have Morris and Pearl as our Virgil on this journey to enhancing our children's lives.

For us as parents, at the core of Morris and Pearl's work lies a rarely spoken reality hidden in a question so deep it cannot be plumbed. How can we integrate the materialization of another's dreams—the financial wealth of another—into the dreams of our children and grandchildren so that such wealth does not dampen their capacity to dream and bring their own dreams to life? Too much education on this subject gets its purpose wrong by teaching inheritors of financial wealth about stewarding someone else's dream instead of teaching them to nurture their own. Who among us, as a young spirit, wouldn't be at risk of drowning in the vast expanse of an extraordinary person's great dream—a John D. Rockefeller or a J. Paul Getty, for example—if asked to steward it? Could we have any hope of success if we had not been, with perseverance and a gentle touch, educated to bring our own small individual dreams to life first?

Sadly, this misdirected process is most often activated by a parent's or grandparent's great love and hope for this young spirit. Equally sadly, this love often comes without awareness of the deep questions and threats posed to a young spirit by another's dream. Many parents have no real awareness of the processes and practices needed to integrate another's dream into the young spirit's dream.

To better understand this concept, parents might consider how the process works systemically. Each of us has our own blessed inner nature and healthy functioning. When some new life form, in this case another's dream, enters that complex system (physical, mental, emotional, intuitional, spiritual), the system doesn't know whether the integration will be healthy or not. So the system responds by seeking to integrate this foreign matter while keeping its T-cells ready to fight.

If the system can safely integrate this new form, then it has adapted to it. Adaptation is the critical action that helps a person change to new situations encountered during a lifetime. The capacity to adapt to a new challenge gives an individual one more quality to call on to survive and flourish. Is the individual—or system—resilient? Every time a system adapts, it changes. Only a resilient person—having courage, gratitude, humility, fortitude, prudence, joy, love, and compassion for self and others—will be strong enough to take in this foreign body—another's dream—adapt to it, and flourish.

A person seeking to steward another's dream, without his or her own having been born and emerged, will be weakened. The dream will certainly submerge and drown the individual. Parents and grandparents, whose love, wisdom, and compassion lead to the nurturance of the human, intellectual, and social capital of their children and grandchildren, reduce the odds of the child's drowning. Such nurturance vastly increases the odds that those they love will learn not only to swim but also to use the vast ocean as their laboratory for the evolution of their creative selves and their dreams.

Morris and Pearl's questions and discussions get to the heart of the process of parents' nurturance. Morris and Pearl offer education, starting with the root issues of how to help the people we love the most achieve happy and productive lives. They do this by helping us learn:

- How to bring to life the dreams of young spirits
- Which practices are most likely to achieve such lives
- How to integrate an earlier generation's dream, represented by its financial wealth, into the life of such a spirit so it enhances that spirit's journey

Thank you, Richard and Jayne, for the gift of your wisdom and compassion. Your questions will help many different families' dreams come true.

JAMES (JAY) E. HUGHES JR.
ASPEN, COLORADO
July 2009

Acknowledgments

This book is the result of a powerful collaborative effort of colleagues, friends, and contacts who cheerfully provided information, referrals, support, encouragement, and constructive feedback.

At the top of the list of people we want to thank is our editor at Bloomberg Press, Stephen Isaacs, who was always accessible and who provided much sage advice. Other Bloomberg Press folks who labor tirelessly behind the scenes include Yvette Romero, Judith Sjo-Gaber, John Crutcher, and JoAnne Kanaval.

We would not have found each other to undertake this collaborative effort were it not for the wisdom and kindness of Howard Muson, former editor of *Family Business* magazine, who introduced us. Any book is only as good as the resources behind it, including the scores of parents, professionals (including lawyers, accountants, psychologists, and academics, investment advisors, investment managers, and family office executives) and individual high–net worth investors, who were generous with their time. These include Mary Jo Barrett, Charlotte Beyer, Thomas Bloch, Bruce Boyd, Jeffrey Brodsky, Ira Bryck, Mitch Cohen, Mike Cohn, Leslie Dashew, François de Visscher, Nancy Donovan, Susan Goldenberg, Fritzi Hallock, Sara Hamilton, Jeffrey Horvitz, James Hughes, Henry Hutcheson, Holly Isdale, Charles Jahn, Dr. Kenneth Kaye, Richard Levi, Charles Lowenhaupt, Teri Lowinger, Doug Macauley, Susan Remmer Ryzewic, Tom Rogerson, Claudia Sangster, Istar Schwager, Jill Shipley, Dr. Kenneth Sole, Michael Sonnenfeldt, and Dr. Kerry Sulkowicz. Our thanks to you all for your insights and candor.

We are very grateful for creative and constructive feedback and some technical advice and help that several colleagues offered, including: Donald Claus, Tura Cottingham, Christopher J. DeMonte, Amy Downey, Phil Gartner, Henry Gorecki, Doug Gourly, Sherri Kole, and Bob and Debbie Render. Special thanks, also to Wolverine Torres, whose inquisitive spirit and laughter are contagious.

We are fortunate for the invaluable contract guidance we received from National Writers Union member Paul J. MacArthur and Authors Guild staff attorney Michael Gross. We would also like to acknowledge our web developer, Roy Plum, whose ability to listen deeply and translate our concepts and style is unparalleled.

The life-long influence of especially outstanding teachers can never be forgotten and should never go unrecognized. Our truly inspiring teachers include Ernest J. Barry, Professor Emeritus at Lake Forest Academy; Diane Gayeski, Professor at the School of Strategic Communication, Ithaca College; Sandra L. Herndon, PhD, Professor Emerita at the School of Communication, Ithaca College; and the late and very great Professor Arlene Wolf Goodman, former Professor of Journalism at Hofstra University.

While immersed, engrossed, and perhaps at times obsessed with pulling together the material for and writing this book, we should not ignore the moral support and patience we received from family and friends, including Mortimer B. Pearl, Robin Pearl, Ellen Pollen, Ryan Hommel, Linda Morris, Aaron Morris, Allison Morris, and Charlie Morris. Thank you for not divorcing or disowning us!

KIDS, WEALTH,
AND
CONSEQUENCES

Introduction

CHILDREN WHO GROW UP in a wealthy household are bound to encounter mixed feelings, mixed messages, and mixed blessings. That's because parents who provide a charmed lifestyle and leave behind substantial money to their children do not guarantee their children's happiness. In many cases, riches have the opposite effect.

For wealthy families, the stakes are high—not just because there's more money to squander, but also because wealth can fuel dysfunction. Money can provide education, comfort, travel, and exposure to high culture, couture, and cuisine. But money can also paralyze people and strip them of ambition and meaning. Some children suffer feelings of guilt over not having earned their wealth; others find themselves mired in a toxic brew of entitlement and numbing ennui.

These problems affect a growing portion of our country. The estimated number of households with at least $10 million in net worth doubled between 1995 and 2004, from more than 200,000 to more than 500,000, according to Federal Reserve surveys of consumer finance. Households with at least $25 million jumped from 50,000 in 1995 to more than 100,000 in 2004.

Of course, a fair number of the country's and the world's wealthy are worth significantly less as of this writing as a result of the stock market meltdown that began in 2008. In fact, as of March 2009, the richest of the rich who made it to *Forbes* magazine's list of World's Billionaires found their average net worth had fallen 23 percent, to $3 billion, from the preceding 12 months. *Forbes* reported that the world now has 793 billionaires, compared with 1,125 the previous year. American billionaires fared a bit better than their global counterparts, snatching 44 percent of the slots, up 7 percentage points from the year before.

The financial crisis has created a new set of financial and emotional issues for wealthy families. Some who saw almost half their net worth disappear were arguably less experienced than middle- and lower-class folks in cutting spending. Families who have inherited their wealth and who have no current wealth creator among them may have an even tougher time weathering the current economic storm, both financially and emotionally.

Many wealthy parents worried even before the economic melt-down about how to raise children with a sense of groundedness and balance: how to impart a strong work ethic, how to counter their sense of entitlement, how to prevent them from remaining depen-dent, how to help them separate their identity from their wealth, how to help them develop confidence in themselves, how to instill a desire to give back to society, and how to be good stewards of wealth for future generations. Suddenly, there's a greater urgency about guiding and teaching children these financial values and lessons.

Moreover, those who count themselves among the elite slice of society found their sense of security shattered. Money had protected them from many of life's harsh realities. They were caught utterly off guard and unprepared to adjust their expectations and lifestyle.

When we began researching and writing our book in the fall of 2008, just as the stock market plunged, we, along with our editor and publisher, felt we might out-date this book if we gave more than a cursory mention of the market meltdown. But as the country and much of the rest of the world began to spiral into a deep and poten-tially prolonged recession, we all agreed that even if a miracle were to effect a major turnaround, the shock waves wealthy families were experiencing were having a profound effect. These world events had the high–net worth community questioning their values, spend-ing habits, and children's future in a profound way. The economic downturn has brought these issues to the surface and made explor-ing them impossible to ignore. We have folded in facts, examples, and quotes that describe how these economic woes impact the many issues our book addresses.

Readers should also be aware that the authors of this book bring very different experiences, skills, and perspectives to this project.

Richard Morris has a background in marketing and education. He worked his way up in his family's auto parts manufacturing company, Fel-Pro, where he worked in marketing and later in acquisitions, until the family sold the eighty-year-old business in 1998. Morris's "liquidity event" prompted him to rethink his life. He wanted a work life that provided a sense of belonging and a chance to give back to society, and he soon created ROI (Resources for Ownership Intelligence) University, which provides certificate courses for private owners in management, marketing, retail, sales, and human resources management. Even though he and his wife decided not to change their standard of living substantially, they found that the liquidity of their assets provided new challenges in bringing up their children as well as managing the families' finances. Many questions needed answers, and they found no one resource to address those questions. Morris devoted substantial time to studying not only how to manage his financial assets but also the psychological and social challenges new and sudden wealth can bring.

Jayne Pearl has been a financial journalist since 1980, when she started as a reporter-researcher at *Forbes* magazine, where she helped research and fact-check the premiere *Forbes* 400 "Rich List" of the wealthiest Americans. She later worked as editor of a syndicated daily financial public radio program, then launched a successful newsletter for management guru Tom ("In Search of Excellence") Peters. In 1989 she helped launch *Family Business* magazine, to which she has contributed for twenty years. She wrote a highly acclaimed book, *Kids and Money: Giving Them the Savvy to Succeed Financially* (also published by Bloomberg Press), in 1999, and has been writing and speaking about financial parenting ever since.

The authors' different professional and socio-economic backgrounds resulted in enlightening brainstorming, challenges, and some creative tension as they periodically wrestled over how to address many of the issues they have covered. Without either one receiving or delivering a single black eye (which would have been difficult not to avoid, as they live a couple thousand miles apart), each difference or hurdle led them to deeper insights and solutions that far exceeded either of their initial positions and preferences.

The authors hope that the resulting book will help readers increase the odds that their family wealth will enhance their children's ability to succeed under any economic circumstances. We will describe the skills children need to obtain successful, happy lives. We will look at how we define success and explore the extent to which money might bring or hinder that success. We will evaluate how spending, financial management, and estate-planning choices today affect what we will leave behind. We will also consider an array of ways that parents can discuss money with and in front of children, to teach them how to spend, invest, and manage it responsibly.

There are many choices that determine how wealth will affect your children. This book arranges these choices into three categories: Financial Choices, Intellectual Choices, and Spiritual/ Emotional Choices, as depicted in **Exhibit O.1.**

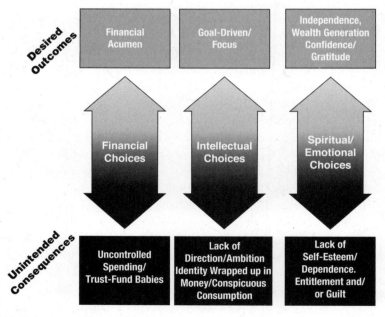

Exhibit O.1 Kids, Wealth, and Consequences Model

Each of these categories of choices comprises one section of the book, with a fourth section focusing on integrating the different types of choices into an action plan.

■ **Section I: Financial Choices.** The three chapters in this section cover somewhat technical concepts, while Chapters 4 through 10 deal with the softer topics. If you are not a numbers person, you may prefer to skim the first chapters or even skip them, although optimally, you would benefit from at least familiarizing yourself with the technical concepts in this section (**Exhibit O.2**).

Our decisions about spending, estate planning, and portfolio management dramatically affect our own future, as well as that of our children.

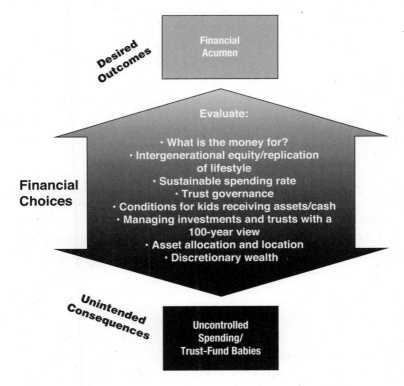

Exhibit O.2 Financial Choices

When wealthy parents neglect to think through these issues, making sure to structure trusts, spending, and investing to meet their goals and values, the unintended consequences for the children can include uncontrolled spending and dependence in the form of trust-fund babies. But when there is careful consideration and preparation, the family will develop the financial acumen, create estate plans that match their long-term values, and maintain their resources so that the children will live independently and responsibly.

In Chapter 1, "Calculating Your Family's Future," we describe the spending choices "Bob" faces, how various spending scenarios affect his net worth in future years, and the legacy he wants to leave behind to his children. How will these decisions affect his children? Will his financial decisions enable his children to enjoy future "intergenerational equity"—the ability to replicate his lifestyle? If intergenerational equity is not available or desired, then at what rate should he spend?

Chapter 1 also includes a spreadsheet calculation about the variables (expected return, inflation, income taxes, number of children) few people consider when they decide the percentage of their net worth that they can spend each year. Many wealthy individuals believe that, as in the case of endowments, they can spend 5 percent of their net worth per year and still preserve their capital. Our calculations demonstrate that such an approach may not allow their children to maintain the same standard of living as the family presently enjoys. What are the unintended consequences when adult children cannot match the standard of living they enjoyed growing up?

In Chapter 2, "To Trust and How to Trust," we focus not only on how to select trustees and make sure they understand and honor the grantor's wishes, but also how to structure the trust for the best financial and emotional benefit of the children—specifically, how to avoid creating a sense of entitlement and the "trust-fund baby" syndrome. In this chapter, we explore the best intentions of parents who work with their lawyers to create trust language that can actually lead kids to become dysfunctional and lack direction in their life. We also present alternative ideas about how to leave a legacy with legal language that will help kids to realize their potential before receiving the money. Chapter 2 illustrates that there is no one right approach, but each approach comes with its own set of unintended outcomes. We explore the pros, cons, and alternatives of incentive trusts, flexibility devices, handing over trust control, trustee selection, and oversight that can all help us to integrate the values and goals that we hope to pass down to our children along with our assets. It is not all about taxes and control.

Chapter 3, "Portfolio Management," provides insights from many professionals and high–net worth investors as to how choices of asset allocation, asset location (which trust the asset should be put in), tax ramifications, and risk tolerance affect our ability to achieve intergenerational goals, or the ability to pass down the most value possible to our children. The interplay of these elements can affect our portfolio even more than our specific investment choices. The financial crisis that began in 2008 has brought to the surface some unexpected lessons about asset allocation, which we discuss along with the scams that have come to light during this economic downturn. They provide us with insights as to how important it is to stick to guidelines for choosing and firing managers and advisors.

■ **Section II: Intellectual Choices.** The previous chapters dealt with how to prepare the wealth for family. In this section we delve into how to prepare the family for the wealth. Providing children with financial education is an important responsibility for any parent in today's complex economic world. But for wealthy families, the stakes are much higher—not just because there's more money to squander, but also because wealth can fuel dysfunction and at-risk behaviors such as substance abuse (**Exhibit O.3**).

Chapter 4, "Financial Literacy," explains that, regardless of how sophisticated (or not) they are about personal finance and investing, parents have a responsibility to prepare their children to live in our complex economic times. We guide parents through the process of instilling the five important financial values: tolerating delayed gratification, understanding the difference between wants and needs, practicing making tradeoffs, telling oneself "no," and developing a healthy skepticism about ads, fads, and conspicuous consumption.

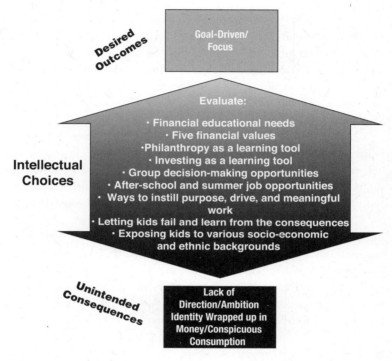

Exhibit O.3   Intellectual Choices

Chapter 4 also addresses specific issues that come up in wealthy families. For instance, will allowance work for high–net worth kids? Should wealthy teens get a summer or after-school job (especially if their parents do not choose to work)? In addition, how can parents prepare children to invest and develop healthy spending and saving patterns early?

Chapter 5, "Skills and Experience," presents a framework to assess the current financial skills both parents and children possess. This chapter is filled with suggestions for preparing children to handle the money they may receive in the future. Experts share their findings about how having dinner with your children can dramatically reduce the chances of an array of at-risk behaviors, including abuse of drugs. For those parents whose kids are less than fascinated with finance, we suggest games specifically for high–net worth families that will make learning more fun.

We will describe creative ways parents can present children the opportunity to practice investing and handling money early so that they can make and learn from their mistakes early, before they inherit significant wealth.

Dealing with advisors is another important skill children will need once they take possession of significant money. This chapter suggests various ways to involve children at different ages with the family's financial advisors and describes how to use a philanthropic family foundation to provide children real-world experience in investing. Often, the first exposure siblings have with financial planning is after the parents die, and they suddenly have to make big decisions with big consequences, without any experience working together. We explain how a foundation can help the family practice making financial decisions together. We also introduce family projects that will allow children to practice investing with real money and learn how to make financial decisions as a family.

Chapter 6, "Goals and Purpose," focuses on how money can bring pleasure as well as problems. While money can provide education, comfort, and travel, it can also paralyze people and rob them of ambition and meaning. In this chapter, we explore how some kids suffer feelings of guilt over not having earned any of what they have or will inherit, while others feel entitled to get everything they desire and yet find themselves bored by it all.

In Chapter 6 we also look at how parents can help guide their children to find their purpose and set meaningful goals that will make them productive. This chapter also illustrates how parents of means can motivate their children, using simple techniques, to find their own path. We also consider ways to encourage children to take sensible risks and experience failure as an important part of their journey.

Many people build their identity around their work or professions. Many wealthy people who do not have to work find it difficult to find a purpose or sense of identity. Parents help their children develop a healthy sense of identity and purpose by exposing them to entrepreneurial and philanthropic activities, and by teaching them that wealth is a responsibility to pass down from generation to generation, not just to buy expensive things.

■ **Section III: Spiritual/Emotional Choices.** Among the many concerns of wealthy parents are how to raise children with a sense of reality and balance, how to prevent them from being dependent, how to help them separate their identity from their wealth, how to help them develop self-confidence, how to instill in them a desire to give back to society, and how to teach them to be good stewards of their future wealth for later generations (**Exhibit O.4**). Parents want their children to develop the capacity to engage in meaningful

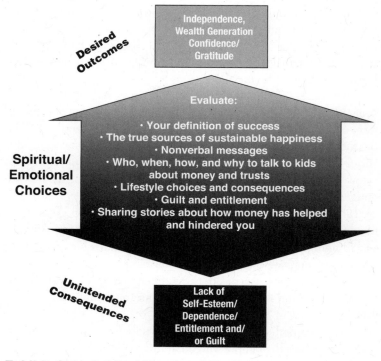

Exhibit O.4 Spiritual/Emotional Choices

friendships, to love and to be open to others loving them—for who they are, not because of their family's balance sheet. In this section we see how parents can enhance the values they hold close and discourage values that may impede living a happy and productive life.

Chapter 7, "Success and Happiness," delves into the issue of entitlement and the insidious effects it can have on children of any age. Entitled people do not appreciate, or even enjoy on any deep level, the possessions and other advantages they receive, which can lead to anxiety and depression when too much is never enough. We look at studies and talk to experts about the age-old question of whether money can buy happiness.

The flip side of entitlement is guilt. Some children feel they do not deserve the advantages they have and will inherit. They are plagued with guilt, which can also lead to anxiety and depression. While money will not necessarily make us happy, we can be happy with money. And while wealthy people can't buy immortality, they can leave a legacy built around healthy values and exposure to the many facets and faces of the outside world. We describe the traits of happy people and consider what "drives" drive.

In Chapter 8, "Communication," we ask: what attitudes and values have served you well in your own life? Which ones have hindered you in your work, relationships, and family? Are you comfortable talking honestly with your children about your own foibles and flaws? The messages we send our children come not just from our words but from our actions. While many wealthy people believe that their legacy to their children is their money, the larger legacy is actually the attitudes and values we pass along with that money. This requires a fairly high degree of open, honest communication, so we also explore in this chapter different communication styles, and how one type of communicator can best communicate with other types of communicators.

Our children derive their financial values and their expectations about what kind of lifestyle they will be able to maintain into adulthood—a topic not often discussed overtly with our children—from what they observe about how much and the way we spend. When is it appropriate to discuss with children what, when, and how they will inherit? Should parents tell their children how they expect them to spend, save, invest, and donate the money they'll inherit? How can they help their children develop a positive identity that is not defined by money?

In Chapter 9, "Navigating the High–Net Worth Environment," we examine the messages children may glean from parents' choices about how to live and spend, and the emotional impact that is likely to have on children. The media have a large impact on our children. It may be difficult for them to distinguish between the values of the media, your values, and the consumption they see all around them. Just because you or your family members have enough money to live in a palace, travel by limo, and jet around the world without traditional employment doesn't mean that you have to do so. Nor should you or your children feel guilty about wealth and enjoying some of the benefits.

But with constant traveling and consumption of massive quantities of clothes, electronics, art, wine, jewelry, and—fill in the blank with whatever your passions or poisons include—children may come to believe their family is better than "those" people who don't achieve the same lifestyle. They may believe it is not fun or safe to live differently. Yet many families have had more fun at a roadside hotel or have met interesting people and learned important skills having to deal with a canceled plane flight than they have living it up in a cocoon. More bonding memories result from the time spent together than from the time spent in a "great place." Such situations teach us that what is important is family and community, not the money things can buy. This chapter will explore some of the unintended consequences children have suffered from being cocooned in the trappings of wealth and how to navigate around it. With the financial outcome of 2008, many parents are rethinking what is truly important about the money they have, the things they own, and the places where they live. Will the high–net worth environment protect wealthy families from new realities of a potentially changing world?

■ **Section IV: Integrating Your Choices.** By examining the unintended consequences of your lifestyle, you can figure out how you can best match your lifestyle choices with your life values. By integrating the strategies and techniques we have presented in the first three sections—Financial Choices, Intellectual Choices and Spiritual/ Emotional Choices—you can greatly increase the chances of raising happy, well-adjusted children who appreciate and know how to manage the wealth they will one day inherit.

"The Family Glue" is the subject of Chapter 10. Studies have found that many families that create even the most sophisticated estate plans but do not prepare their children to inherit their wealth will end up in a generation or two with little or no wealth. This chapter presents techniques for working together as a family toward common goals and values. Business owners and managers invest countless time and money teaching employees to work as a team, yet they do not teach their own families to do so. Business owners and managers also invest heavily in creating vision and mission statements that articulate their values and goals; yet they rarely if ever do so with their families. How can or should the family use its wealth to accomplish the family's mission and vision in a way that complements its values? We will focus on how to begin to execute these goals at home to strengthen the family glue.

In Chapter 11, "Pulling It All Together," we review how the issues, decisions, and challenges we have grappled with in previous chapters come together. We explore the likely outcomes—intended and unintended—of parenting and lifestyle choices, investing and trust decisions. One set of parents may decide to give their child a BMW at a young age but make other choices that offset the possible "spoiling" that may otherwise result. We help parents align their communication, trust documents, work expectations, and spending choices with their personal and shared family values.

This is not about judging or making all the "correct" choices but about understanding how the combination of our choices will affect each individual child. This chapter will also describe choices about what kind of legacy, beyond the dollars and cents of your wealth, you have an opportunity to leave future generations.

If 2008 has taught us anything, it is to prepare for the unexpected. All the chapters in this book raise—and we hope, help answer— some critical financial parenting questions, such as how we can plan and protect our children for the unknown and how can we prepare our kids to survive any potential lifestyle.

There's no substitute for good basic, active parenting. Three of the many ingredients behind good parenting are clarity (setting clear rules and expectations), consistency (imposing consistent consequences for breaking those rules), and communication (about your family values, your expectations, and the lessons children learn from their successes and failures, whether at home or at school).

We are delighted you will join us on this journey and hope you visit our Web site, www.KWandC.com, where you will find many financial and parenting tools, updates, and links.

SECTION I

Financial Choices

1

Calculating Your Family's Future

MANY WEALTHY PEOPLE have worked hard to amass their wealth, while others have been fortunate enough to inherit a large sum of money. In either case, most wealthy people do not take the time to answer the most important question this book will ask: What is money for? After answering this question, the next step is to calculate how much money is needed to reach your goals. Many wealthy people run out of money or leave far less to their kids or grandkids than they had imagined. The first section of this book, "Financial Choices," helps you consider what you want your money to be for, and helps you set a strategic course to meet your money goals. The three chapters in this section pose hard questions and introduce financial techniques to help you understand the realities of what happens to money through the generations. Although this section of the book may seem very technical, it is the first step to increasing the likelihood that your money will help, not hinder, your children's success, emotional health, and happiness.

The amount of money you decide to spend each year can have far-reaching consequences, both intended and unintended, on your children's future. It can affect the legacy you leave behind, not only in terms of how much financial capital they will eventually inherit, but also in terms of the lifestyle to which they have grown accustomed, the messages your spending patterns send to them, their expectations (which may not be realistic if you outlive much of your wealth), and their career decisions. In addition to spending patterns, inflation, return on your investments (net of fees), the number of children you have, and the amount of wealth your children will create in the future will all affect the extent to which you will be able to meet your expectations for your children and future generations.

Self-Survey for Intergenerational Equity

Every chapter of this book presents a self-survey so that you can assess your assumptions and beliefs before you read about the subject matter. Please write your answers in the column to the left of each question. Then, after you read through the chapter, turn back to this page, and consider each question once again—this time, writing your answers in the column to the right of each question. By noting any questions you answer differently the second time, you can pinpoint areas of your lifestyle, parenting, and planning that you may want to reconsider and discuss with your spouse, advisors, and children. Perhaps this will lead to changes, subtle or profound, in the way you handle your wealth and improve the chances that it will enhance your family's healthy attitudes, expectations, and decisions concerning money.

Self-Survey about Intergenerational Equity

1 = Strongly Agree, 2 = Agree, 3 = Neutral, 4 Disagree, 5 = Strongly Disagree

BEFORE   AFTER

_____   I expect to leave my children enough   _____
            assets to enable them to live at the same
            lifestyle our family currently enjoys,
            regardless of what kind of work they may do.

_____   My children should have to work to support _____
            themselves at whatever lifestyle to which
            they may aspire.

_____ percent	... is the approximate amount of my liquid assets I spend on average each year.	_____ percent
_____ percent	... is the approximate annual return my portfolios have returned, on average over the past ten years.	_____ percent
_____	At the rate I currently spend each year to support my lifestyle, my net worth will continue to appreciate in spending power over time.	_____
_____	My children will be prepared to manage the money they will likely inherit.	_____
_____	My children will be prepared emotionally to handle the assets they will eventually inherit.	_____
_____	My children will be prepared to adjust their expectations and standard of living regardless of whether they inherit substantial wealth or have to make their own way in the world.	_____
_____	I have communicated to my children my plans and expectations about the lifestyle they can expect to achieve (or not achieve) through their future inheritance.	_____
_____	I have considered what kind of legacy I want to leave future generations.	_____

What Is Money For?

There's no single correct answer to this question. Some feel their money is there to spend during their lifetime, and that their children should work to support themselves. Others believe their children should be entitled to the same standard of living as the parents enjoy. Most of us fall somewhere in between. For instance, some feel, especially if their money was inherited rather than earned, that they are stewards, not owners, of that money.

You may want your children to find fulfillment in a meaningful, successful career and the pride that comes from earning their own keep, but you may not want them to have to bear the financial burden of paying for their home, vacations, retirement, or their children's education.

Some feel compelled to use their money to help society. For instance, some wealthy people decide to bequeath all or a significant portion of their net worth to a foundation, as Microsoft founder Bill Gates and entrepreneur/investor Warren Buffett have done. Buffett's estate, for example, will leave his children enough that so they would never starve; some of the excess has been designated for foundations partly for them, which they manage; the rest he has donated to Bill Gates's foundation.

We recommend that you sit down, preferably with your spouse (if you have one), to sort out what you want your estate to provide the next generation:

- The ability not to have to work, or to take a meaningful but low-paying job
- The ability to give back to society
- The ability to pay for their college education and that of their children
- Some amount of extravagance, such as travel or a vacation house

Whether or not you believe your children are entitled to inherit your wealth, they will need to know your intentions, which will affect their life decisions. If you live lavishly, they may assume they will be able to do so as well once they are on their own. If you live frugally and your children have no idea that they will eventually inherit vast sums, they will need to be prepared emotionally and intellectually to handle that wealth.

One unprepared young woman, Kathy, became enraged when she learned she would be inheriting enough money that she

TEACHABLE MOMENT

If your kids are old enough, which could mean when they know who they are and what they want to be—probably sometime in their twenties—you might want to include them in this discussion about what money is for.

UNINTENDED CONSEQUENCES

The lifestyle you choose to live will create certain expectations in your children as to what lifestyle they will maintain. Communication with your children about this, even when they are mature enough, may be uncomfortable or unpalatable, but it is one of the best gifts you can give them, regardless of how much or how little they may ultimately inherit.

would not need to work to maintain her lifestyle. She had chosen to get an MBA and had pursued a career on Wall Street rather than her passion for art. Had Kathy had any inkling she would not need to support herself, she would have taken a completely different path.

If you have $2 million in assets, your ability to create *intergenerational equity* so that your children will be able to replicate your lifestyle without having to work is not realistic. But perhaps you could create a more modest level of intergenerational equity in terms of providing a roof over your children's head—maybe not a palace, but a modest home in a nice community, or a down payment for a more upscale abode. Or you could supplement what your grown children earn so that they can enjoy a higher standard of living than they otherwise might.

Current Spending versus Future Intergenerational Equity

If you want your children to enjoy intergenerational equity, calculate whether your annual spend rate (as a percent of your net worth) will preserve enough capital for them to enjoy the same standard of living as your family currently enjoys. If you do not work, will they need to? Would you have answered this question the same way in 1929, 1960, 1985, 2005, 2008? What world events might make you think differently?

We talked with many high–net worth investors who analyzed the ability to create intergenerational equity and pointed out what they think most investors fail to see. Richard Levi, age sixty-one and a father of two children, recalls a presentation he attended several years ago at which the presenter mentioned how rare it is for a family fortune to last past the fourth generation. Levi says the presenter explained that "estate and income taxes along with inflation (and occasional spendthrifts or imbeciles) play a role, but the real killer is that assets expand arithmetically and families expand geometrically."

Even if parents do everything right (however you define "right"), Susan Remmer Ryzewic, who has worked with her family for twenty years, points out unforeseen events can play a big part. "My thoughts are clouded by recent market events [the financial crisis that began in 2008]. No matter how much 'financial and family' planning one might engage in, there are events and mistakes that can change it. It is critical that we all know that the best-laid plans are subject to six-sigma events and may change."

Jeffrey E. Horvitz, who manages his family's third-generation wealth as vice chairman of Moreland Management Company in Beverly Farms, Massachusetts, explains, "I had tried to formalize the spending rate questions for taxable investors with my 'four horsemen' concept: fees and costs, taxes, inflation, and consumption. Lawyers and insurance salesmen have these huge projections where you own California by the third generation. Most get the tax part, sort of, and underestimate the fees, but completely miss inflation." Horvitz has found that compounding of inflation is the secret killer of wealth preservation and growth that most of us, and our investment managers, miss.

Fritzi Hallock, a principal who manages investments for her family office, believes achieving intergenerational equity "is just not possible without some active wealth creation in each generation. My grandparents were one couple in one household. They had two children in two households. Each child had three children (including me)—that's six more households. The next generation has eight children (at this point). How can we all live as well as the household who lived or lives the highest unless we are working ourselves or the wealth is grown?"

The following section presents the example of Bob, a forty-year-old man with a net worth of $10 million. We will create a spreadsheet calculation of Bob's intergenerational equity using several variables. The results of this calculation may help you understand how these variables impact future intergenerational equity with the wealth you have amassed. Keep in mind a long-term view over several generations. We focus on the spend rate, as that is the only variable fully under your control that may allow you to achieve intergenerational equity. Few wealthy people consciously consider the ramifications of their spending. Even those who do tend to grossly overestimate how much they think they can spend without eroding their principal. For instance, many wealthy individuals believe that, like charitable endowments, they can spend 5 percent of their net worth per year and still preserve their capital. Our calculations demonstrate that a more realistic spend rate is closer to 1 percent to 2 percent.

What follows is a fairly technical explanation of how we arrived at the 1 percent to 2 percent spending level. If you are a numbers person, the remainder of this chapter will show how we come to our conclusion. If you are not a numbers person, you may simply want to skim this chapter and go to our Web site (www.KWandC.com), where you can plug your numbers into our intergenerational equity calculator to see your personal results.

The point of this section is to calculate whether or not your current annual spending will allow you to meet your intergenerational equity goals, whatever they may be. If you find you will not be able to meet those goals, it's better to learn that sooner rather than later so you can weigh your options: finding ways to cut back on your spending, creating additional wealth, or lowering your intergenerational equity goals (and your family's expectations about that).

Here's how to make these calculations:

■ **Write down the current value of your assets.** You may want to read this chapter with your browser opened to our Web site (www.KWandC.com), where you will find a calculator that will enable you to plug in your actual numbers to figure out where you stand vis-à-vis intergenerational equity.

■ **How much are you actually currently spending?** We are going to assume, for this exercise, that our hypothetical Bob is spending about 5 percent ($500,000 per year) to support his current lifestyle, which includes a nice primary residence, a lovely vacation home on a lake with a beautiful boat, a ski trip to Aspen, Colorado every winter, a couple of long weekends in the Caribbean or Mediterranean each year, a few cars, and a nanny for his kids.

■ **Select a reasonable rate of return.** Of course, at the same time Bob is withdrawing funds to maintain his lifestyle, the balance of his portfolio is accruing interest or appreciating. For instance, if he has invested most of his assets in the stock market, his expected rate of return, pre-tax, will be in the neighborhood of 10 percent.[1] That's the annualized rate of return the S&P 500 has produced between 1926 and 2007. Your first impression might be that this is not a good number to use. In 2000 or 2008, people would have definitely felt that 10 percent was too high. However, remember that we want to take a long-term look over 100 years, or several generations. The years 1926 to 2007 include the Great Depression as well as the boom times of the eighties and nineties. During those times 10 percent may have seemed too low. It is important not to be swayed by current events but to use them as a guide. Estimating over a long period is best. In any one year, the numbers will not reflect current conditions. We will suggest numbers, but you should choose what you think is correct given your current understanding of what the future might bring. Then go to our Web site and enter your information based on those assumptions.

We picked the average of the S&P 500 over a long period because, even with the best, brightest, and most expensive investment advisors, the average wealthy member of the Institute for

---

1. According to http://www.moneychimp.com/features/market_cagr.htm (accessed July 6, 2009), the average return of the S&P 500 since 1950 has been 8.66 percent. Between 1996 and 2007 the rate was 8.83 percent. Money Chimp argues that the average may not be the right thing to look at and suggests, instead, using the real Compound Annual Growth Rate. The number is about 1 percent lower in both periods above.

Private Investors (IPI) has not done much better. In fact, as **Exhibit 1.1** illustrates, for each year between 1996 and 2008, this group was asked what their return was. The average for the group during the first eleven years (1996 through 2007) was 10.3 percent. Interestingly, the S&P 500 returned 10.6 percent during this same time period. So an average portfolio of this highly sophisticated investor group as a whole achieved about the same return as the S&P 500.

Many wealthy investors believe they are smarter than the market. In 2005 this group was asked to predict how their portfolio would perform that year. The following year, they were asked to compare their previous expectations to their actual results. How did this group actually do? The Institute for Private Investors Family Performance Tracking® 2006 – Part I survey found that almost half—47 percent—of their portfolios returned less than the 9.4 percent expected benchmark return, 27 percent came in right at 9.4 percent, and 26 percent achieved more than what they expected. We often over-estimate how our portfolios are performing or how they will perform in the future.

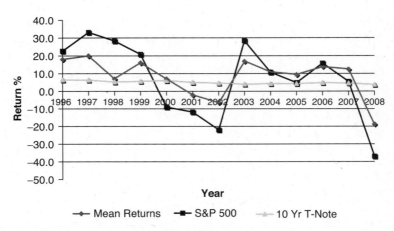

Exhibit 1.1   Return Trends 1996–2008

Source: Institute for Private Investors Family Performance Tracking® Survey Data.

However, this group tended to under-perform during up years and outperform the S&P 500 during down years. Exhibit 1.1 bears this out during the 2000, 2001, 2002, and 2008 bear markets. If you insist that you do better, that's great. But remember, during down years, you may need to dig into principal. If you have a down year and lose 20 percent of your portfolio, to make that up you will need several years of 14 percent to 15 percent returns. The most pronounced example is that if $100 drops to $50, you would need a 100 percent rate of return to get back to even.

Collin, an acquaintance, claimed his portfolio had been returning 14 percent over that same period. When prodded, he admitted that he was boasting only about his winners, not his losers, and that some investments, such as bonds and cash in the bank and money market funds, returned far less. After further thought, Collin realized, in fact, his total portfolio indeed earned about 10 percent.

Therefore, whether you are a passive investor or you get up every day and trade, over the long term it's difficult to make more than the S&P benchmark. The main exceptions are those who own an active business. Therefore, plug in whatever rate of return you want (on our online calculator or your own spreadsheet).

■ **Subtract investment fees**, which can include banking fees, management fees, family office fees, and accounting or legal investment advice. An estimate of these fees is 1 percent, which brings Bob's return down to 9 percent.

■ **Subtract taxes.** For our calculations, we will only consider two forms of taxes: federal and state income taxes.

State income tax rates vary depending on where you live. We'll assume a combined federal and state income tax for a high–net worth person to be about 25 percent. Tax rates periodically change and different investments have different tax consequences; if you've invested a large portion of your portfolio in long-term tax-free bonds, your income taxes will be lower than someone who puts the lion's share in the stock market.

Your tax advisor can recommend which rate is best for you to assume in the long term. Bob's 25 percent will further erode his 10 percent investment returns (9 percent after investment fees) by 2.5 percent. That leaves him with just a 6.5 percent rate of return.

We are not factoring in inheritance taxes for this calculation. We assume that you'll be savvy enough over your lifetime to mitigate that tax rate as much as you can by using all the tools available to transfer your money during your lifetime into estate tax-free trusts. If you've purchased life insurance to cover any estate taxes that are not protected in such trusts, you should include your annual premiums in your annual spending budget to figure out how much you can spend each year to meet your intergenerational equity goals. You should also include any fees you pay professional estate planners, including lawyers and accountants, each year into your annual spending budget.

■ **Factor in inflation.** History tells us long-term inflation averages 3 percent to 4 percent per year. In the seventies, inflation was at double digits, while in 2008, during the spike in gasoline prices, the CPI (consumer price index) was running at about 3.8 percent. If your purchases are weighted heavily on food and fuel, your personal inflation rate would have been higher that year. In mid-2009 the CPI went down to about 3.3 percent. You should factor in a different inflation rate than the government reports, based on the goods and services you consume.

Inflation means $1 today will be worth about 97 cents in one year (at the long-term inflation rate of 3.15 percent),[2] or, to put it another way, you will need $1.03 next year to buy the same goods you bought this year for only a $1.00. Depending on our calculations, we will look at inflation using one of these perspectives. Specifically, when we are looking at the value of a portfolio, we will use the descending numbers to reflect how inflation erodes future value. When we are looking at how inflation erodes spending power, we will use the ascending numbers to reflect how much you have to spend after inflation to maintain a steady lifestyle. Just a 2 percent to 4 percent

---

2. Based on data obtained from http://www.bls.gov/cpi/#tables July 2009.

TEACHABLE MOMENT

Will saving money in a one-year certificate of deposit (CD) provide the same buying power, after inflation, when it comes due? Try an experiment with your kid. Find something she wants to buy and have her put the money in a one-year CD. See if she can afford it after a year. Is there money left over to reinvest?

inflation rate can be a large hurdle to keep up with your spending rate even if you want to leave nothing behind. For the purposes of our calculation, we'll use 3 percent.

Let's say Bob spends 5 percent of his portfolio every year. **Exhibit 1.2** shows what his portfolio will look like over time. His assets, in forty years, would double to $20 million, and his spending rate would be about $1 million. That sounds wonderful.

Exhibit 1.2 Portfolio Growth

SPEND RATE @ 5% OF ASSETS	CURRENT YEAR	20 YEARS	40 YEARS
Age of Person	40	60	80
Projected Investment Return after Fees	9%	9%	9%
Tax Rate	25%	25%	25%
Inflation Rate	3%	3%	3%
Value of Liquid Assets	$10,000,000	$14,147,782	$20,015,973
Annual Increase/ Decrease to Portfolio after Taxes and Spending	$175,000	$247,586	$350,280
Actual Annual Spending @ 5%	$500,000	$707,389	$1,000,799

However, if we look at his annual spending in **Exhibit 1.3**, we find that to keep up with inflation, his buying power has actually been reduced. At age eighty he would only be able to live at 61 percent of his current lifestyle. That's because, to keep up with inflation, Bob would need to spend $1.6 million, and he will only be spending $1 million per year in forty years.

To keep up with inflation and maintain his buying power, Bob's spending will have to increase by 3 percent per year. He may have more dollars to spend due to future growth of his assets, but that will only

Exhibit 1.3   Inflation Erosion

SPEND RATE @ 5% OF ASSETS	CURRENT YEAR	20 YEARS	40 YEARS
Age of Person	40	60	80
Projected Investment Return after Fees	9%	9%	9%
Tax Rate	25%	25%	25%
Inflation Rate	3%	3%	3%
Value of Liquid Assets	$10,000,000	$14,147,782	$20,015,973
Annual Increase/ Decrease to Portfolio after Taxes and Spending	$175,000	$247,586	$350,280
Actual Annual Spending @ 5% of Assets	$500,000	$707,389	$1,000,799
Inflation-Adjusted Annual Spending @ 3% Per Year	$500,000	$903,056	$1,631,019
Future Buying Power (Lifestyle)	100%	78%	61%

buy him the same amount of goods as it does today. We will continue to use 3 percent as our buying power inflator. As **Exhibit 1.4** illustrates, Bob's $500,000 dollar spending rate would have to grow to about $900,000 in twenty years, and almost $1.6 million in thirty-nine years, to maintain the same buying power as today. We use thirty-nine years instead of forty, as Bob's portfolio will not last him forty years.

This is because Bob's spending and inflation would greatly erode his future portfolio value. As **Exhibit 1.5** illustrates, even after factoring in his portfolio return (less taxes and investment fees), his assets would be negative $354,989 in thirty-nine years.

So much for intergenerational equity! If he spends more and more each year to keep up with inflation, not only will our Bob not have anything to leave his children, he will, in fact, run out of money in thirty-nine years, when he is seventy-nine years old.

How could this be? After all, his portfolio is growing at 6.75 percent, after investment-management fees and taxes. That leaves him with $675,000 to spend and reinvest. The problem is that in reality, he is spending after-tax dollars, not pre-tax dollars. For instance, in year one, his $500,000 spending is 5 percent of the value of his portfolio. However, his $500,000 spending equals 74 percent of his after-tax investment returns—that leaves only $175,000 to be added to the portfolio to be reinvested. Bob is adding less then 2 percent to his portfolio each year while inflation is at 3 percent. The problem gets worse each year if he increases his *spending* to keep up with inflation.

For Bob's *assets* to keep up with a 3 percent inflation rate, he will need to reinvest about 3 percent back into the portfolio. This will allow

Exhibit 1.4   Inflation-Adjusted Spending

INITIAL 5% SPEND RATE, THEN KEEP UP WITH INFLATION	CURRENT YEAR	20 YEARS	39 YEARS
Age of Person	40	60	79
Spending to Keep up with Inflation @ 3% Per Year	$500,000	$903,056	$1,583,513

Exhibit 1.5 Running Out of Money

INITIAL 5% SPEND RATE, THEN KEEP UP WITH INFLATION	CURRENT YEAR	20 YEARS	39 YEARS
Age of Person	40	60	79
Projected Investment Return after Fees	9%	9%	9%
Tax Rate	25%	25%	25%
Inflation Rate	3%	3%	3%
Value of Liquid Assets	$10,000,000	$11,772,096	$(354,989)
Annual Increase/ Decrease to Portfolio after Taxes and Spending	$175,000	$(108,439)	$(1,607,475)
Inflation-Adjusted Annual Spending @ 3%	$500,000	$903,056	$1,583,513
Future Buying Power (Lifestyle)	100%	100%	100%

the portfolio to compound and increase in value at the same rate as inflation. **Exhibit 1.6** shows that if Bob spends about 3.75 percent of his portfolio each year instead of 5 percent, he will be able to sustain that spending rate into perpetuity as long as taxes, investment fees, and investment returns stay the same on average over the years.

At this rate, what will Bob have left to leave his children?

■ **Consider how many children you have.** The U.S. Census calculates that today, a woman can expect to have in her lifetime an average of two children.[3] If Bob has two children and wants to achieve perfect inter-generational equity for both of them, he will need to spend less than the

3. *Source:* U.S. Census (http://www.censusbureau.biz/Press-Release/www/2006/cb06ff07-2 .pdf).

Exhibit 1.6   Adjusting Spending to Preserve the Portfolio

SPEND RATE @ 3.7% OF ASSETS	CURRENT YEAR	20 YEARS	40 YEARS
Age of Person	40	60	80
Projected Investment Return after Fees	9%	9%	9%
Tax Rate	25%	25%	25%
Inflation Rate	3%	3%	3%
Value of Liquid Assets	$10,000,000	$18,237,274	$33,259,816
Annual Increase/ Decrease to Portfolio after Taxes & Spending	$305,000	$556,237	$1,014,424
Actual Spending @ 3.7%	$370,000	$674,779	$1,230,613
Inflation-Adjusted Annual Spending @ 3%	$370,000	$668,261	$1,206,954
Future Buying Power (Lifestyle)	100%	101%	102%

3.7 percent we arrived at to maintain his buying power and pay taxes and investment fees. If he has three children, he would need to spend even less to achieve perfect intergenerational equity by age 80.

Because no one knows at what age they will die, or when they may want to begin future distributions to their children, **Exhibit 1.7** uses a 1 percent spend rate to demonstrate how this may plays out.

Note that the buying power is truly the ability to achieve inter-generational equity. At 1 percent, Bob could almost support three adult children at the original buying power he had when he was forty. Because his kids will want or need cash before he dies, Bob will want to share this intergenerational wealth while he is alive. For Bob to

Exhibit 1.7   What You Can Leave Behind

SPEND RATE @ 1% OF ASSETS	CURRENT YEAR	20 YEARS	40 YEARS
Age of Person	40	60	80
Projected Investment Return after Fees	9%	9%	9%
Tax Rate	25%	25%	25%
Inflation Rate	3%	3%	3%
Value of Liquid Assets	$10,000,000	$30,591,975	$93,586,896
Annual Increase/ Decrease to Portfolio after Taxes and Spending	$575,000	$1,759,039	$5,381,247
Actual Spending @ 1%	$100,000	$305,920	$935,869
Inflation-Adjusted Annual Spending @ 3%	$100,000	$180,611	$326,204
Future Buying Power (Lifestyle)/ Intergenerational Equity	100%	169%	287%

maintain his $100,000 lifestyle (a 1 percent spend rate), he will not need to spend the almost $1 million he can draw on at age eighty or the $300,000 that he will have at age sixty. He can distribute to his children some or all of the excess of his 1 percent spend rate in any given year.

Other Factors

If you are in the money-making mode, and you therefore have not completed your "endowment," you can add how much you expect your saved earnings will add to your estate during your remaining expected work years. Or, perhaps you know that at some point you will inherit a large sum. (Our Web site will include a separate calculator that will allow you to factor in any ongoing wealth creation or eventual windfalls.)

Let's look at how that might affect future intergenerational equity. Let's say your current net worth is $5 million, and you are currently making $1 million a year from your active business endeavor or your salary. Assume you are supporting your lifestyle from your business earnings and are putting away 25 percent or $250,000 per year. When you retire, what will you start off with in your "endowment?" Here is the calculation: the $5 million you had in savings and the amount you add to it will grow on average 9 percent per year from investments. (As we discussed earlier in this chapter, you will have to subtract the taxes you will have on your investments and add to it the $250,000 contribution from your active business or employment to savings each year.) As **Exhibit 1.8** shows, your current net worth will grow to almost $12 million. However, if we adjust that wealth to today's buying power, it will be worth more like about $10 million after inflation in ten years.

Therefore, you will have to decide how much to spend and how much to save or give to your kids during your lifetime to achieve the intergenerational equity you may want to leave behind, and at what age.

Getting back to Bob, so far we have assumed that he will never spend any more money than his current spend rate. But people can end up spending more money during some periods of time. Bob may have more children. A divorce could cost him big time. Plus, older kids tend to cost more. Then again, perhaps in Bob's later years he pares back his lifestyle: he may decide to travel less, reduce spending on "toys," and sell one or more of his homes, lowering his annual expenses. You can play with different assumptions about your future spend rate on our online calculator (www.KWandC.com) or your own spreadsheet.

We have also assumed thus far that future generations' assets depend solely on the current generation's net worth. As we mentioned earlier, that wealth will unlikely be able to support the growing

Exhibit 1.8   Factoring in Wealth Creation and Windfalls

YEARS	START	10	15	20
Current Net Worth	$5,000,000	$11,964,350	$18,016,029	$26,405,127
Investment Return @ 9%	$450,000	$1,076,791	$1,621,443	$2,376,461
Annual Taxes on Investments @ 25%	$(112,500)	$(269,198)	$(405,361)	$(594,115)
Annual Contri- bution to Net Worth (Savings)	$250,000	$250,000	$250,000	$250,000
Annual Increase in Wealth	$587,500	$1,057,594	$1,466,082	$2,032,346
Reduction in Buying Power Due to Inflation @ 3%	$-	$2,304,197	$4,619,827	$8,044;432
Inflation- Adjusted Wealth @ 3%	$5,000,000	$9,660,153	$13,396,202	$18,360,694

family, as your children have children, and each of them have children. Even if every member of future generations lives a moderate lifestyle and manages the family money wisely, your descendants are unlikely to maintain that affluence without each future family member generating further wealth. That may or may not trouble you. If it does, you would be wise to try to motivate your children to pursue a profession, learn how to invest and manage wealth, and develop

---

UNINTENDED CONSEQUENCES

One family office director was concerned for one client's children. The family always flew on their private jet. At the parents' current spend rate, it was clear there wasn't going to be any money left for the kids to maintain that lifestyle, and they would be ill-equipped to deal with the emotional baggage and basic skills when they eventually have to fly commercially. Growing up with a wealthy lifestyle can leave offspring clueless about how to handle a different lifestyle.

TEACHABLE MOMENT

How did you make your money? Is most of your wealth from your own earnings, investing acumen, entrepreneurial expertise, luck, or inheritance? What stories—with lessons learned along the way— can you impart to your children about your successes and failures along the way? Do you expect your children to make their own way even if eventually they will inherit significant money?

---

at least some limits to their lifestyle—which we cover in Sections II (Intellectual Choices) and III (Emotional/Spiritual Choices).

Comparing 1929 and 2008

It's not hard to get a bit depressed and wonder how you can possibly create intergenerational equity when the market tanks the way it did in 2008. But few people consider that during a market crash, other variables change—some to our advantage:

■   Inflation usually goes down or becomes negative (which economists call *deflation*).

■   You can use tax losses to cover future gains, reducing the tax you will need to pay in the future.

■   If you are not making money in the market, you may owe no tax at all on your portfolio.

■   There may be great investing opportunities for those who won't lose too much sleep before their picks have a chance to reward them.

Remember, our model for Bob is based on long-term equilibration back to financial norms since 1926. Even if the rate of return changes, it is likely that other numbers will change in the calculation and that plugging in new assumptions for all of the numbers may help you create intergenerational equity for at least a portion of the lifestyle you want to hand down to your children.

Where to Go from Here

If you find that based on your current spend rate, you will not be able to leave your children enough assets to enjoy the same lifestyle, you have some thinking to do. Many wealthy individuals believe that their children will be much happier and emotionally healthier if they are forced to make their own way in the world. Perhaps you'd like to leave them some start-up capital to finance their own business or provide them with a rainy-day fund to protect them from some of life's inevitable crises, be they financial, medical, or emotional.

It makes sense to take time to evaluate your values and goals about intergenerational equity and then have the information to figure out if your current lifestyle will enable you to achieve those goals.

This is a feedback loop. You start with an assumption about the lifestyle you want to maintain with intergenerational equity. If the formula shows it's not possible to achieve your initial assumptions about full intergenerational equity, you may have to adjust those assumptions or consider other choices. For instance, you may in your heart want your kids to live your lifestyle, but ultimately you may realize the best you can do is provide them with a vacation home and an education. Or you can find ways to reduce your own spending. Or you can find ways to earn money so your net worth will grow enough to achieve complete intergenerational equity.

There's no right or wrong goal concerning intergenerational equity. You can have a different set of rules for yourself than for your kids — you can enjoy spending what you want and leave behind whatever is left over, if anything. The only real mistakes are:

■ unconsciously assuming, and leading your children to assume, that they will be able to achieve the same lifestyle you currently live, without realizing that at your current spend rate, that will not be possible;

■ not preparing your children financially and emotionally for living a much more modest lifestyle, if they will need to; and

■ failing to prepare them financially and emotionally if they will inherit significant wealth.

Whether or not your children will be able to live off of your estate eventually, they will be able to decide what kind of education and career they want and feel they need, based on an accurate picture about future intergenerational equity.

In the United States, our children have generally always ended up better off than their parents were. Our ancestors came into this country with nothing; they worked and managed to save a bit; maybe they started a business that the next generation built up, or their children went to college and entered lucrative professions.

In many cases, parents who inherited all their wealth may feel differently than parents who built their own fortunes. One third-generation family business owner, for instance, feels he should be a steward of the wealth that his family spent eighty years amassing. Another parent, an entrepreneur and brilliant investor, decided his grown children would, for the most part, be left to their own devices to achieve any lifestyle they wanted. He left most of his fortune to various charitable organizations and a relatively modest amount for his children so that they would never have to worry should they encounter serious problems. He also created a family foundation for his children to manage, to enable them to support causes that reflect their values and passions. In case you haven't guessed, this person is Warren Buffet.

The next chapter will present important issues about trusts and trust. Before moving ahead, please return to the beginning of this chapter and re-take the self-survey. Note which questions you answer differently now, and consider what the ramifications could or should be in terms of the parenting and lifestyle choices you make day to day and the plans you have made for your family's future.

2

To Trust and
How to Trust

I N CHAPTER 1, we encouraged you to test different assumptions: your annual spend rate as a percent of your net worth; your portfolio return; taxes; inflation; and how many children you have. We considered how those assumptions may affect the amount of your estate that you likely will be able to leave to the next generation or two, whether you need to adjust your current spend rate to achieve some desired degree of intergenerational equity, and the potential unintended consequences your children may suffer as a result of inheriting such wealth. In this chapter, we explore how to begin minimizing those unintended consequences by setting up estate plans and trusts that will likely result in the best financial and emotional outcome for the children.

This chapter will not consider the tax issues involved in estate planning. There are many books devoted to this topic and many experts who can guide you. But many of those books and many legal and financial advisors may not consider it within their purview to discuss the personal consequences or considerations involved in preserving and transferring wealth, which is our mission in this chapter. In fact, attorney James E. Hughes Jr., author of *Family Wealth—Keeping It in the Family* and *Family: The Compact Among Generations* (both published by Bloomberg Press), pointed out during our telephone interview with him, "It's well-known, which attorneys never tell anyone, that many of their clients who created and funded trusts, particularly these modern things called GRATs [grantor-retained annuity trusts], show up five or ten years later having tremendous remorse. Their GRAT is working perfectly, but their child, now 25, has just come into a million bucks and they know the chances of that child living a fulfilled life are small. The trust they created did not enhance the lives of the beneficiaries." Hughes, who comes from six generations of counselors of law, explains, "The great risk of trusts is that they create people dependent on the trust for all their lives."

A Little Disclaimer

Before making any changes to your trusts, we urge you to explore the ideas we present in this chapter with your lawyer, as laws vary from one state to another and may change from the date of this publication. Depending on the kinds of trusts you have and your circumstances, some of the ideas we describe may or may not apply or be appropriate for you.

Self-Survey about Trusts

A quick self-survey will help you to take stock of the assumptions and attitudes you bring to the topics explored in this chapter. After you finish reading the chapter, you may be surprised to find that some of those mindsets have shifted. We suggest you answer the questions again after you finish this chapter, and consider how you might want to adjust some aspects of your own trust documents to reflect your new thinking.

Self-Survey about Trusts

1 = Strongly Agree, 2 = Agree, 3 = Neutral, 4 = Disagree, 5 = Strongly Disagree

BEFORE		AFTER
_____	I believe it's important to specify certain conditions my children must meet in order to receive distributions from trusts I have set up for them.	_____

_____   I believe it's important to specify how,   _____
where, and when my beneficiaries may
spend distributions from trusts
I have set up for them.

_____   I believe it's important, to maintain   _____
family harmony, to bequeath the
same amount of assets to all the
children, and with the same restrictions
and rules.

_____   The trusts I have established are flexible   _____
enough to adapt to potential future
changes in tax laws, my family's
circumstances, or my children's needs
and life choices.

_____   The trustee(s) I have named understand   _____
my wishes and intentions regarding
how trust assets are to be invested and
distributed. The trustee(s) I have named
share my values.

_____   When my kids reach a certain age,   _____
I would prefer that they become trustee
and control their own destiny.

_____   My beneficiaries know the trustee(s)   _____
I have named and interact with trustee(s)
on a regular basis.

_____   My beneficiaries have been, or are   _____
being, prepared to make or share
investment decisions concerning trust
assets so they can eventually manage
those assets wisely.

_____   I have told (or intend to tell) my children   _____
about the existence of trusts I have
established (or plan to) establish for
them, but have not yet divulged the
amount of assets in such trusts.

Age _____   ... is when I believe my children should   Age _____
be informed about the specific amounts
they will receive, when they will receive
those distributions, and the conditions
they may have to meet to receive
such distributions.

Tom Rogerson, director of Bank of New York Mellon's Family Wealth Services in Boston, tells wealthy clients that tax-minimization planning has much less effect on the well-being of the next generation than integrating family values with wealth planning. The "shirtsleeves to shirtsleeves in three generations" paradigm is universal, Rogerson says, but don't blame estate taxes. He points out: "The oldest Chinese proverb is 'rice paddy to rice paddy in three generations.' China has no estate tax, yet it has the same problems, and it has nothing to do with taxes or estate planning."

Rogerson explains that many families "focus so much attention on the estate tax, as if that's the reason this happens in families." Indeed, based on interviews with 3,025 wealthy individuals in many countries over four decades, Roy Williams, the dean of post-transition research and planning, has estimated that 70% of wealth transitions fail. His book, *Preparing Heirs* (Authors Choice Publishing, 2003), co-authored with Vic Preisser, concludes that wealthy people in countries with an estate tax had no greater incidence of successfully transferring wealth to the next generation than those in countries without an estate tax.

"So something else is going on," concludes Rogerson. "Traditional planning is failing. It's failing miserably, and people continue to think that's the only thing they can do."

He should know. His great-grandfather, Charles Rogerson, was very wealthy. He owned and operated a large investment trust company in the Boston area. He also started the Boston Foundation, the third oldest and one of the largest community foundations in the United States. Rogerson says, "Although his estate plan was designed to get the bulk of his money down to the family, it's gone, I'm sorry to say. His son was one of the best estate planning attorneys in Boston. I don't think you can estate-plan or tax-plan your way out of this problem, which is news to a lot of wealthy people." In fact, Rogerson finds that successful use of philanthropy as a family-building tool may be more helpful at solving this problem. "I'd rather see a family using philanthropy effectively and have no estate plan at all than have the best estate plan money can buy and not use philanthropy."

Intelligent Trust Design

Our point is not that trusts are evil or unnecessary. High–net worth families obviously need to create trusts to protect their assets from creditors, nuisance law suits, and taxation—and the majority of wealthy families is no stranger to trusts, as evidenced by a Spring 2008 survey, "Trusts, Trustees and Trust Advisors," sponsored by the Institute for Private Investors (IPI). Three-quarters of the investor respondents have set up a family trust, and 85 percent are either a trust beneficiary or trustee for a family member's trust, with a little more than half serving as a co-trustee. High-net worth families and their advisors have lots of expectations about what trusts and trustees can accomplish, as you can see in **Exhibit 2.1**.

However, trusts cannot accomplish, especially by themselves, another task many wealthy parents hope or expect them to achieve: protecting their assets from their children. Some wealthy parents are looking for a silver bullet in trust planning that will magically turn their children into thoughtful, responsible, and productive citizens. Even your hard work in transmitting and modeling your values and knowledge cannot guarantee your children will turn out the way you hope they will—although it certainly increases the odds significantly. Nonetheless, many people and their advisors try to structure trusts to aid or detract from some of the most troublesome possible outcomes inheritances can have on your children.

■ **Incentive trusts.** Exhibit 2.1 also shows that a little more than half of the individuals agree with the statement, "Trusts are used too often as a way to control children, or worse, to control 'from the grave,'" while just under half of advisors agreed. That leaves a lot of people—wealthy individuals and their advisors—who do not agree; who believe trusts can control their children's behavior.

Indeed, many parents often want to build into their trust certain distribution conditions and incentives. Incentive trusts attempt to ensure any number of goals, such as ensuring that beneficiaries will be financially responsible, will lead productive lives, will obtain certain

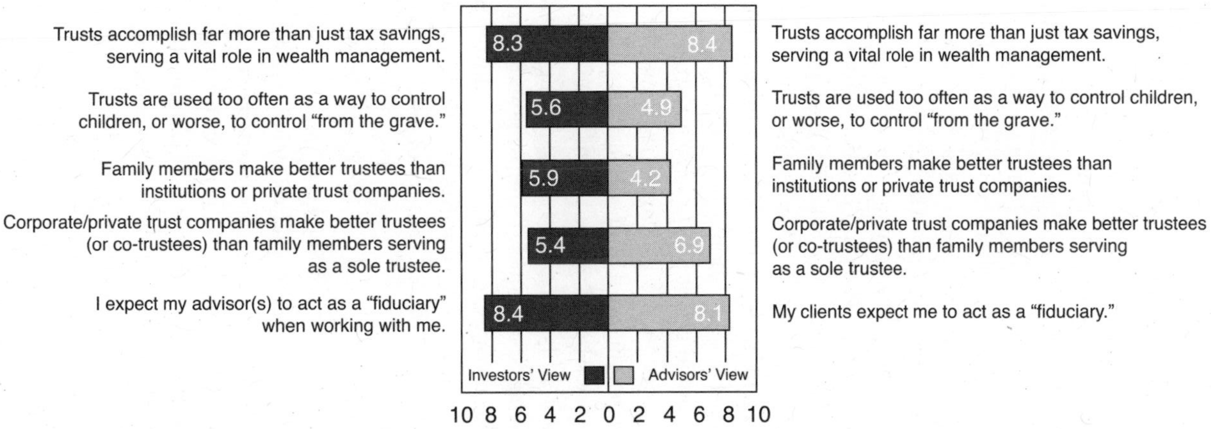

Investors' View statements (left):
- Trusts accomplish far more than just tax savings, serving a vital role in wealth management.
- Trusts are used too often as a way to control children, or worse, to control "from the grave."
- Family members make better trustees than institutions or private trust companies.
- Corporate/private trust companies make better trustees (or co-trustees) than family members serving as a sole trustee.
- I expect my advisor(s) to act as a "fiduciary" when working with me.

Advisors' View statements (right):
- Trusts accomplish far more than just tax savings, serving a vital role in wealth management.
- Trusts are used too often as a way to control children, or worse, to control "from the grave."
- Family members make better trustees than institutions or private trust companies.
- Corporate/private trust companies make better trustees (or co-trustees) than family members serving as a sole trustee.
- My clients expect me to act as a "fiduciary."

Investors' View: 8.3, 5.6, 5.9, 5.4, 8.4
Advisors' View: 8.4, 4.9, 4.2, 6.9, 8.1

Exhibit 2.1 Views from Both Sides: Trusts and Trustees

Source: Institute for Private Investors Survey, "Trusts, Trustees and Trusted Advisors," Spring 2008.

types of jobs, will be charitable, or will accomplish certain tasks or reach particular life milestones (such as earning a college degree, marrying (or marrying a person of a particular religion), or having children)—before the trusts will pay out any income to them.

Billionaire Leona Helmsley, who died at age eighty-seven in 2007, placed one stipulation on two of her grandsons' inheritance of $5 million apiece: they must visit their father's grave (Leona's only son, Jay Panzirer, who died in 1992) at least once a year.

Stacey Vanek-Smith reported on "Marketplace Radio" in late 2008 that her parents had just informed her about a generation-skipping trust for her children. The problem: the thirty-one-year-old unmarried journalist has no children. She interviewed her mother, who informed her, "It was set up for your thirtieth birthday, the idea was to have everything in place by the time you were thirty." One financial planner suggested she should have a kid. "It only takes nine months, so you should go for it," he said (we hope in jest!).

As she dug a little deeper, Vanek-Smith realized her situation was less troubling than some of the incentive trusts other parents had devised. Los Angeles-based estate planning lawyer Jon Gallo related the example of a "Twinkie trust," which was structured to factor in the beneficiary's weight. "If she weighed more than a specified amount, the income from the trust would be cut back, because her father was always concerned that she was going to be obese," explained Gallo, co-author of *Silver Spoon Kids* (McGraw-Hill, 2001).

A 2007 PNC Financial Services Group "Wealth and Values" survey of adults with assets more than $500,000 found that 30 percent of respondents said that their heirs had to meet certain conditions to receive their inheritance. Fourteen percent put restrictions on how the heirs can use the money. "With incentive trusts you can promote beneficial work and a valuable contribution to society as opposed to treating family assets as an entitlement," says Martyn Babitz, JD, senior vice president of PNC Wealth Management and a senior trust advisor for Hawthorn, the PNC division that serves clients with $20 million or more in investable assets. The wealthier the respondents, the more likely they were to apply such incentives.

For instance, 57 percent of those with $10 million in assets require heirs to satisfy certain age, education, or job requirements before they can gain access to their inheritance, compared with 42 percent of those with $5 million to $10 million in assets.

Exhibit 2.2 shows the stipulations respondents to the study have attached to their will or trust.

However, many estate-planning experts are not particularly enamored with incentive trusts. The problem is that "they all have incentives that make sense socially and philosophically at a certain time in history, but might not make sense at a later time," says Charles Lowenhaupt, CEO of St. Louis-based wealth-management firm, Lowenhaupt Global Advisors, and managing member of Lowenhaupt & Chasnoff, LLC the first U.S. law firm to concentrate in tax law, which his grandfather established in 1908. "I don't think they ever work in the long term. There's always a tension between control and freedom."

Jeff Brodsky, director of Midwest Area Personal Financial Services for Ernst & Young, affirms, "In my experience working with clients and their families, the best way to have your children grow up and be good citizens is to raise them the right way. And there's no one right way. I've always felt that the integrity behind documents is more in terms of people and actions they take than the legal document. The parenting factor is so critically important, coupled with an education process."

Brodsky adds, "I've had very few clients, if any, who have used trusts to motivate people to do certain actions, although that's

Exhibit 2.2   Conditions on Trust Distributions

77 percent	for education
46 percent	for basic needs such as housing
29 percent	for the next generation
28 percent	for business or career-related expenses
16 percent	for specific charitable donations

Source: 2007 PNC Financial Services Group "Wealth and Values" survey of adults with assets more than $500,000.

sometimes talked about. Having trusts, especially with parents still living, and having money controlled to motivate [the children], may create resentment in the child." More often, he finds it's helpful to leave such decisions to the trustee's discretion, within the guidelines of a nonbinding statement of intent or desire.

■ **Fair versus equal.** Many parents believe that, to maintain family harmony, it's important to bequeath the same amount of assets to all their children, and under the same restrictions and rules. Leona Helmsley ignored this rule when she excluded two of her four grandchildren from her will, which read, "I have not made any provisions in this will for my grandson Craig Panzirer or my granddaughter Meegan Panzirer for reasons which are known to them." Helmsley did, however, leave $10 million to her brother, Alvin Rosenthal, and $12 million in trust for her pampered pooch, Trouble. The result was anything but family harmony. The court ultimately whittled Trouble's trust down to $2 million and provided $4 million to grandson Craig and $2 million to Meegan.[1]

But often, each child within a family displays very different skills, sophistication, responsibility, needs, and behaviors. Some of Brodsky's clients want to impose equal criteria on all beneficiaries, which will either impose unnecessary restrictions on children who don't need them or fewer restrictions on those who do need them. "When the terms are not equal, I do not suggest putting siblings in charge as trustees. That can create a bad family dynamic."

Equalization can also get tricky when a family business is part of the estate, especially if some next-generation members work in the business while others are inactive shareholders. In such cases, Brodsky says, "It's not unusual to have different voting control even though asset ownership is the same. That's often accepted and understood. My concern in that case is to create some degree of flexibility or liquidity to allow children with ownership without votes, to have an opportunity to get paid out for their stock, and

---

1. Source: "Leona Helmsley's Dog Loses $10 Million of Trust Fund," Fox News, June 16, 2008 (http://www.foxnews.com/story/0,2933,367257,00.html).

balancing that with the financial needs of the corporation." He explains that doing so cuts down on inactive shareholders resenting the active family shareholders who make a large salary or objecting to certain business strategies when outside shareholders have different risk tolerance and liquidity needs than inside shareholder relatives.

■ **Flexibility devices.** In addition, family circumstances and needs may change over time. As Lowenhaupt points out, "The best written trusts are the ones that are flexible, because trusts are intended to govern situations down the road when we have no idea what will happen."

For instance, if a trust restricts beneficiaries from using distributions for anything other than college tuition or housing, what would happen if in the future a beneficiary were to obtain a full scholarship, or if tax laws governing housing deductions were to change? Or what happens if the child develops emotional or cognitive problems that rule out a college education and requires some sort of support instead? The possibility of such contingencies means it's important to build in a certain degree of flexibility, either formally through the language of trust documents or informally with a nonbinding letter of intent to trustees that accompanies the trust document.

One formal way to build in flexibility is to assign individuals—such as the beneficiary or other family members—a "power of appointment" to effectively amend the terms of the trust. For instance, Brodsky says, if a trust's distributions are specifically intended to pay for college and then the beneficiary gets a full scholarship or has special needs that preclude attending college, the trust can say that, while the assets are intended for college, if the child doesn't go to college the holder of the power of appointment can move the assets into another trust to pay for other needs of the beneficiary or to support a charity.

"You can have the holder of the power of appointment direct the trustee to take assets from one trust if and when the provisions are no longer appropriate as [they were] at the time of creation, and move those assets to a new trust that doesn't have those restrictions," says Brodsky. Similarly, the beneficiary can be given a power of appointment to rewrite the terms of the trusts to be created for the beneficiary's descendants upon the beneficiary's death. This is similar to revocable living trusts that change as clients see children mature. Even irrevocable trusts can build in flexibility to change as appropriate in the future, for instance to deal with changes in family circumstances or tax laws.

An example of an informal form of flexibility is a nonbinding statement of intent that guides the trustee about how the grantor desires distributions to be made under different future circumstances. Brodsky explains, "If your trust document limits distributions to a certain fact pattern that no longer exists, then you're limited to that fact pattern. So your trust can give more flexibility and discretion to the trustees, while giving them nonbinding guidance in the statement of intent about how you want them to implement their flexibility."

For instance, instead of specifying that distributions can only be made if the beneficiary is working a full-time job, the trust can say that distributions are intended for the education and welfare of beneficiaries, while the nonbinding letter of intent would explain that you would like distributions to be contingent on your beneficiary remaining productively employed unless for some unforeseen reason the beneficiary becomes physically or emotionally incapable of working or chooses to take an unpaid, volunteer position. In that case, you would like the trustee to decide how best to continue distributions for the child's benefit. This letter of intent preserves the trustee's latitude while providing some guidance.

UNINTENDED CONSEQUENCES

There is a tradeoff between writing too specific a trust that allows the trustee to control the beneficiaries and make them feel impotent and writing a trust that permits so much discretion that potentially irresponsible beneficiaries could use trust assets to support risky behavior, such as gambling or alcohol or drug abuse.

Rogerson recommends that, instead of designing estate plans that *distribute* to people, the focus should be on plans that will *invest* in people. "If you're in a business, isn't there a natural law of reinvesting in the business you own?" he asks. "If you're the beneficiary of a trust, is there a natural law of reinvesting in the trust you're a beneficiary of? Not even a remote concept! No wonder trusts designed to preserve wealth long term often have the opposite effect." He describes one family that created what it calls a "Family Endowment" that allows family members to apply for funds to support only four areas: human capital (such as adopting a child); intellectual capital (such as obtaining an advanced degree); social capital (such as donating to help victims of Hurricane Katrina); and financial capital (such as making an investment in a business). Rogerson points out that "none of these are to pay for family members' lifestyles, but they're to invest in them so they can enjoy their lifestyle."

Trustee Selection and Oversight

"Clearly, the person who doesn't need a trust doesn't mind having a trust because if you're living responsibly with your wealth and trustees are following fiduciary practice, you're getting along with the trust," says Lowenhaupt, while "the person who needs a trust really resents having a trust."

One important quality for trustees is flexibility. Hughes notes, "The great reason beneficiaries dislike their trustees and their trusts is because they don't function for them. It does not function in a collaborative way for the beneficiary. Many trustees manage the trust to the letter of the law to avoid trustee's liability. But for a trust to function, the trustee has to be willing to make the decisions about the trust's assets that will cause the beneficiary's life to be better, rather than having a wooden, formulaic relationship, in which his or her liability is the highest concern."

The selection of trustees can make or break the intention of a trust. Is it best to name a bank trust department, a lawyer, a trusted professional, or an individual? What happens if that person proves to be incompetent or divisive, or dies? Who gets to select a successor trustee, and with what rules and criteria? What role and responsibilities do beneficiaries have in relation to the trustee?

■ **How to select a trustee.** In the 2008 Institute for Private Investors survey, "Trusts, Trustees and Trusted Advisors," 59 percent of individual respondents said that they agreed with the statement that family members make better trustees than institutions or private trust companies, while 42 percent of advisors who participated in the survey agreed with the same statement.

Brodksy acknowledges that the choice is complicated. "Historically," he says, "many of my clients have used individual trustees rather than corporate fiduciaries. Now there's more of a trend within my client base to use corporate fiduciaries, but not a big push. There are a lot of reasons for that, such as increased magnitude of wealth, more complicated investments, or the grantors don't want to vest too much control in one trustee. In families where there is a bad dynamic and the grantor doesn't feel comfortable with any one family member, clearly that's a case for a corporate trustee."

When you have one child who is responsible and one who is not, you may want to name neither, not even the more responsible one, as trustee. Otherwise, you are bound to cause resentment and friction between the siblings. However, you could have the responsible child serve as trustee of her own trust and a corporate or other individual trustee over the irresponsible child's trust.

Typically, a corporate trustee will have more depth of experience on the administration and investment sides, while individual trustees are more likely to understand and share the grantor's personal values. Ideally, the main qualification you should look for is that the trustee should know and understand the grantors' wishes, and care about the family.

An individual trustee may need the assistance of outside advisors such as attorneys and accountants to help them meet administrative responsibilities. Your trustee does not have to be an investment expert. Susan Goldenberg, a partner at the Chicago law firm Neal, Gerber & Eisenberg LLP, points out, "Even the child you think would be great managing the money may not have enough investment sophistication to do that, so you can put someone in place alone or with the child to make investment decisions, including hiring and firing money managers."

Unless you hire a bank as your trustee, the best thing a non-expert trustee can do is to hire a professional to manage the money, such as a bank trust department or independent investment advisor. Otherwise, the trustee may be at risk of being sued by the beneficiaries for mismanaging the money.

Brodsky adds, "I think it's important, where there's a trusted family friend or advisor, that kids understand why that person is there and interact with them at family meetings and such, so they have trust in that person as well, and that they understand the grantor's goals and desires. It's not unusual that beneficiaries have some degree of choice of who's trustee of the trust."

Even if you choose an individual as trustee, you may want to name a bank trust department as a trustee of last resort in the event that your list of trustees and trustee successors happen to become incapacitated, get "voted off the island," or meet their demise.

It's not necessary to hand over complete control to a corporate or individual trustee. **Exhibit 2.3** lists several ways to dilute or distribute trustee responsibilities beyond one person.

Exhibit 2.3   Spreading Out Trustee Powers

■ Name two or more co-trustees, whether two family members, one family member and one trusted advisor, or one family member plus a corporate fiduciary.

■ Designate separate people to make investment, distribution, and trustee successor decisions. You can even have a separate trustee responsible for making decisions on the family business if there is one in the trust.

■ Create investment, distribution and charitable committees comprised of beneficiaries and/or trusted personal or business advisors (see "Trustee Governance" section below).

■ Grant beneficiaries the right to fire the trustee or trustees and select another so the trustees can't get too comfortable in that position.

■ **Trustee succession process.** In the event that the beneficiaries are unhappy with decisions the trustee has made, it can be very difficult to oust that person unless the grantor has specified under what circumstances the trustee can be removed and a new one selected.

Especially in light of the banking crisis that erupted in 2008, Lowenhaupt says, "Only a fool would think Bank A will look like Bank A over the next 100 years. Much more important than who trustees are, is the process by which they are designated or removed, and processes under which they are acting."

Goldenberg explains that the trust document can include language stating "when a trustee can be removed and who has the power to make that decision. Often, the trust agreement will allow the beneficiary, assuming the intent is for the beneficiary to have significant control, with the right to remove the trustee, even without any restrictions. They can have the unilateral right to remove a trustee. There may or may not be restrictions on whom they can appoint as successor. For instance, restrictions can be to comply with certain tax rules. When a beneficiary possesses the unilateral right to remove a trustee and absolute discretion as to whom the successor can be, there could be estate-tax implications, and the assets could be deemed to be in the beneficiary's estate."

In such cases, Goldenberg recommends imposing some restrictions, such as, "if they exercise that power, the successor trustee can't be someone who is 'related or subordinate' to the beneficiary. That's the test." "Related or subordinate" is a technical phrase defined in the tax code specifying that the successor can't be the beneficiary's spouse, parent, sibling, descendant, or employee. In addition, Goldenberg says, some people restrict selection of a successor trustee to someone sophisticated in the business world, whether a lawyer, money manager, investment banker, accountant, or executive of a business with a certain number of years of experience—so the beneficiary can't just appoint her best friend.

■ **Trustee governance.** Phoenix-based family business consultant Mike Cohn, who holds both CLU and ChFC designations and is a psychologist, believes it's critical to involve the next generation into the relationship with trustees. He points out, "You have a wealthy family whose lawyers say, 'You need to put your growth assets into generation-skipping or irrevocable trusts' and no one thinks much about it. Then death [of the parents/grantors] occurs. Suddenly, the assets are in entities with banks and trustees that are in charge of the beneficiaries' lives. The game changes because trustees have fiduciary responsibility to the beneficiaries, but not an emotional one. Disempowered beneficiaries may become angry at the trustee." Beneficiaries who have a bank telling them what they can spend and where they must invest funds are liable to feel impotent and angry.

Obviously, at certain ages we need trustees to handle money for our kids. But at some age they should be able to take care of themselves. Even if they have no financial abilities, they should be brought into the trust-management process to learn as much as they can. But Cohn points out that education about the trust alone won't alleviate all the beneficiaries' resentments over having to be subordinate to their trustee. "You can be informed, but if you don't have a voice, what's the point? And the bank trustee may not be motivated to listen to your input."

Thankfully, Cohn suggests another way. "What if you engage beneficiaries and design the trustee relationship so it meets parents' as well as next generation's goals on wealth and wealth management—through committees?" He refers to this as "trustee governance." Cohn explains that usually, beneficiaries have no legal voice. But he helps many of his clients create trustee investment, distribution, and charitable committees and has the beneficiaries participate in those committees. Beneficiaries can then have a vote on asset investment, mandatory and discretionary distribution, and charitable donations.

Estate planner Brodsky has seen such committees attached to trusts and agrees they can be helpful. "You can build that into a trust agreement," he says. "One of the benefits is that the beneficiaries, along with others, may get experience for some time period while they serve on the committee. Then the committee can go away and the beneficiary can take over." He has also seen committees comprised of some people in the family and some non-family members—which is no different than having an outside board member or advisory boards. The committee can "have an individual, such as a special business advisor or family business executive, whose role is to vote the securities in the family business but not make other investment decisions."

"All the sudden," adds Cohn, "the trustee is empowered more as an administrator, and decision making is pushed to committees and family members. The trustee is obligated to act at the direction of the committee. It's a cool way to get the family involved in estate planning so they don't all go nuts and sue each other."

He cautions that in many trust structures, certain members of the distribution committee should not be related or subordinate to the grantor. "There are certain rules you have to be careful about so you don't give too much power back to the grantors and wind up with assets back in their estate."

Cohn believes that involving beneficiaries on committees won't give them a total voice, but it does give them a forum for participating and building consensus.

When and How to Tell/Involve Beneficiaries

"When your children are married and have their own family, they may need to take action in their own estate plan to implement their goals and objectives," Goldenberg points out. "If they don't know the terms of trusts that name them as beneficiaries, they won't be able to make informed, wise decisions about their own children who may have different needs."

But when's the right time to tell them?

Half of the respondents to the U.S. Trust survey of people with $5 million in investable assets, 20 percent of whom had inherited their wealth, report that they have not communicated their estate plan to their children. Goldenberg notes that many parents think that if they "have incredibly mature, responsible kids, they can tell them at age 18. I think this is wrong because they haven't left home or experienced the world." When *is* a good time to spill the beans? "No earlier than their mid 20s; ideally after school or grad school."

There are as many risks in telling them as there are in not telling them, and parents need to consider the best time and amount of information to divulge based on the most important factor: who their children are. Of course, there's telling them, and then there's telling them specifics, points out Goldenberg. Based on their lifestyle, she says many children are likely to figure out the family has money and assume that eventually at least some of it will be theirs. Goldenberg recalls one client whose child told her friends, who then told everyone in school, that her parents' company sold for X million dollars. Some kids will come right out and ask, "are we rich?" or even "how much money do we have?" Even if you don't intend to make full disclosure to your kids, what should you do when they ask such questions?

She recommends telling children enough basic information to satisfy their curiosity and emphasizing to them that it's not appropriate to discuss such information with anyone outside the immediate family. "Also, parents may want to say we're fortunate because mommy and daddy have worked hard and done well. Or our family worked hard (if that's the case). You have to tailor the message to the circumstances."

Different states have laws that entitle beneficiaries, once they reach the legal age of majority, to see the trust agreement, the accounting, and their legal rights with respect to the trust. Many parents are not aware they are supposed to do so. Beneficiaries at that age are not likely to know they have such rights, so some parents who do know this law choose not to offer them such information. They may feel it's best not to disclose details, lest the information squash their children's motivation to study, complete college, and become productively employed, responsible, and independent. We do not suggest you break the law. One alternative is to set up a trust in a different state that gives you flexibility as to when to tell the children so that you can tell them when they are ready, not when the state mandates it.

Lowenhaupt disagrees. "It's always a mistake when parents don't disclose," he says. "Wealth secrets never work. They make the wealth too important or too unimportant. If you keep it a secret, the secret becomes the focus of attention, not the business aspects of the trust." He points out that if parents don't say anything about what's in the trust and it's a $600,000 trust, their children may think it's a $10 million trust—or vice versa.

Once the children know about the trust, says Brodsky, they can consult with the family advisors or attorneys who can explain the trust, what powers they may have over the trust, the legal implications of the trust, and under what circumstances they can exercise their rights and receive distributions. Children—at any age—are often more willing to listen to a third party than to their parents. In general, it's helpful to start educating kids in their mid-twenties about the basic concepts of trust planning and the reasons for trusts and prenuptial agreements. We will have much more to say in Chapter 8 about the best ways to communicate this information.

While both Brodsky and Goldenberg agree advisors can help explain some of the details, Goldenberg warns, "Parents need to control the process of disseminating the information, not the advisors, although they need to clear all this in advance with the advisors. Don't just set everyone loose. I've seen that, where the parents tell the kid to meet with the lawyer and accountant … it's a bad, bad idea. Parents should be there every step of the way."

She recalls one client who brought in her thirty-one-year-old daughter just before her wedding to have "the talk" and to reveal

TEACHABLE MOMENT

The time to bring up the topic of prenuptial agreements is before your child becomes involved in a serious relationship so he or she does not believe you dislike or distrust the romantic partner. It's best to discuss prenups with your children as soon as when they're in their early teens. You might want to wait for the subject of money or wealth or someone's recent marriage or divorce to come up to mention that, in families with some degree of wealth, it's necessary to tell an intended spouse that it's the family's custom to have a prenup.

TEACHABLE MOMENT

Ask beneficiaries to put in writing their understanding of what the trust money is to be used for. They should list what needs of theirs they think it will and will not fulfill. This way, parents can correct any misconceptions before the trust goes into effect, minimizing potential future conflicts between beneficiaries and trustees.

that she was the beneficiary of a $12 million trust. "She had no idea whatsoever. Her parents had never told her anything. She cried in my office because this knowledge was overwhelming to her. She knew her parents [had been] putting X dollars a month in her checking account and were paying her mortgage, but she was a responsible, productive person. She had her own small business. I think the family did a disservice to her. It was an emotional time, as she was getting married, and this added knowledge put her over the edge. It's better to let children know gradually, imparting some knowledge along the way, telling them there's money set aside for them."

Handing Over Trust Control

As with giving information, there's no one proper age when you should set up the trust to be controlled by your children. It's about maturity, and it's not easy to predict when they will acquire that maturity, as you create the trust.

If the parents placed assets in the trust from their annual exclusions, then the trust must, by law, distribute those assets to the beneficiaries once they reach the age of majority in their state. Lowenhaupt says parents usually want their children to put that money into a new trust. "It's not unusual for a father to take the kid out at age twenty-one to treat him or her to a few drinks and have him or her sign a new trust." With or without the parents using booze, he says his company has never had a case in its 100-year history where a twenty-one-year-old has refused to put assets back into trust.

Parents can then direct that trust to be managed by trustees until after the beneficiaries figure out what they want to do in life. What you disclose should be congruent with what your children need to know and not risk upsetting their life. When considering who should control the trust, think about whom you can trust. If parents put an outsider in control, they may be giving their children an unintended message that they do not trust the children, that they are not responsible enough to handle the money. At eight years old, that's just a plain fact. But what about at thirty? If they become trust-fund babies, they might be just fulfilling a prophecy the parents set up with an "untrust." In cases where the trust cannot allow you to put your kids in control in the long term because it would violate a tax provision, appointing someone else does not send this message.

"I know some kids who are ready for the world at twenty-four, others who don't get ready for the world until thirty-five or forty," Lowenhaupt says. "At the very least, I like to say my trustees can bring on my children when the trustees feel they are ready. But importantly, there is no formula to fit every trust. Trustees must be considered in the context of the trust's purposes."

Hughes recommends that grantors sit down before they make a tax move of any kind and ask themselves: Can I create a trust that's a gift of love? Can I create a trust that will enhance the life or lives of its beneficiaries? "If they can't answer those questions, they should not act. They should have a deep awareness of the consequences of their actions on the persons in the future. It's a courageous act to create a trust, not an act to save taxes. But that's not what's going on in many attorneys' offices."

Now that you've completed this chapter, we encourage you to go back to pages 39 and 40 at the beginning of this chapter and re-take the self-survey. Examine your original responses. Wherever you have revised your thinking, what are the implications for your estate and trust plans? This might be a good time to meet with your advisors to make any changes. Also, what changes might you make regarding what and how you communicate these issues with your children? This might also be a good time to hold a family meeting to start a conversation about wealth and your family.

3

Portfolio Management

N OW THAT WE HAVE considered your intergenerational equity goals (Chapter 1) and how to structure trusts that will help support those goals (Chapter 2), we will consider how to manage your portfolio so that your investments will achieve those goals.

This chapter is not meant as a primer on investing, but it will present concepts and approaches that you may want to consider and discuss with your investment advisors and/or managers.[1] Some high–net worth people possess the interest, education, and experience to oversee their own portfolios, from assessing risk tolerance to creating asset allocations, selecting actual securities and other investments, and tracking their returns. Others prefer to entrust all those decisions to investment professionals. Somewhere in the middle are individuals who essentially act as their own general contractors, finding and assessing the right blend of investment experts to create and manage different portions of their portfolio.

Wherever your comfort zone may be on this scale, understanding how best to manuever within the maze of the high–net worth

---

1. We define an investment manager as one whose role includes hands-on management of a portfolio, and an investment advisor as one who helps investors select and monitor managers for each portfolio.

investment world will enable you to work more effectively with
the people you hire to meet your personal and intergenerational
equity goals.

Self-Survey about Portfolio Management

First, here's a self-survey to help you assess any assumptions you
bring to this exploration. We encourage you to revisit this self-survey
after you read this chapter to identify areas where your thinking
may have changed and where and how you may want to adjust your
investment approach.

Self-Survey about Portfolio Management

1 = Strongly Agree, 2 = Agree, 3 = Neutral, 4 = Disagree, 5 = Strongly Disagree

BEFORE		AFTER
_____	I believe good asset allocation should include a wide variety of stocks, bonds, international, and alternative investments.	_____
_____	Although I know asset allocation is a good idea, I think it's best to invest in what I understand and in what I'm confident will give me the best return.	_____
_____	The least risky way to invest is to hire people I know as investment advisors.	_____
_____	It's important to do due diligence on managers and investment advisors and take emotions and feelings of friendship out of the equation.	_____
_____	It's best to structure each trust with its own separate asset allocation.	_____
_____	It's prudent to look at all trusts and assets as one family asset allocation.	_____
_____	Asset-allocation needs ought to be structured to support the family's consumption (living) expenses/distributions in a down market.	_____

Asset Allocation

"I don't jump immediately into pie charts when I work with new clients," says Holly Isdale, a tax attorney and managing director of Bessemer Trust in New York City. "I start with their goals and objectives: What do you have? How do you hold it? What do you want to do with it? It helps us unpack what the client needs to think about." Isdale goes over each investment entity the prospective client owns to get a sense of a client's risk before developing her investment policy statement.

If your investment manager or advisor does not do this with you, then you need to develop your own investment policy, which ideally should factor in your intergenerational goals as well as all the trusts your family holds, when they become available to beneficiaries, tax consequences, and so forth. Some people also include policies about whether or not to avoid "sin" stocks such as tobacco, alcohol, and firearms, or whether to focus on socially responsible investments. Risk tolerance needs to be included, such as the maximum amount to be invested in any one stock, manager, or asset allocation.

The stock-market meltdown in late 2008 reminded investors how impossible it is for any risk-management strategy or technique to protect one's portfolio perfectly from losses in any and all economic scenarios.

"The ground rules don't apply anymore," says Sara Hamilton, founder and CEO of the Family Office Exchange, a network of more than 500 wealthy families, family office members and advisory firms. "The framing principles we've been taught have let us down and don't seem to apply in this market environment. Investors are numb and frozen about what they've been through, angry about the fact that no one could see it coming, and are hesitant about what to do next."

James E. Hughes Jr., author of *Family Wealth—Keeping It in the Family* and *Family: The Compact Among Generations* (Bloomberg Press, 2004 and 2007, respectively), says the 2008 financial "blizzard" affected those clients who are primarily second-generation wealth owners and beyond differently than it affected first-generation wealth creators. "Their problem is to dynamically preserve the fortune. The blizzard has proven that almost no investment advisors who promised to dynamically preserve the fortunes of their clients have, in fact, done so." Hughes believes that many advisory institutions forgot that if the family members are not first-generation wealth creators, they may lack the skills to recreate their wealth, as entrepreneurs, professionals, and high-level corporate executives are better able to do.

It is not all the advisors' fault. Many investors spent their time looking at what their neighbor's portfolio was returning and searching for institutions that would provide them with that golden ticket. They did not stick to their investment policy or did not reallocate their investments. Instead, they invested in bond alternatives and other products that caused what Hughes calls "equity creep," which resulted in a riskier portfolio. Many investors shared an ill-fated belief that risk had been nearly eliminated and that one could not lose half or more of one's portfolio—that was a concern of the past, before asset allocation. Hughes told us "those in second and later generations of wealth would be very wise to learn the lessons—to ask their advisors to focus on dynamic preservation, which is entirely different than trying to make a fortune."

Isdale adds, "One bright spot to this market is that people understand there's a downside."

Many investment managers, trained in classical Capital Asset Pricing Model (CAPM) asset allocation techniques, also called Modern Portfolio Theory, which was developed in the 1950s by Harry Markowitz (for which he earned a Nobel Prize in 1990), will approach their clients' portfolios first by assessing their risk tolerance, then by divvying up the portfolio pie into assigned asset classes to reflect that risk level, and finally by plugging in specific investments for each class. In general, the higher the potential return an asset may produce in a given time period, the more risk that it may experience a lower, or even a negative, return in that period. It's all about the tradeoff between expected risks and expected rewards.

A middle-class young professional working couple with young children and a presumably long investment horizon may have a higher risk tolerance than a middle-class older, retired couple with grown children. The first couple's portfolio may be weighted heavily in riskier equities that are projected to enjoy long-term appreciation, while the second couple, no longer in their wealth-creation stage of life, may prefer higher income-producing assets. High–net worth investors at any age or stage of life may look at risk more as an endowment fund manager does. Wealthy investors and endowment funds generally need their assets to produce cash flow and moderate growth. Age may have more to do with the non-wealthy investors' choices about risk, while the wealthy will focus more on meeting intergenerational goals and current cash-flow needs.

Exhibit 3.1 depicts a fairly standard view of the risk associated with different asset classes.

Many of the Classical Asset Pricing Model (CAPM) assumptions— such as the absence of transaction costs, changes in inflation or interest rates, and the ability of any investor's securities transactions to affect the price of a security—happen to be false. However, experts justify basing their portfolio projections on such assumptions by pointing out that they have minimal impact on the model's

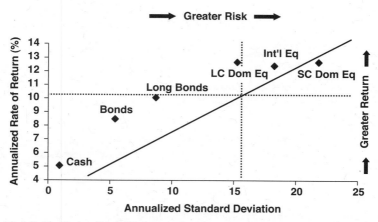

Exhibit 3.1 Risk/Return Relationship 25 Years Ending 12/31/2007

Source: Consulting Group at Morgan Stanley Smith Barney.

outcome and that omitting them allows portfolio managers to simplify their simulations.

For at least a decade (from mid-1998 through mid-2008), the average endowment managers have outperformed the stock market by 390 basis points (3.9 percentage points). In fact, as **Exhibit 3.2** shows, the Yale University endowment fund has beaten the S&P 500 benchmark by more than 1,340 basis points (13.4 percentage points)—which it achieved in no small part by moving significant assets into alternative investments.

Curiously, the Yale endowment fund reported that it had declined at about the same 25 percent as the S&P 500 in the second half of 2008.

Jeffrey E. Horvitz, vice chairman of Moreland Management Company in Beverly Farms, Massachusetts, believes that "asset allocation has not only outlived its welcome, it has become counterproductive. It gives people the misguided sense that all you have to do is follow these rules and it works out." His main complaint is that the way assets are typically classified incorrectly assigns assets with *similar* patterns of behavior to different asset classes. The entire

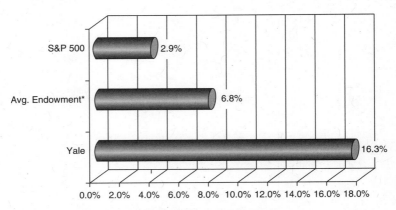

Exhibit 3.2   Endowment Returns June 30th, 1998–June 30, 2008

Sources: Based on 2008 NACUBO Endowment Study, © 2009 National Association of College and University Business Officers and The Yale Endowment Annual Report 2008.

point of asset allocation should be to create classes that behave quite *differently* from each other, so that when one asset class falls, another class may rise, thereby minimizing potential losses (the tradeoff is it will also minimize future potential gains). Horvitz explains, "Asset allocation gives people the illusion that somehow if you have mid-Cap and small-Cap stocks, you have two asset classes and you can diversify your risk, and if you rebalance somehow life gets better." The problem is that correlations between these two asset classes are extremely high. When one rises or falls, the other is likely to do the same, resulting in no risk protection.

In March 2009, Bank of America and Merrill Lynch put out an Investment Strategy Update that looks at the correlations of asset classes to the S&P 500 from 1995 to 2005. Correlations are not static, as many investors assume; they fluctuate—sometimes dramatically. In some market scenarios, asset allocation does its job and reduces volatility; at other times even assets like bonds, often thought to have little positive correlation with equities, can become highly correlated. Fixed-income substitutes, which some advisors suggest provide the same diversification benefits as corporate bonds but with higher returns, may correlate even more with equities than bonds themselves—the cause of equity creep. As Hughes explains, "There is not an alternative to bonds. Bonds are bonds, cash is cash. REITs are not bonds. There are other asset categories that might perform like bonds, but they have an equity correlation." Investors who were told otherwise paid a huge price when the market tanked in 2008. "The problem is, when you actually look at their actual asset allocation, it was actually 80/20, not 60/40," says Hughes.

If asset allocation is so problematic, then why even bother with the whole processes? Wouldn't it be easer to just plunk all of your wealth into an exchange-traded fund (ETF) such as iShares or S&P 500 Spyders, when the S&P 500 index has returned an average of about 10 percent from 1926 to 2007, instead of hiring an expensive investment managers and advisors who will design an asset allocation based on your risk profile? The answer is that you need cash flow. If you sell out of the market to meet your spending needs when stocks are down (as they are as we write this in early 2009), you will not likely end up with that 10 percent return over time that you need to create intergenerational equity. By selling part of your portfolio at the low end of the market, you would need your ETF to return an average of 12 to 13 percent over time to recover from what you sold. The volatility of the S&P 500 and its return over time cannot deliver the stability, safety, and cash flow you need to pay your bills. In other words, you need part of your portfolio to return to you what you will live on—your consumption spending needs, as some professionals will call it.

Therefore, to keep some of your portfolio safe, stable, and providing cash flow, you will need to purchase bonds, CDs, Treasuries, or some form of debt—the asset classes that produce cash flow. These investments will produce far less than the 10 percent S&P 500 over time. To offset this lower yet needed safer return, you need investments on the other side that will do better over time, which comes with some risk, to give you that average 10 percent return. That's why asset allocations are constructed to make the portfolio less volatile over time. Indeed, asset allocation strategies account for 91 percent of return variability, Roger G. Ibbotson and Paul D. Kaplan report in their article, "Does Asset Allocation Policy Explain 10, 90 or 100 Percent of Performance?" in the January/March 2000 *Financial Analyst Journal* (pages 26–33). Ibbotson and Kaplan found that security selection accounts for 5 percent, market timing 2 percent, and other factors 2 percent of the variability of returns.

The other question you might ask is why not just invest in bonds and be done? Why take the risk of the S&P 500 or even riskier assets such as hedge funds, private equity, or real estate? To find the answer, go back to your intergenerational equity calculations and put in zero for taxes and whatever you think you can get on a tax-free bond (probably 4 percent), and you'll see that after inflation, you can't get to an intergenerational equity return.

Asset allocation also helps save investors from the risks of basing investment decisions on emotions, which might tempt them to chase whatever securities are performing well at the moment, resulting in buying high and selling low. If an investor puts all of her assets in stocks and then when the stock market falls apart switches her entire portfolio into municipal bonds, she may find that municipalities may lose value just as equities start to rebound, and that she's in all the wrong asset classes at all the wrong times.

After a rebound period, she will also likely miss all or the majority of that rebound, as few investors ever get in at the bottom of the stock market. In fact, most often they miss most of the upside or even get in near the peak of an upswing. **Exhibit 3.3** shows that if you were not invested in the market and missed just the top ten up days between 1980 and 2008, your average return for the S&P 500 would fall from 11.8 percent to only 7.4 percent!

If, instead, she maintains an asset allocation in different classes, and she regularly rebalances to keep those allocations stable, when equities rise she will transfer some of her profits into classes that are currently performing poorly. When the stock market crashes, she will have other investments propping up her portfolio. If those things that held you up start to go bad, the stock market may start to improve.

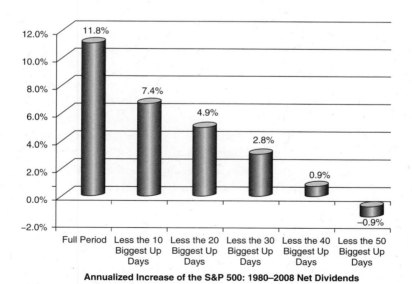

Annualized Increase of the S&P 500: 1980–2008 Net Dividends

Exhibit 3.3   Missing a Few of the Up Days

Source: Consulting Group at Morgan Stanley Smith Barney.

So instead of throwing out asset allocation altogether, tempted though some investors may be, Horvitz more or less turns it upside down. He says large-cap, small-cap, mid-cap, value, and growth stocks are not sufficiently different to comprise separate asset classes, "until you go to the extreme of the biggest five and smallest two companies traded anywhere. They might be sufficiently different." In some periods, real estate investment trusts (REITs) are highly correlated with stocks; in other periods they are more closely correlated with bonds or real estate. It's therefore crucial to consider the point in time you're planning to purchase such securities. He says asset classes must be seen in a context of how they change.

Doug Macauley, managing director of investment consulting at advisory firm Cambridge Associates, LLC, cautions, "There has been lots of press about hedge fund blow-ups and private equity calls. This [the financial crisis that began in late 2008] is essentially a credit and liquidity crisis, which doesn't mean the market has broken. It changes nothing in my view. From an asset allocation standpoint, since its first client, Cambridge Associates has believed in the model of broad diversification across all asset classes. It continues to believe this model holds true. All those assets offer diversification away from U.S. equities, and provide a better risk-reward profile."

Horvitz conceives of a portfolio as a large bucket of water, representing the entire value of his literally liquid available investment money. Then he imagines a set of glasses each of a different size, representing every possible asset class. The size of each glass represents the risk limit he is willing to commit to that asset class, which may be filled to the brim, empty, or partially filled at any given time. The idea is to "pick the most attractive glass first and fill it up, and then go to the next glass and fill that up, until you've used up all the water. Then periodically, you can pour water from one glass to another, but not so much that it spills over (in other words, that it exceeds your risk tolerance)."

Bessemer's Holly Isdale treats her clients' "core" investment needs differently from the remainder of their assets. For instance, she explains, "By the time a client is worth $30 million or $50 million, she has increased her lifestyle, but has also now achieved a substantial nest egg. She can put that to one side and still have $20 million to

$30 million to invest in a broader diversity of investments that might include private equity deals. At that point, she says, "the questions are more sophisticated: clients often create a core portfolio (sleep-at-night money) and opportunistic money (cocktail-chat money). But the core doesn't have to sit in muni bonds; it should be growing over time. So instead of looking at your portfolio as one bucket of money, maybe there should be three buckets: 'sleep at night,' 'core market beta,' and 'opportunistic.'"

Another option, instead of focusing on protecting your core, or corpus, is to think about how to protect your cash-flow/spending needs. If you're seventy years old and put all your assets into bonds, and you don't expect to leave anything behind, even in hyper-inflation you'll be okay. But if you're twenty-five years old and you expect to fund a certain segment of your future lifestyle, not to mention some degree of intergenerational equity, there's no growth factor in there. So rather than the first bucket being about protecting what you have, perhaps it should be about protecting your current cash-flow needs. And the second bucket can focus on creating some element of growth with stocks or ETFs. No matter what, says Isdale, the three buckets can include protection, growth beyond inflation, and opportunistic money.

While the core needs to be funded first, you need the opportunistic portfolio to bring your core up to the market. In theory you could just have core and get the same return as an ETF, which is the market. So when you're thinking of asset allocation and amount of safety you want, you have to decide how much growth you're willing to give up for safety and how much safety you're willing to give up for growth.

We must interrupt this discussion to make yet another plug for active wealth creation. Investing is a passive activity, unless you're in the investment business. Without some active, ongoing wealth creation in each generation, the family wealth will erode and eventually disappear as the family expands and the wealth disseminates among more and more members, even with the best asset allocations, an absence of extended bear markets, and the selection of the cream-of-the crop investment advisors and managers.

We have deliberately presented many different opinions in this section to expose you to a range of perspectives and provoke you to consider diverging approaches to investing and asset allocation. Additionally, some viewpoints may favor higher–net worth portfolios; for instance, some investment advisors and managers recommend that only families with upwards of $100 million take positions in private equity.

Asset Location

After exploring the pros and pitfalls of asset allocation, investors would be wise to consider asset location—which accounts and trusts will hold the various assets. The drivers of asset location decisions include the family members' ages, a variety of tax considerations, and cash-flow needs.

Traditional investment managers and advisors create an asset allocation for each trust a client has. One drawback to this method is that each individual trust may not meet the investment minimums that many of the better managers require.

Some advisors recommend creating investment entities, limited liability companies (LLCs), or corporations, where each trust can pool their investments in each asset to meet those minimums. They often solve the minimum problem, but when family members need or want to withdraw from a trust, these entities can create tax problems for many of the trust beneficiaries or cause the entity to fall under the minimum investment requirements. Cambridge Associates' Doug Macauley says, "This is a tricky issue. Most of our families are multi-trust, multi-generational. Each trust has a different term life, different beneficiaries and different goals." Before implementing an investment entity, it's wise to talk through such drawbacks with your accountant and lawyer.

Another way to look at asset location is to consider all the money in the family as one big pie and then do an asset allocation that factors in the risk of the family, as an endowment might do. When you get to location, consider tax ramifications, age, and cash-flow needs, and then place assets in the appropriate trusts with an eye toward balancing those issues.

For example, consider Bob, from Chapter 1. Say he has three sets of trusts: one set consists of three trusts, one for each of his three children. The second set consists of generation-skipping trusts (set up by Bob's father) that are outside his estate, which he can access during his life, with any leftover proceeds going to Bob's children. The third set of trusts is in his estate. When Bob created his asset allocation, he focused on all the assets in all the trusts from the intergenerational perspective of what would be best for the family as a unit.

When he purchased short-term, income-generating assets such as bonds, Bob recognized that he needs the cash flow but his children do not, so he placed those bonds in his own trusts. He consciously avoided placing any assets that were likely to appreciate in trusts in his estate, to avoid future estate taxes. (Bob wisely does not let tax issues drive his asset allocation decisions, but taxes do drive his asset location decisions.) He places any investments that are likely to produce long-term growth into his children's trusts.

The result of this asset location method is that each year the percent of the family's assets outside of Bob's estate grows. This works quite well, until the market experiences a six-sigma event,[2] which would disproportionately affect the assets in the trusts for Bob's children. To recoup such losses, Bob would have to put back $2 for every dollar those trusts lost because of gift taxes. But Bob is forty years old and still has a good twenty-five years left of productive earning, and his children are still young. Assuming the market will eventually rebound, those trusts are likely to still come out ahead of where they would be had he used a more traditional, trust-by-trust asset allocation and location.

Isdale raises another point about asset allocation and location: timing. She says, "Quants can create beautiful pie charts with asset allocations, but do we implement all those asset classes at the same time? For new wealth, usually we should start off being conservative and increase risk over time. I might not go into private equity funds now or funds that can have significant capital call requirements. So if my asset allocation shows $5 million should be devoted to private equity, I won't fill it all out today in secondary funds. I would

---

2. A six-sigma event is a price drop of six times the volatility (or standard deviations) of an asset.

UNINTENDED CONSEQUENCES

If a trustee were to look at your family's assets as one big allocation and then locate the assets, this may not be considered responsible from a fiduciary perspective. Depending on who the beneficiaries are, the laws surrounding the trust, the state in which you live, and the lawyer you consult, this asset location approach may not be suitable.

slice it differently and say, when will I move into that asset class? Otherwise, some people find the process so overwhelming. We'll fill that asset class out over a five-year period. It also makes it more understandable to clients."

Portfolio Manager and Advisor Selection

Choosing portfolio managers and advisors is as difficult as selecting stocks. Many investors find comfort in turning over their portfolio to a trusted friend, neighbor, relative, or golf partner who happens to be in the investment field—and many also feel an obligation to do so. You may believe that such people understand your values and goals, that only they truly have your family's best interest at heart, and that you are more comfortable sharing personal financial information with such people than with strangers. One problem with turning your fortune over to a personal friend or relative, however, is that if their performance is disappointing, it can be emotionally difficult to let them go. And perhaps it's actually better for your golf partner not to know your financial particulars.

Tom Rogerson, director of Bank of New York Mellon's Family Wealth Services in Boston, puts it this way: "If I've got a broker who's a brother-in-law, a neighbor who's a hedge fund manager, and a golfing buddy who does some other stuff ... I won't want to tell each one what the other has, because then they're going to fight over it. I'm going to keep it secret. It's amazing how often they don't know what their consolidated return is or their risk in terms of the portfolio, or taxes, because they have multiple advisors. We see that about 60 percent of the time. I'm also amazed at how often I find high–net worth people in this situation, who admit they have advisors they feel they've grown past and they don't know how to bring in a new relationship."

Just one name should make anyone shy away from entrusting your fortune to a "trusted" friend or personal colleague: Bernie Madoff. How many wealthy investors, some extremely sophisticated, based their decision to invest with elite investment manager Madoff on personal connections to him, or on recommendations of their friends or relatives who were connected to him, only to watch him abscond with $50 billion of his clients' money? Count Michael Sonnenfeldt among them. He's founder and CEO of Tiger 21, a network of peer-to-peer learning groups for more than 150 high–net worth investors. Sonnenfeldt invested with Madoff based on the recommendation of his father. "For a number of years Madoff was our number-one performer," he says. "Now I like to call it our number-one illusion." He did, however, resist temptation to increase his concentration in Madoff's fund. They benefited by exercising "discipline of limiting our exposure, so the loss was not devastating."

Horvitz says, "I can excuse people who invested with Madoff, but I can't excuse people who invested a huge percentage of money with him." That's because Horvitz believes that in addition to diversifying asset classes, it's crucial to diversify by having more than one manager within each class. He explains, "You never know where your risks will come from. The worst risks are those I can't imagine. No amount of due diligence will protect you." Therefore, limiting your exposure to any individual asset or manager will limit your risk.

Charlotte Beyer, founder and CEO of the Institute for Private Investors (IPI), which provides education and networking to 1,200 wealthy private investors and 200 professional firms, points out, "People who were just a little in denial and were drawn to it, were

UNINTENDED CONSEQUENCE

Splitting up managers can create extra costs, even if you can invest enough with each manager to meet their minimums. That's because it costs more to follow twenty managers than to follow ten.

essentially abdicating their own responsibility to do a minimum amount of due diligence and know what the questions should be. Instead they trusted someone who said, 'I have this fantastic investment, it returns this amount year in, year out. Everyone around this board room table are in it.' The whole exclusivity of 'I can get you in' made this a perfect stew of irresistible allure for some. But just as many members were throwing out red flags, saying, 'I couldn't get comfortable with this.' That was in a 2002 IPI discussion online."

Beyer says before engaging in due diligence concerning an investment manager or advisor, it pays to engage in some due diligence in oneself. Specifically, she recommends asking how much sophistication you have concerning investments and how much control you wish to exert. She suggests creating a grid to identify the quadrant where you belong, as illustrated in **Exhibit 3.4**.

Beyer explains, "If you're willing to go to a Wharton or Stanford investment program for five days and figure it out, you're clearly

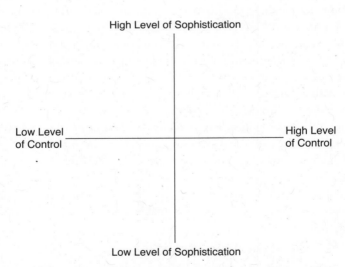

Exhibit 3.4   Quadrants of Control and Sophistication

Source: Charlotte B. Beyer, "Understanding Private Client Characteristics," ICFA Continuing Education, Investment Counsel For Private Clients, October 1992.

motivated. If you find reading the *Wall Street Journal* or listening to CNBC like drinking castor oil, then you're probably not interested. That creates a treacherous situation for a smooth salesman or charismatic advisor to convince you not to bother—'I'll take care of it.'"

Even if you possess a high degree of investment knowledge, you may not want to spend an equal amount of time searching for managers in each asset allocation class, suggests Sonnenfeldt of Tiger 21. He believes, "Within each major asset allocation, the range of performance between the very best managers and mediocre managers in that allocation can be very large or relatively small. As an example, the very best public equity managers tend to outperform the public equity average by only 1 or 2 percent over time, if at all. With bond managers it may be even less, relative to average bond returns. Therefore, you may want to accept an 'average' public equity manager or bond manager—or even better, just buy the relevant index. However, as but one example, the very best private equity managers can outperform the private equity average by 5 to 10 percent or more." So in Sonnenfeldt's opinion, it pays a lot more if you can find one of the best private equity managers.

What can you do if you are not interested in or sophisticated about investing and are about to inherit money? Beyer uses a medical metaphor, explaining, "I have a certain responsibility for my own body. I need to know what's good to eat and drink, how much I need to sleep and exercise, how often I should go to the doctor, what blood tests I need, and what they mean. I could choose to ignore that, gain forty pounds, take drugs to minimize the effects of that, or I can take responsibility without becoming a doctor. So a person has to get into it enough to pick the right team of advisors. If you pick an advisor who put all your money with Madoff, that was not a good decision." She recommends finding out the important questions to ask each advisor, comparing their answers, and checking references. You need to do your own due diligence as well. Don't rely on other people's due diligence. "There was such an enormous distraction, called the greatest global bull market," says IPI's Beyer. "We all were lulled to sleep by it. It's a classic behavioral finance thing. If Rich

Morris invested with Madoff and I know he does due diligence, then it must be safe." That may be a dangerous assumption.

Sonnenfeldt adds that there's no getting around taking an active interest and responsibility. "If you don't have a point of view, then you don't have a point of view about what your manager is doing and if it is consistent with your point of view. That takes a lot of work. It's not easy. I don't think most people who inherit money were trained to have a point of view, they were trained to rely on advisors. Mom and Dad said, 'these are our trusted advisors, if something happens to us, rely on them.' That's a recipe for disaster. At Tiger 21 we say you're not just a shareholder; you're the CEO of your own investment company and you need to hold everyone accountable, make sure you're keeping them aware that you're looking at what they're doing, and have them justify what they're doing in ways you can understand."

Among the considerations that Macauley evaluates when recommending investment managers for his wealthy clients are what he calls the five Ps: philosophy, process, people, performance, and price.

■ **Philosophy.** "If they say they're a small-cap value shop, do they show consistent holdings in small-cap value?" Macauley asks. Chemistry is very important. In other words, a firm's philosophy should match that of the client in terms of risk tolerance and level of aggressiveness. If a firm has a bit of value bias, and the client comes from a growth background, such as technology entrepreneurship, that may not be a great match.

■ **Process.** Is their process consistent with their philosophy? Some management firms look at companies by scanning every industry from the top down to find an industry first, then the best company in that industry. Others look at price-earnings ratios and then determine if a company meets other criteria in their "screen." In either case, if the manager finds a company that seems like a great investment but does not jibe with their firm's process, he should not invest in that company. However, one benefit of having multiple managers is that each may pick up promising investments that might not emerge through the others' approaches.

■ **People.** Is the investment firm's staff stable, with low turnover? Macauley also looks for managers who are highly incentivized. "We want organizations, to the extent possible, that are as independent as they can be found. Generally, those that are owned by huge insurance companies and investment banks may have good products, but their incentive structures may not always be good," he notes. Also, look at the depth and breadth of the firm's research efforts, staff knowledge, and global coverage. For example, we're in a global world now, and when looking at investments, you should not be U.S.-centric and just sprinkle in a few international equities. When looking at firms that invest in international or global stocks, ask whether they have offices in Asia and Europe and research teams to investigate overseas opportunities.

Chemistry is equally important. For instance, says Macauley, some families like to be spoken to directly and like to be told when the consultant disagrees, while others prefer to seek advice rather than to be told.

■ **Performance.** Macauley believes performance is not the top criterion for hiring an investment manager, although certainly if a manager has terrible long-term performance, he would not even be on his radar. Mostly, he's concerned that performance be consistent over time. For performance to be repeatable, the investment manager must have a competitive edge. For example, does the firm have the special ability to identify distressed securities in their niche? "Obviously any manager goes through cycle periods," says Macaulay. "That's understandable. But what's the source of their returns?" This would have been important to know if one had invested with Madoff. Many believe his volume was higher than the whole market at times.

■ **Price.** There is a wide range of fees across different types of products, says Macauley. "Pricing is all over the map with hedge funds and private equity, for a given level of expected alpha we're hoping to achieve." If you can get a 10 percent return after fees from manager A, who charges 1 percent; and a 10 percent return from manager B who charges 3 percent, that means manager B may have to take more risk to get that same return. If manager A has a 10 percent return with a 1 percent fee and manager B has 20 percent return with 3 percent fee, you may be willing to accept that higher fee.

Another criterion investors should weigh is bias. Every investment manager, advisor, firm, and institution has some degree of bias. IPI's Beyer says, "We are all, every last one of us, a product of our environment. We're all potted somewhere. We began as a little plant in a pot. You might have been potted as a trust and estate attorney, as an equity manager or analyst, a consultant in family dynamics, a CPA/tax advisor, or just an extraordinary people person who happened to land in financial service because it's so lucrative. Given that every advisor has biases and conflicts of interest, the big job is to name them and be aware that the transparency is more important than the fact that they have them [biases]. If I'm working at xyz firm and I say you should invest 60 percent in global and 40 percent in munis, that might be because I don't know about ETFs or gold or the shopping center down the street that might be a lucrative investment." If an advisor is honest about her biases, investors can be fairly comfortable and try to balance those biases with other advisors who have their own, but different, biases.

So, you may wonder, where are the authors "potted"? We believe that you need to take responsibility for yourself and the outcomes you wish to achieve. There is no guarantee of those outcomes, but at least you tried. Abdicating responsibility for the investment outcome to someone else is very risky. Even if you hate finance, we believe you should learn the basics and take control of your hiring decisions. We believe that your children also need to become their own general contractors, quarterbacks, or CEOs—however you want to frame it.

In many cases, you won't be selecting investment advisors and managers in a vacuum. You will likely need buy-in from relatives who may be co-beneficiaries of one or more trusts, trustees, or sit on a family office's investment committee or family foundation board. As a result, Family Office Exchange CEO Hamilton has watched a room filled with thirty-five family members while they discuss their portfolio objectives. "Any time you get a large group of people together in a room who share investment assets, there will be disagreement about investment performance. The disagreement centers on how they view risk taking and its impact on liquidity—their ability to spend money. Some in the room will think a particular investment advisor is doing a good job, and the rest will wonder if he's doing enough." She explains that the solution is not "to hire another portfolio manager, because then the other half of the family will think that one's not doing a good job." She says that one way to try to avoid locking horns is to "agree together how much risk we want to take for the return we want to get, and how much income we need. And of course they never agree because they tend to spend at different levels. They also need to reach consensus about their goals, including the investment goals." That dynamic can become exaggerated in an extreme market environment such as the one that began mid-2008. More than ever, Hamilton says, "consulting work is much more challenging because it brings that question to the forefront. Clients thought they were doing fine. What does fine mean anymore? Someone who lost 40 percent might think it's life-threatening; another might think that's a bummer but we'll survive. And if those two people are using the same portfolio manager, you've got trouble because they have different goals."

Sara Hamilton believes the definition of due diligence will change dramatically as a result of the 2008 market meltdown and the shockwaves from the Bernie Madoff scandal. "When the market started to melt down in October [2008], it was about the time we do our annual meeting for our 350 family members. We got thirty experienced advisors in the room together and asked them what will change about the definition of a trusted advisor in the future. Everyone in the room felt because of the trust issue and an inability to predict the markets, everything you were expecting of your advisor and how you viewed them was going to change."

Exhibit 3.5 maps out what those changes will be by type. Hamilton says it's about trust more than performance. One negative

Exhibit 3.5 Fall Forum 2008—Strategic Advisors Group Discussion

How do you think the client will define the role of the trusted advisor in the future?[3]

■ **Quality Advice.** This includes the advisors' ability to provide cross-discipline strategies, to customize solutions, and to re-evaluate conventional wisdom.

■ **Communications.** Solid people skills to understand clients and their needs; better interpersonal skills; being open, honest, and able to learn from events to be better prepared in future; greater ability/depth in counseling in family dynamics and family governance; understanding the goals and consequences of decisions (e.g., good decisions can lead to bad outcomes); educating clients about all the different roles their advisors play; and better information management and communication to clients.

■ **Collaboration with a team of advisors.** Providing a strong, diverse network to offer integrated advice/services; more of a team approach; more opinions; more checks and balances; a long-term partnership with the client; a commitment to be with clients through it all.

■ **Objectivity.** More independent, objective investment advice; pressure to educate clients on the outcomes of possible scenarios; more examination, evaluation, and documentation; pushing against conventional thinking; more creative thinking and scenario thinking.

■ **Risk Management.** A true focus on risk control/better understanding of risk; new definition of risk and clarity on what the client really has; better education of what risk means and how it is allocated in clients' portfolios; more scrutiny of underlying analytics.

- Going back to the fundamentals, understanding the plan with more specificity—more reviews of the plan—understand all the risk factors really well
- More explanation of what is being recommended and how it works
- More conversation/focus on exit strategies and their implications
- Being conversant in asset-protection strategies
- Strong plans/tactics in place for global events like 2008 in the future

Source: Excerpted with permission from the Family Office Exchange. For a full version go to http://www.foxexchange.com/.

---

3. Family Office Exchange Strategic Advisor Group Discussion Contributors: CTC Consulting, LLC; Deutsche Bank Private Wealth Management; Fiduciary Trust Company International; GenSpring Family Offices; HUB International Personal Insurance; Morgan Stanley Trust, NA; Nease, Lagana, Eden & Culley Inc.; Threshold Group; U.S. Trust, Bank of America; Wells Fargo Bank; Wilmington Family Office.

consequence, she says is that cautious, nervous investors "will move much more slowly, even when they shouldn't."

In addition to Macauley's five Ps (philosophy, process, people, performance, and price), many experts, such as Horvitz, say it's as important to diversify portfolio managers as it is portfolios. Although Sonnenfeldt did invest with Madoff, he at least limited his exposure by restricting the amount; you should likewise restrict your investments with any one manager to a small percentage of your assets.

The better financial institutions and independent investment advisors ensure that their clients' different managers truly invest in different securities and strategies to avoid overlap. However, many advisors and managers prefer that their clients entrust the lion's share of their assets with them.

Exhibit 3.6 illustrates that among IPI members surveyed, the larger an investor's net worth, the more investment managers they hire. While respondents employ a mean of fourteen managers, investors worth more than $200 million utilize an average of thirty-one managers, while those with less than $50 million work with an average of seven managers.

While 92 percent of the IPI respondents to the "Absolute Risk and Relative Return" survey in 2007 use benchmarks such as the S&P 500 for at least some of their managers, two-thirds hold all

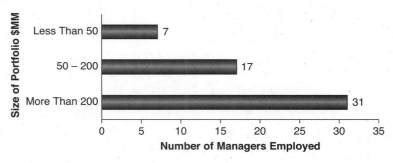

Exhibit 3.6   Multiple Managers

Source: "Absolute Risk and Relative Return," Institute for Private Investors member survey, Winter 2007.

of their managers to some benchmark. More than two-thirds also favor a longer-term time frame for evaluating their managers. Yet the high–net worth investors answered "yes" when asked if their commitment to the "long term" would change in the event of a big drawdown. The study conjectures, "Here again is an example of what happens when circumstances (read returns) change. Volatility (fear?) can override a longer-term perspective in the minds of many investors."

Some experts recommend encouraging, or even insisting that your portfolio managers meet one another and collaborate so that they can avoid overlapping investments in any one asset or security, thereby skewing your desired aggregate allocations and risk. If you offer an investment advisory firm half a billion dollars, and you're worth a billion, they'd say sure, but they'll charge you a fee for that, so you may end up with fees upon fees. Part of those fees would represent an actual expense they would incur, but part might be a tactic to encourage you to hand over that other half a billion for them to manage.

Sonnenfeldt believes that asking advisors and managers to collaborate would not be one of his highest-priority concerns. "If you're doing your job, you come up with an asset allocation strategy and if you want to hire managers, you identify who the managers for each allocation are, and depending on size of your portfolio, within each asset allocation, you may have a manager for each one. I'd instinctively have two or three private equity managers. Within an allocation, figuring out where there's overlap is reasonable. But that's the client's work."

Breaking Up Is Hard to Do

When is it best to take all your marbles to a new investment manager or advisor? A 2003 study, "Manager Firing and Hiring," conducted by Cambridge Associates, LLC, finds fault with the all-too-common approach to hiring and firing managers: firing those who have underperformed peers or the benchmark, hiring those who have outperformed both peers and the benchmark, and emphasizing the prior one-to-three years of performance. The study, which analyzed 92 Cambridge Associates clients since 1996, tracked the hiring and firing of an initial base in 1996 of 639 traditional marketable managers through March of 2003, and found a 61 percent attrition rate, with only 249 of the original managers in place in early 2003. That turnover proved costly, as hired managers substantially lagged the fired managers in the one- and three-year periods following the change. In fact, 80 percent of the fired managers outperformed the benchmark over the following three years. It is hard to escape the allure of recent performance though. Cambridge Associates notes that many investors feel pressured to consider managers with stellar recent records and any attempts to focus on longer-term results are often unavailing.

Macauley says that when the portfolio starts to degrade, he does not necessarily bail out. He just monitors the key factors he uses to select the manager to see what may have changed. In fact, sometimes his regular monitoring helps him see warning signs even before performance has slid. "Maybe people change or stop being value oriented, or the firm was bought out by a larger company that elected not to offer any retention incentives to key personnel. So we put them on an internal watch list. Any good consulting firm would track all those factors, not just say, is the manager producing 200 basis points above the benchmarks."

Exhibit 3.7 presents Cambridge Associates' guidelines for hiring and firing managers.

We hope this chapter has provided new ways for you to consider developing an investment policy, including: how you evaluate your risk-reward tolerance, the relative benefits and drawbacks of asset allocation, often-overlooked asset location factors, investment manager and advisor selection and firing. Before continuing, please turn back to the beginning of this chapter and take the self-survey once more. Again, consider any answers that have changed and the implications of those changes. We encourage you to discuss these self-surveys with your spouse, family members, and advisors and investment managers.

Exhibit 3.7 Manager Hiring and Firing Guidelines

BEFORE HIRING A MANAGER	BEFORE FIRING A MANAGER
■ Define objectives and success criteria.	■ Identify your real concerns.
■ Be clear about your tolerance for risk/volatility.	■ Compare the results against your criteria for success.
■ Meet the portfolio manager.	■ Understand risks that the manager is taking and compare them to what you expected.
■ Educate yourself about the managers' experience, skill sets and personal fit.	■ Compare your results against agreed benchmarks and peers of same style.
■ Understand the portfolio managers' competitive advantage.	
■ Understand their likely behavior in different market environments.	■ Look to see if there have been fundamental changes within the managers' team or firm.
■ Do not be influenced by good recent performance.	■ Be confident that you can select a replacement whose performance will cover the costs of change and outperform the current manager.
■ Be sure remuneration and rewards are designed for your benefit.	

Source: Copyright © 2008 Cambridge Associates LLC. Reproduced with permission.

SECTION II
Intellectual Choices

4

Financial Literacy

B Y ADDRESSING INTERGENERATIONAL equity, estate planning, and portfolio management in Section I, you have taken important steps toward getting your financial house in order, which is a necessary step in preparing your wealth for your family.

It's equally important to prepare your family for that wealth. An important part of that requires teaching kids the financial facts of life. Regardless of how sophisticated (or not) you as a parent are about personal finance and investing, you have a responsibility to prepare your children to live in our complex economic times.

Self-Survey about Financial Literacy

First let's assess the assumptions you are bringing to this discussion with your self-survey about teaching your children to be financially literate.

Self-Survey about Financial Literacy

1 = Strongly Agree, 2 = Agree, 3 = Neutral, 4 = Disagree, 5 = Strongly Disagree

BEFORE		AFTER
_____	Allowance is not necessary for high–net worth children.	_____
_____	I don't need to bother encouraging my children to get after-school or summer jobs.	_____

____   It's not necessary to force kids to live
within a budget when the family
does not have to do so.   ____

____   There's no purpose to encouraging my
children to save because they will inherit
enough money to cover their needs.   ____

____   My children do not need to learn
about investing because professional
advisors will be managing their
trusts and other family funds.   ____

____   I believe it's important for my children
to create their own wealth, regardless
of how much I may be able to and
choose to leave them.   ____

____   My children are savvy about and
responsible with money.   ____

____   My children would be financially
and emotionally prepared to survive
even in the unlikely event that the
family fortune were lost.   ____

____   I believe I set a pretty good example
for my kids when it comes to modeling
positive financial values.   ____

Financial ABCs

There are many books available to help parents teach the financial
basics to their children, including *Kids and Money: Giving Them the
Savvy to Succeed Financially,* by Jayne A. Pearl (Bloomberg Press,
1999). However, wealth can complicate parents' efforts to teach
their children about money, as the self-survey questions indicate.

Obviously, there's no one right answer for every wealthy family
in all circumstances. Some parents who run through the intergenerational equity calculations will be shocked to discover that they
will likely not be able to leave their children enough assets to replicate the family's current standard of living. In the financial chaos
that began in late 2008, many families who never questioned their
spending habits were shocked to watch the value of their portfolios

plummet along with the S&P 500's 38.49 percent drop that year. For the first time, many wealthy families began to worry about whether they, let alone their children, would be able to maintain their current lifestyle. One lesson has come into sharp focus: it's no longer a safe bet to assume anything. Therefore, it's wise to prepare ourselves and our children to survive and thrive under *any* financial circumstances. No matter how much money the family may have today, circumstances can change.

Even if the parents' calculations reveal that they should be able to leave their children enough assets to enjoy the same lifestyle, without proper preparation, what are the chances that the children will not fritter away the family funds? Most parents we know and have interviewed hope that the financial assets they have overseen will be a part of the legacy they leave to the next—and many future—generations. It's imperative that their children become good stewards of their wealth. Therefore, job one for parents is to teach their children how to survive and thrive in various financial circumstances.

A good place to start is by adopting healthy financial values and instilling those values in the next generation.

Financial Values

We have identified five financial values that parents may find very useful. **Exhibit 4.1** lists those financial values.

■ **Learn to handle "no."** This includes teaching children how to hear and accept "no" from parents; how children can learn to tell themselves "no," and how to say "no" to others. Do you find that you feel guilty when you say "no" to your children when they ask you to buy something? Many parents hate to deprive their children of things they want, especially when they know their children know they can afford to buy them pretty much anything, and when they know their children watch them spend liberally on their own material desires.

While it's important to pick your battles, parents must not take the easy way out by caving in to every whim their children may have.

Exhibit 4.1   Five Financial Values

Make sure your children learn to
- Handle hearing "no"
- Differentiate between wants and needs
- Tolerate delayed gratification
- Make tradeoffs
- Develop a healthy skepticism

Children desperately need to understand boundaries around their behavior and their expectations. When they never hear "no," they will bump up against the outside world's boundaries and encounter problems in relationships with friends, teachers, bosses, spouses, and eventually their own children.

Some parents feel guilty when you say "yes" when their children ask them to buy them things. Many parents also know that giving into their kids' every whim is indulging them and feeding their sense of entitlement. Also, they know that children are less likely to appreciate their possessions when everything is handed to them on a silver platter. More importantly, giving them everything robs their children of the pride and self-esteem people derive when they work hard to earn and save up for things they want.

"It is when riches go well beyond the point of comfortable subsistence and preoccupation with acquiring more persists that there can be some threats to mental health," writes Prof. Suniya Luthar, a psychologist and professor of education at Columbia Teachers[1] College, who has conducted a ten-year study on affluence and adolescents.

A 2007 study by Waterbury, Connecticut-based market research firm Harrison Group found that almost 75 percent of parents gave in when their kids nagged for new video games. Half of those parents caved within two weeks.

---

1. S. S. Luthar and C. Sexton, "The High Price of Affluence," in R. V. Kail (Ed.), *Advances in Child Development*, p. 144. (San Diego: Academic Press, 2005).

If your children are not accustomed to hearing the word "no," there may be an uncomfortable transition once you start strategically doing so. "Parents are suddenly saying 'no' and their kids are saying, 'What do you mean?'" Robert D. Manning, an economist at the Rochester Institute of Technology and author of *Credit Card Nation* told the *New York Times* in its October 10, 2008 article, "Frugal Teenager, Ready or Not."[2] "The sooner we have these conversations in the family and as a society," adds Dr. Manning, "the sooner we can focus on core values, and have a more realistic dialogue about the meaning of happiness and money."

It seems like a no-win situation. But there *is* a way out of this vicious cycle. Simply take yourself out of the equation by helping your children tell themselves "no." The more kids can decide that they can live without that brand or getting yet another toy, the less you will have to say "no." Later in this chapter, we will suggest specific ways you can help your kids learn to say "no" to themselves.

Children also must learn how to say "no" to others, including their friends, who may ask for loans if they know your children come from a wealthy family. When they get older, they will begin dealing with bankers, lawyers, accountants, investment advisors and managers, and even charitable organizations that may approach them with deals or schemes. They will need the common sense, good instincts, confidence, and fortitude to decline high-pressured come-ons.

■ **Learn to distinguish between wants and needs.** It's fine to want stuff. We all do. But it's important to know what essentials we need to survive (our "needs"). Everything else is "gravy." The line between discretionary goods (wants) and nondiscretionary things (needs) is often blurry. When large sums of money are involved, the line can barely seem discernable. For instance, in families with modest means, the majority of household spending consists of nondiscretionary goods and services (needs). The lion's share of the family's limited resources will have to cover a roof over the

---

2. http://www.nytimes.com/2008/10/12/fashion/sundaystyles/12teen.html (accessed July 31, 2009).

family's heads, food in their bellies, a few basic articles of clothing, medical care, and transportation. In contrast, wealthy families may have a harder time distinguishing whether or not the house constitutes a want or a need. Homes of the rich and famous are often so opulent that for the most part, their home (or homes) can be considered discretionary. Similarly, when transportation consists of a BMW versus the subway, one could argue that their car is more discretionary than not.

"Individuals will get some kind of high from an addictive behavior like shopping," writes Ruth Engs, EdD, a professor of applied health science at Indiana University, in an article on WebMD.com, "Shopping Spree, or Addiction?"[3] "Meaning that endorphins and dopamine, naturally occurring opiate receptor sites in the brain, get switched on, and the person feels good, and if it feels good they are more likely to do it— it's reinforced."

Distinguishing between wants and needs gets down to personal values. Again, there's nothing wrong with purchasing luxury items you can afford, but it's very important that you and your children understand the difference between wants and needs.

This is a great conversation to have with your kids. Here are some questions you may want to ask them:

- Is a BMW a want or a need?
- Is our 10,000-square-foot home, with all its expensive furnishings, a want or a need?
- Are our designer clothes and latest electronic gizmos wants or needs?
- When is it fine and appropriate for our family to spend on luxuries, and when might it be okay, or even better, to choose less expensive items?
- Do we choose to buy luxury items based on quality (some higher-priced goods last longer or perform better) or a desire to impress and keep up with our friends?

---

3. http://www.webmd.com/mental-health/features/shopping-spree-addiction (accessed July 31, 2009).

■ What would it be like to wear a $16 pair of jeans from the GAP instead of the $500 pair you may own?

■ What are some categories of purchases for which we would not mind spending much less, and why? Why should we think about spending less when we can afford the more expensive things?

As we'll see in the section on instilling financial values, these issues relate to how much intergenerational equity you plan to leave to your children. If your children consider everything as a need, and you don't plan to provide them enough money to support those "needs" when they're adults, they will likely be ill-equipped to live within their means, and may become depressed or frustrated by a life that does not fulfill what they perceive to be the "needs" of life. They will also likely spend out of control to fill some desire that money can't truly buy. Even if we were to count the value of such luxury versions of necessities in the "needs" column, affluent households' spending would generally consist mostly of discretionary goods and services (wants).

■ **Learn to tolerate delayed gratification.** We all need to develop this, if the current credit card debt in our country is any indication. Kids especially need to be able to leave a store without buying something, if only to check out prices at other stores.

In the 1960s, Stanford University researchers studied a preschool class of four-year-olds, and followed up when they were teens. The researchers put them alone in a room with a marshmallow and told them they could either eat one now or wait and receive a second marshmallow a little while later. One-third of the class was able to wait fifteen to twenty minutes for the second marshmallow. By the time they were eighteen, students who could not wait had a significantly higher incidence of dropping out of high school, problems with the law, alcohol and drug abuse, and teen pregnancy. They also scored about 200 points lower on SAT tests and were less emotionally stable than those who could wait.[4]

---

4. Daniel Goleman, *Emotional Intelligence: Why It Can Matter More Than IQ.* (New York: Bantam Books, 1995). There are several more recent re-enactments of the marshmallow test on youtube, such as http://www.youtube.com/watch?v=amsqeYOk–w&NR=1.

Are kids born with this skill, or can parents teach it to their children? Dr. Istar Schwager, a New York educational psychologist, says it's a little bit of both: "Some children by nature are more patient than others. But it can be learned."

■ **Learn to make tradeoffs.** Children need to understand that money is a limited resource, no matter how wealthy the family might be. Teaching them that they can have some things, but not everything—even if the parents can afford pretty much everything—helps them understand and accept limits to their material appetite. Children who do not learn to make tradeoffs are likely to become uncontrolled in other aspects of their lives, whether it be eating, alcohol consumption or drug use, or even seemingly innocuous obsessions such as videogame playing.

Children who cannot accept limits are likely to develop an exaggerated sense of entitlement, which is more than just an unpleasant personality trait. Entitlement gets in the way of developing healthy relationships with friends and, eventually, their mate.

■ **Develop a healthy skepticism.** Kids are besieged with ads and come-ons almost every waking moment. They need to learn not to believe everything they see and hear. The more our children are exposed to ads that feed their desires, the more they will develop an appetite for material goods. Ads don't just hurt our wallets; they also hurt children's ability to be happy and emotionally healthy. Ads entice our children to smoke, drink alcohol, and eat unhealthful food, and try to convince them that the right clothes, toys, and food will make them popular or happy. Ads breed insecurity, not to mention lethargy and obesity. Take, for instance, the recent craze to turn our teeth unnaturally white. With so many people buying tooth-bleaching products or having their dentists give them expensive whitening treatments, those with natural off-white colored teeth look unhealthy or dirty in comparison. Watch enough ads without the proper skepticism and your self-image and self-esteem may suffer.

Children are exposed to an average of 40,000 television commercials each year according to Dr. Victor Strasburger, professor of pediatrics and author of a December 2006 report, "Children, Adolescents and Advertising," for the American Academy of Pediatrics. And that figure does not include the barrage of advertisements shot at them in other media, including radio, the Internet, billboards, mass transit, logos on clothes and sporting events, and product placements in movies, television shows, and even textbooks. Sweden and Norway have banned television commercials directed at children under twelve, based on research studies indicating that young children cannot distinguish between the program they are watching and the commercials. Such a ban is not likely to happen in the United States, but parents can certainly limit how many ads their children are exposed to by reducing the time they spend watching television or surfing the Internet. Later in this chapter we'll suggest ways to help them develop a healthy skepticism about the ads they do watch.

In addition, as mentioned earlier, kids must be prepared to deal with unscrupulous people eager to take advantage of them. But, warns Sara Hamilton, CEO and founder of the Family Office Exchange, too much skepticism can also be dangerous, especially in adult children who have inherited their wealth and do not work. "Often, healthy skepticism in people who don't have a working career turns into second guessing if you're not careful. Asking probing questions is good risk analysis to check if we have thought of everything we should have. If there has been no business context, that second-guessing becomes totally ineffective. I think it's hurt more families than helped them. The core issue is whom you should trust, and whether you have the ability to take sound advice from your advisors."

Imparting Financial Values

Helping your kids learn the five financial values described above will likely get them on a cycle of success. **Exhibit 4.2** presents techniques that will help you impart these important values.

■ **Allowance/budgets.** Many wealthy parents don't see the value of giving their children allowance because they take care of all their

Exhibit 4.2   Tools for Imparting Financial Values

VALUE	TECHNIQUES
Tell themselves "no"	Allowance: based on financial responsibilities Spending policy: who pays for what
Differentiate between wants and needs	Budgeting: how they afford what they pay for Jobs Modeling and talking about wants versus needs
Tolerate delayed gratification	Saving: setting goals, offering incentives
Make tradeoffs	Investing Experiencing a bit of discomfort
Develop a healthy skepticism	Watch television/commercials together Charitable giving

kids' expenses. In the 2007 American Express Platinum Luxury Survey (of 1,100 U.S. parents with an average net worth of $4.3 million), about half of the respondents' children receive allowance.

But allowance can be a useful tool for helping children learn how to tell themselves "no" to every whim. When parents base allowance on clearly defined expectations about what they can and cannot use it to buy (in other words, when it's tied to a budget), children will also learn the important value of differentiating between wants and needs. This list should include discretionary items (wants) and non-discretionary things (needs). Once you determine what's on that list, they will take over responsibility for taking care of those expenses. The idea is that they learn how to stretch out a finite amount of money to cover very specific expenses, and then you need to stop paying for those things.

Some affluent parents give their children an extravagant sum to spend however they wish, or just drop them off at the mall and hand them a credit card on weekends without any spending limits. That

TEACHABLE MOMENTS

Imparting financial literacy and values to children is not a one-time event, say Sara Hamilton, founder and CEO of Family Office Exchange (FOX), and Joline Godfrey, founder and CEO of Independent Means Inc. (a provider of financial education products and programs) in their 2007 white paper, "Responsibilities of Ownership":

"Distinguished from the conventional 'water hose approach' to education, in which a young person, on coming of age, is sent to the trust officer to receive instruction, the drip, drip, drip method utilizes a carefully designed education plan employing family members, nannies, mentors, advisors and family office staff members in the education of children."

This "drip, drip, drip" method includes:

■ family talk (in a plane, car or over dinner);

■ family traditions (such as retreats, meetings, foundations, gifts, and benefits);

■ family mentoring (by aunts, uncles, professionals and friends); and

■ education programs (financial camps, tip sheets, newsletters, e-mails, activities, products, nanny training, family coaching).

may solve the problem of arguing with your children about whether or not they can get whatever they ask for, but it does not help them appreciate the value of money, understand reasonable limits, or learn to be cautious and smart about spending.

Helping your kids to be frugal is important no matter how much money you have. Giving kids an allowance—whether $20, $500 or more a week—with no rules about what it's for just teaches them to spend without thinking. Instead of teaching important financial values, it will likely reinforce a constant desire for conspicuous consumption. It may help to base allowance on your values and your calculations and conclusions about intergenerational equity, discussed in Chapter 1. Design allowance and experiences that will teach your kid what you want them to learn. For a grade-school child, you can include school lunches, videogames, and DVDs, and

TEACHABLE MOMENT

The best way to teach kids to be frugal is to model frugal behavior. Many wealthy parents may not be willing to rein in their own spending. However, giving children less allowance than their peers receive challenges them to choose doing without some things their friends have or earn money to pay for things they want.

perhaps sports fees. For teens you can factor in daily, weekly, and monthly expenses such as toiletries, haircuts, music lessons, and entertainment (a weekly movie and snack, for instance).

Think about allowance in terms of your children's futures, not the environment in which they live today. For instance, if you expect your children to work after college and want their entry-level salary to cover most of their living expenses, it may be a mistake to give your high school or college children a huge allowance that may provide them a lifestyle that is more extravagant than their first job will enable them to replicate. They will likely have a hard time reining in their spending and living within a budget once their smaller income must cover their expenses, both discretionary and nondiscretionary.

If you've set up trusts to cover most of their living expenses when they turn twenty-one, the amount they earn from their job may seem trivial and make them feel working is pointless, which can squash their ambition. As we'll see in the section about jobs, having a sense of confidence and meaning in life very much depends on being able to be productive at work.

UNINTENDED CONSEQUENCES

Giving your kids an allowance to spend money however they want instead of tying it to some financial responsibility, to pay for some needs, not just wants, may backfire in terms of teaching them how a budget works. When children only need to choose between, say, a pair of $500 jeans one month and going to five rock concerts, they are not learning how to make trade-offs between wants and needs. If there is no pain, there will likely be no gain.

We don't wish to judge how much is too much. But it's important to be thoughtful about your decisions about what allowance you give your kids and what it is to be spent on if the lesson of budgeting and spending limits is to be learned.

■ **Spending policies.** Children who do not understand, let alone appreciate, what material goods cost will have no appreciation for setting limits on their spending. That's why it's important to base allowance on a set of age-appropriate expenses they will now have to pay for. As they get older and better at making allowance last the full week without blowing it on whimsical things outside that budget, you can give them a raise in their allowance. With that raise, though, should come an increase in their own financial responsibilities, for purchasing items you now pay for directly.

When you stop purchasing everything for your children, suddenly they are forced to evaluate whether or not they truly need or even want some things they now take for granted. For instance, one teen felt that even if last year's winter coat was still in style, still fit and was still in good condition, she "needed" a new one. Once her parents gave her a clothing budget and left her in charge of buying all her clothes, suddenly she started noticing the price tag for coats. She realized that maybe she really didn't need a new coat that year, which would enable her to buy other items that caught her eye.

Some teens or adult children have no concept of how much they are spending each year. *New York* magazine's May 2008 article, "Rich Kid Syndrome" relates an extreme case of a twenty-something, nonworking daughter who was spending more than $1 million a year and never saw the bills. She was the daughter of a client of Steve Barimo, CFO of GenSpring Family Offices, who explains, "Our response was, let's first tell her that that's going to be her budget for the next year—$1 million. Let's put it in her account, and let's make her get her own credit card, and let's make sure she lives within that amount for the next 12 months." He says that if her parents had forced her to live with an arbitrarily lower number, most likely "she'd have blown through the money, and she wouldn't have learned anything. The first step, at least, was about taking ownership over the money she's already spending."

■ **Jobs.** Working provides many benefits. Being productive feels, well, good. It provides a compass, helps develop relationships with different types of people outside the adult children's perhaps more insulated high–net worth environment, and instills a dose of humility as they make mistakes or learn how to deal with difficult bosses or co-workers. Another key advantage to kids working is that it enables another generation to become wealth creators, which (as mentioned in Chapters 1 and 3) is a critical factor in whether that wealth will continue on as a legacy in future generations.

Harvard psychiatrist George Vaillant tracked 456 underprivileged, inner-city males from ages fourteen to forty-seven.[5] He found that the "capacity to work" during their youth predicted their future earnings, mental health, and ability to sustain relationships as adults. The men in the study who had been deemed competent and industrious at age fourteen were twice as likely to have warm relationships with a variety of people, were five times more likely to be well paid for their work as adults, and were sixteen times less likely to have suffered prolonged periods of unemployment.[6]

While Dr. Vaillant's study focused on underprivileged children, his findings about the importance of the capacity to work transcend class. The problem for the over-privileged class is how parents can instill a work ethic in their children, when they may have enough money so that they don't or won't have to work. PNC Wealth Management's 2007 survey "Growing Up Wealthy" polled 210 wealthy teens and 272 affluent parents. The study found that while 90 percent of wealthy parents believe their children should learn the value of money through hard work, only 63 percent of the teen respondents hold a full- or part-time job. Eighty-nine percent of

5. George E. Vaillant and Caroline O. Vaillant, *The American Journal of Psychiatry,* Vol 138(11), Nov 1981, 1433–1440.

6. http://www.nytimes.com/1981/11/10/science/work-habits-in-childhood-found-to-predict-adult-well-being.html (accessed 10/8/2009).

the teens said their priorities for having a "perfect life as an adult" include "having a high-paying job," although nearly half expect to have a tougher time making it financially than their parents did. In Chapter 6 we will explore more about why jobs are so important for the mental health and well-being of adults. Encouraging your kids to get a job early helps to establish this important part of their future.

Parents who feel strongly that their children should earn their own way can set up their allowance and structure their trusts and estate plans in ways that will make it difficult, if not impossible, for their children *not* to work. For instance, giving them too much information too early about their future inheritance may make them lose their ambition to work. They may realize, "I can make $100,000 a year by passive investing. Why work for only $50,000 a year at a job after college?" Knowing how much money one has can suck the ambition out of doing what one wants to do for life's enjoyment.

Troy Dunn, who sold his company, BigHugs.com, for many millions of dollars in 2002, does not give his seven children, ages three to sixteen, an allowance. Instead, when they want money to buy things for themselves, all (but the youngest one) have to earn it by starting and running their own businesses, which include making cookies, picking up pine-cones, and a video production service. Multi-billionaire Donald Trump had his son, Donald Jr., then thirteen, earn minimum wage plus tips during the summer at the Trump Castle marina.[7] He and his siblings were only hired at the Trump Organization full-time after earning business degrees. Holly Peterson, daughter of Pete Peterson, co-founder of venture capital firm Blackstone Group, says she had no choice but to work. When she earned $32,000 a year as a researcher at ABC News, her father gave her $600 a month, the difference between a studio walk-up and a safer apartment with a doorman.[8]

While they want their children to hold productive positions in the work world, some wealthy parents believe that one of the benefits of coming from a wealthy family is that they should at least be able

---

7. http://nymag.com/nymetro/news/people/features/10610/index1.html (accessed 10/8/2009).

8. http://nymag.com/news/features/42595/index4.html (accessed 10/8/2009).

to pursue their passions, whether that means a career in the arts or becoming a teacher or social worker. If, as a result, their earning potential is very low, many such parents are happy to supplement their earnings so they can lead more comfortable lifestyles than their salary alone would permit.

Tom Bloch came to this realization in his early forties. He had always expected to work for H&R Block. His own father had gotten him hooked on the family business by taking Tom on business trips starting at age four. By age seven, he wrote, "When I grow up I want to be an income tax man." After earning a degree in economics in 1976, he had no problem starting at an entry-level position and worked his way up to CEO by 1992. However, as the position became more and more consuming and negatively affected his family life, he left the job in 1995 to become an inner-city math teacher. With his savings, he could clearly afford the cut in pay from nearly $1 million a year (including bonus) to $20,000. Then, in 2000, he opened University Academy, a tuition-free charter school. By doing so, he sent an important message to his sons, Jason and Teddy, now ages twenty-four and twenty-one. Bloch, author of *Stand for the Best* (San Francisco: Jossey-Bass/Wiley, 2008), says, "The message my decision gave my sons was that it's important to find your calling, to follow your heart and to do something to repair the world."

Jason, after a year and a half out of college, decided to follow his father's early footsteps and is currently a district manager for H&R Block in Portland, Maine. Son Teddy, a senior at Princeton with a passion for sports, hopes to pursue a career in sports journalism or sports management. Although his sons' trust funds could allow them to live comfortably without working at all, Bloch says he believes the example he and his wife have set, and the conversations about wealth, work, and happiness they have had throughout their sons' lives, contribute to his children's work ethic and sense of balance.

■ **Saving.** Why should wealthy children be encouraged to save when they can probably wrangle anything they want from their parents?

Saving has many benefits, not the least of which is the pride and joy of accomplishing something one values. For instance, if your eight-year-old son develops a passion for skiing, he will enjoy that class ski trip far more if he saves up for some or all of it himself. After your daughter graduates college and gets her first job, letting her save up to furnish her first apartment piece by piece, month by month, will have more meaning than sending over your interior designer with an unlimited budget.

The key is to harness your children's passions to motivate them, and then to help them set goals based on those passions and strategize how to meet those goals. You can certainly offer some financial incentives—such as a challenge grant (they save up some percent of the cost and you will kick in the rest) or a 401(k)-type matching program (for every dollar they save, you will set aside the same amount).

Many of us can remember, with a nostalgic glint in our eyes, some struggles we may have endured to accomplish something that was important to us. No matter how much we may enjoy sipping piña coladas on some Caribbean beach, we take pride in and remember fondly some of our toughest times: having hitchhiked through Europe on a shoestring budget or having launched a business and worked day and night until it broke even and then provided a fortune. When we indulge our children with every material comfort and every high-tech toy, we essentially rob them of such experiences as well as the pride and self-esteem they can derive by working hard to accomplish or earn things on their own.

■ **Investing.** With the stakes so high in wealthy families, parents would be wise to prepare children to invest and develop healthy spending and saving patterns early, and to become comfortable and conversant in the world of investing. It's important to offer children the opportunity to practice investing and handling money early so they can make and learn from their mistakes early, before they inherit significant wealth.

Investing is a complicated and sophisticated art that requires years of education, experience, and making mistakes to get it right. Start young and provide the chance for mistakes. Hope they make mistakes—as that is how they will learn—while the stakes are not very high.

Set aside real money for them to invest. It should be large enough to feel significant and challenging to them, whether they lose it or make great gains. It should not be large enough to risk a significant portion of the family's assets or lead them to believe they do not need to get a job or work. Let them make investment decisions on their own and suffer the positive or negative consequences over years of time.

Some families expose their children, beginning in their teens, to their financial advisors, to listen and learn the ropes of investing; other parents bring their children to meetings with various advisors. Doug Macauley, managing director of investment consulting at advisory firm Cambridge Associates, says there's not enough tagging along. "We get asked this question, 'at what point should I start involving my children in this process?' It's challenging because some families don't want their kids to know [specifics about their wealth] to keep them incentivized. But generally, families that waited too long hurt themselves, as opposed to those who started too early … maybe it's best to err on side of a little too early."

He says one client trickled down some assets to the children when they were in their teens as a test, to see what they do. They monitored the children. One handled the money conservatively; the other went in the other direction. Macauley explains, "It gave the parents a window into how the children think, and insight into how and what they need to do to educate them—seeing where the problems were and addressing them. They brought in outside people to counsel them." He says it's better to make mistakes early, than waiting until they each inherit substantial wealth.

In Chapter 5 we will expand on techniques for introducing kids to real-world investing, including involving children in family foundation management.

■ **TV time together.** Most parenting experts believe that children watch way too much television. But there may be some value when parents watch a bit of TV with their children, from very young ages all the way through their teen years, so they can have some fun while opening their kids' eyes to some of the most manipulative commercials. Think of it as a vaccine that gives children a little bit of the disease so that they can build up immunity. For instance, challenge your children to spot deceptive ad techniques such as fast talk, small type, and camera special effects. Explain that the point of the commercial is to make you want to buy the product whether or not you need it or want it. Ask them if they think that toy is as easy to use or as big or as much fun as the commercial makes it seem. Ask how they feel about advertisers who try to trick them with such gimmicks? Share memories about times when you saw a product advertised, bought it, and ended up disappointed that it was not as good as the commercial made it seem. Ask if products they've used are really as terrific as they looked in the commercials and how they feel when they've bought something that didn't measure up. Did it seem bigger, higher quality or easier to use on television? When an ad implies that buying a particular product will make them popular, do they think that message is really true? If they wear the most fashionable clothes, if their breath smells minty enough, or they possess every latest fad, are they more likely to find love? As ridiculous as it sounds to say, that's exactly what commercials do—they try to make us feel insecure about ourselves and convince us that if we buy their products we'll find true happiness.

■ **Charitable giving.** Family philanthropy is a fabulous way to help kids develop compassion for others, learn about the world outside their privileged bubble, acquire practical financial skills as they research charitable organizations, and become involved in how family foundation funds are invested and distributed. We discuss this in much greater detail in the next chapter.

Financial Boot Camp for Teens

Many private wealth management firms, trust companies, bank wealth departments, multi-family offices, and other financial institutions offer financial education classes and seminars, also known as boot camps, for the children of their high–net worth clients. These boot camps are designed to help children learn how to manage and invest the money they are destined to inherit. Many of the programs are free, as their sponsors hope to snag business in the future from another generation. While the best ones don't actually include sales pitches, some classes are taught by sponsoring company executives who may describe the benefits of their products and services.

Some high–net worth people question whether such "rich camps" reinforce a sense of entitlement among attendees, or whether the purveyors of these classes are just preying on wealthy parents' concerns and fears in an effort to pry some of their money from them. Some such financial camps teach valuable lessons, but just as no amount of brilliant estate planning or investing acumen will supplant active and thoughtful involvement and guidance from parents, no amount of high-priced financial literacy classes can compensate for what only parents can and should provide: modeling and communicating solid financial values for their children.

In 2007, reporter Frank Rich attended IFF Advisors' three-day Financial and Life Skills Retreat at the University of California-Irvine's Paul Merage School of Business. The syllabus included managing credit, debt, and cash flow; managing an investment portfolio; protecting wealth and managing risks; understanding property and marital rights; enhancing interviewing skills; learning negotiating skills; improving leadership and communication skills; and understanding the psychology of money.

In his *Wall Street Journal* article, "Richie Rich 101: More and More Camps Are Teaching Trust-Fund Kids to Handle the Wealth Headed Their Way," Rich realized that many of the eighteen- to thirty-five-year-old über-affluent attendees (of which there were about twenty) lacked important skills to enhance their wealth or land a top job. "Raised in a bubble of privilege and insulated from the competitive pressures of the everyday world, many tend to have low self-confidence, little drive and few of the necessary tools to succeed in today's global economy," says Rich who is also author of *Richistan: A Journey Through the American Wealth Boom and the Lives of the New Rich* (New York: Three Rivers Press, 2008). In fact, few of the teens understood the difference between a stock and a mutual fund. He concludes, "These kids wouldn't be tomorrow's chief executives and billionaire entrepreneurs. Most would probably drift through life spending their parents' money and hoping it would last. Tomorrow's economic superstars will more likely come from the striving middle class, just as they have for much of American history."

When used as one piece of ammunition in a family's arsenal of financial parenting, some such boot camps may be a good place to fill in some gaps in the parents' own knowledge or comfort zone. Still, it pays to check out a few providers to make sure you know what you're getting. For instance, New York wealth advisor Kathryn McCarthy recommends that the speakers should not all be from the sponsoring organization, that program materials should be more than company brochures, and that programs should meet more than once, as they enable participants to build on their knowledge. It always pays to ask for references of parents who sent their children who attended before to ask how well the program was run and what their children learned.

It's time now to return to the beginning of this chapter to take another stab at the self-survey about financial literacy. Again, note any areas where your beliefs and feelings have changed. Consider discussing ways to improve your children's financial savvy with your spouse, advisors, and children.

In the next chapter, we'll explore how your children and family can apply many of the new fiscal skills you have been imparting in your children by involving them in stock market simulation games, family philanthropy, and business and financial advisory meetings.

5

Skills and Experience

IN THE LAST CHAPTER we started down the path of financial literacy—giving children the framework and foundation for learning about finance. As important as it is to talk to your kids about financial values and teach them the basics of financial management, at least some such discussions are bound to go in one ear and out the other unless their learning includes plenty of hands-on experience. People—children as well as adults—require many forms of education, including experiential learning, to develop the skills for managing the high-net worth financial world.

Professor David A. Kolb and colleague Roger Fry have developed a model that explains why experiential learning has such great value. The elements of their model consist of concrete experience, observation and reflection, the formation of abstract concepts, and testing in new situations. These elements will enable your children to evaluate new situations and test them against experiences they have encountered in the past. This skill set is especially important when it comes to navigating the fast-changing financial world.

This chapter will present several ways to involve your children in first-hand learning experiences. We will suggest simple ideas for connecting with your children to bring up issues; activities that expose them to your real-life financial and business activities; games that simulate business, investing, and personal financial management;

and opportunities to include them directly in family philanthropy and investing using relatively modest amounts of money.

Of course, you don't need to do every activity we present. However, as we noted in the previous chapter, financial education has to be consistent and ongoing. We cannot emphasize this enough. Select activities that reasonably fit your schedule, proclivities, and family culture. Also, don't be afraid to try a few that may seem a bit outside your comfort level but are likely to offer the most learning and growth opportunities. As you work with your kids on the projects you choose, you are bound to identify misconceptions and gaps in their knowledge and perceptions.

Before we start exploring ways to provide your kids with skills and experience, take a few moments to answer the questions in this chapter's self-survey so that you can record any assumptions you bring to the discussion that follows. It will be helpful for you to return to this self-survey after reading the chapter and reconsider your answers, as we have suggested you do in previous chapters.

Self-Survey about Skills and Experience

1 = Strongly Agree, 2 = Agree, 3 = Neutral, 4 = Disagree, 5 = Strongly Disagree

BEFORE		AFTER
_____	My children understand the basics of money management.	_____
_____	My child has learned most of what she needs to know about finance from a program she attended.	_____
A _____ B _____	Children learn the most about personal finance from: A: School B: Parents	A _____ B _____
_____	My children will not need to learn about finance, as they will hire trusted advisors to invest for them.	_____
_____	Financial experts such as my advisors or family office professionals can best assess my children's financial educational needs.	_____

_____   Getting the kids together to discuss finance and   _____
investing is a good way for them to learn those subjects.

_____   I need to be involved in teaching and modeling to my   _____
kids the basic as well as the more advanced points
of finance.

_____   If my kids do not show an interest in finance, they will   _____
not be able to learn what they need to handle their own
financial affairs

_____   Kids do not belong in the family foundation as active   _____
participants, although they can attend meetings to
listen and learn.

Let's take a look at the common assumptions about where financial knowledge comes from. JumpStart Coalition for Personal Financial Literacy, a clearinghouse for K–12 financial curricula, has found that 87 percent of parents believe their children learn everything they need to know about money at school. Clearly, that's not the case. But when you ask students, 90 percent say they learn everything they know about money from their parents. So it should not be surprising that JumpStart's financial literacy tests have found that 62 percent of high school seniors failed a personal finance exam, with only 12 percent scoring a C or higher. Not only are parents not adequately teaching their kids about money, many adults in the general U.S. population max out their credit cards and cannot afford to pay the minimum balances. Clearly, such adults are not modeling restraint or responsible behavior—which may partially explain why the fastest-growing age group filing bankruptcies are eighteen- to twenty-four-year-olds.

Some readers will argue that's not the case in high–net worth circles. Our experience has shown us that the amount of money you have has nothing to do with your ability to control spending or use credit cards wisely. Many high–net worth people carry large balances on their credit cards. Even if you do not do so, your kids will see uncontrolled spending modeled by other people in your neighborhood. The high–net worth environment is filled with examples of over-consumption. It is difficult for young adults to understand the need to rein in spending when it appears the family can afford just about anything. We will talk much more about how this affects your kids in Chapter 9, which focuses on navigating the high–net worth environment.

Assessing Financial Skills

Young adults who are raised and continue to live lavishly, who do not understand how to manage a credit card or balance a checkbook, and who develop sloppy financial habits may not realize or appreciate that however much wealth their families may possess, money is still a finite resource.

The question we hear most often from high–net worth parents is, "What do I need to teach my children and at what age?" Age can be a tricky thing. Different children display varying degrees of interest, ability, and need. Therefore, there's no one order in which to present information, and not all children even need to know all aspects of personal finance or investing. "Functional families constantly assess at each age how much we tell, how much we show, how ostentatiously we live, and how public we are about our wealth," notes Chicago psychologist Kenneth Kaye, who also wrote, with son Nick, *Trust Me: Helping Our Young Adults Financially* (iUniverse, 2009). "At every stage they're thinking it through in relationship to the age and maturity and trustworthiness of their kids. They pay attention to the developmental level and readiness of each child in the family. It's a very big task."

For instance, if your child shows interest in a more advanced topic such as investing in stocks, is it okay to teach them that before showing them how to balance a checkbook? Absolutely. In fact, we would encourage you to do so. People learn best when they have an interest in the subject or need to use the information. We suggest that you let their interest or need drive when you teach theses subjects.

On the other hand, it's important to expose children to most of these subjects on a regular basis, no mater what their interest. Kids' interests change over time. They will not have an opportunity to become interested in an aspect of personal finance unless you expose them to it periodically.

You may find it helpful to have a list of lessons your children need to learn and a set of experiences that will teach those lessons. Appendix 1 provides just such a checklist. We suggest you start by checking off which items in the "outcome" column you think your children already know, and circle items that you'd like them to learn in the next year or two. Be sure to add to the chart any other financial topics you'd like your kids to learn. If you find a subject or learning tool that was helpful to you, please post it to the "community" section of our Web site, www.KWandC.com, to share your knowledge with others. If your children are old enough, you may want to use Appendix 1 as a quiz. You may also want them to read Appendix 1 and see what interests them and what they think they already know. Go back to what you have circled and determine what you feel comfortable teaching and what you may need to find someone else to teach them.

Financial education does not have to involve formal training alone. This chapter introduces several ways to engage your kids in financial learning. We hope you come back to this chapter at least once a year and review the learning techniques and Appendix 1. Sometimes sophisticated high–net worth parents skip the basics because they assume their children already know those things. We encourage you to evaluate the entire spectrum of what your child may need to be a good financial steward.

Schedule Spontaneous Time

Scheduled spontaneity? Isn't that an oxymoron? Not really, because without scheduling time to hang out with your children in casual settings, you won't find those spontaneous moments in which some of the most honest, deep and bonding conversations—about issues surrounding wealth as well as other aspects of your and your children's lives—tend to occur.

There's no getting around it. The best chance you have of helping your children become responsible wealth owners and wealth creators is to be involved in the process. The more time, effort, excitement, and creative energy you invest in the process, the better the likely outcomes. For one thing, only by being present will you be able to identify where your children are motivated (and where they are not), what they know (and where there are gaps in their knowledge), as well as any misconceptions they may harbor that could trip them up once they're out in the world.

The problem is that in some wealthy households, individuals conduct very busy, separate, lives. A nanny may assume responsibility for most day-to-day child-rearing activities, including overseeing mealtimes, the logistics of getting children to and from their after-school activities, and even bedtime routines. Parents may be consumed with work, travel, and social or philanthropic-related events. As a result, many such families will rarely sit down to a single meal together in a typical week. That's very unfortunate because downtimes—such as meals, driving to and from activities, or running errands together—can be extremely powerful opportunities to interact in a somewhat relaxed yet focused way, to share what's going on in one another's lives, to find out what your children are excited or upset about at school or with friends, and to get a sense of where they may need some help from you or a teacher, tutor, mentor, or professional.

Finding—or carving out—such time to engage your children in casual conversation is an important part of helping them develop in all sorts of ways, including forming their attitudes, values, proficiency, confidence, and experience in handling money. As with many endeavors, a good 80 percent of being a good parent is just showing up.

You don't need to have an agenda or a list of questions—just look for those "teachable moments." They are all around you. Think what your kid can learn by accompanying you on a trip to the bank or to purchase something simple such a computer gadget or large such as a car, or even by overhearing a conversation on the radio. These are all opportunities to start a conversation about finance, wealth, consumption, and values. Just let the kids start a conversation about what's going on in their lives and what might be bothering them. Along the way, a topic related to wealth will emerge, which you can use as a springboard into a discussion about how money affects your child, such as fads and peer pressure to keep up with all the latest videogames or designer clothes that "everyone" at school has. When your kids mention that a friend's family bought a new boat or car or is going on a fancy vacation and asks if your family can have one too, you can discuss how you make decisions about what luxuries to buy, and when. Chapter 8 will provide an in-depth look at communication styles and techniques that can help you make conversations engaging, fun, and productive.

So if you do not already have dinner at least once a week together, you may want to start doing so. In fact, the value of family dinners goes way beyond improving communication. Durham, New Hampshire-based psychologist Dr. Kenneth Sole says, "The single predictor of staying out of trouble—which I define as criminality, teen pregnancy, drug abuse, and dropping out of school—is family dinners." Sole, who provides group development and organizational change programs and consulting (www.soleassociates.com), explains, "It's got nothing to do with the food. It has to do with the predictability. It's a powerful lesson." The more dinners the family can have together each week, the better.

If possible, try to also schedule time to take over at least some carpooling and bring your kids to help you run errands and engage in projects you enjoy. Jill Shipley, director of next generation education at GenSpring Family Offices in Jupiter, Florida, says that a large percent of the 600-plus families she helps educate do spend lots of time together. That's probably because most of their clients have already had a major liquidity event, having sold their business, and are not working at building a company. "These parents are the most intuitive about their kids," Shipley notes. "Results are better when parents are involved."

TEACHABLE MOMENT

We sometimes like to turn on some of the financial talk radio shows while we're on the road with our kids, to hear issues and problems people raise. It's an opportunity to discuss the answers radio experts offer, such as Clark Howard, Ken and Daria Dolan, Bob Brinker, or Dave Ramsey.

Rather than have a nanny take them to all their activities, drive your kids to at least some events. Road time can be a good opportunity for discussions without distractions. You may even want to agree that both you and your kids will turn off your cell phones so that you can talk without constant interruptions of incoming calls and text messages.

Take time to be with your kids' friends as well. Carpooling can often reveal incredible insight about who your kids and their friends are and what they think, even if they tend not to be open with you. They often will get involved in a conversation with a friend and forget you are in the car. Just sit back and listen. Feel free to pipe in once in a while to raise questions about what they're discussing. When a topic arises that you have circled on Appendix 1, you will be ready to jump in and talk about it.

For instance, while Jayne was driving her son and his friends to basketball practice when he was in middle school, the boys were arguing about the value of their basketball trading cards. One boy claimed his collection was worth so much he could pay for college with it. Jayne took the opportunity to challenge that assertion. She commented, "Wow, that would be incredible. How do you know how much your cards are worth?" He mentioned a magazine published by Beckett that tracks sports trading card prices. "That's interesting," she said. "Don't the prices change over time? And how do you know the prices will be high enough just when you need to sell them, if you wanted to pay for college?" That started an energetic discussion about the laws of supply and demand (in Appendix 1 under business skills) that lasted until we got to our destination.

While it's always productive to engage in discussions about wealth, you don't need to be an expert in finance to guide them. If you have very young children, you can take the opportunity when you withdraw money at the ATM to ask them why they think the bank (or machine) gives you all that money. You can also initiate discussions about financial values, expectations, stories from your own childhood, or business experiences. In addition, you can access some of the many programs, resources, games, and experts to teach your children the more technical financial facts of life. In fact, maybe you can learn with them.

Create Class Time

If you have a family office or financial advisor, you can ask the professionals to meet periodically with your children, or the entire younger generation of cousins, to assess their level of financial literacy. They can then recommend ways to supplement their understanding with classes, books, and articles, or perhaps develop training programs customized for them. Many bank wealth departments offer such programs such as boot camps, some in conjunction with a university (as mentioned in Chapter 4).

François de Visscher, founder of Greenwich, Connecticut-based de Visscher and Company, which provides financial advice to business-owning families, says his family started Bekaert Academy several years ago to provide four or five education programs each year for the fifth-generation owners of N.V. Bekaert S.A., his family's Belgium-based steel wire company. At Bekaert Academy, company executives describe the $3 billion (revenue) family business, its history, and its products. Outside speakers come to explain various aspects of running a business and financial concepts and tools. The family also participates in the Family Business Network in Belgium, which holds another handful of meetings each year at which Bekaert's chairman and seventy or eighty other Belgian family business leaders lead meetings for all family members fifteen and older.

You know your children's learning style (aural versus visual, for instance), any learning disabilities, or challenges they may have, as well as their passions. Don't force any of the activities listed in Appendix 1 on your children. Try several things to see what sparks their interest, and build on those that seem to resonate and yield the best results.

Play Games

Many families find or develop their own board games or computer games try to simulate starting a business, investing, or running a town or a household. The more fun you can make a lesson or activity, the more eagerly your children will participate and the more information they are likely to absorb.

Such activities are fun and educational for the kids, but parents who play games such as the ones described below are also likely to learn quite a bit about their kids—and reveal a bit about themselves as well. For instance, parents may be surprised to notice which kids take the biggest risks. Will the child who is aggressive in sports take wild risks or be cautious with money?

Be careful to select games that will provide the lessons you intend that your kids should learn. Many online stock market games give players a hypothetical $10,000 or $100,000 to invest over some short time period. As participants play, they learn the basics of investing. One problem is that players who "win" are often those who purchase risky stocks, buy and sell aggressively, and engage in other tactics that in the real world would likely cause their portfolios to crash and burn. You may learn how to beat the game, but not necessarily the most prudent ways to invest. While players may learn about concepts such as price-earnings ratios, dividends, and return on investment, they also pick up unrealistic assumptions about how investing works.

GenSpring's Shipley says that it's possible to play some of these online games—such as Stock Trak and Investopedia (see **Exhibit 5.1**)—without competing with others, but it's a good idea to practice sticking to an investment strategy or allocation. A parent or educator monitoring how well teens follow their own goals and risk tolerance can set up a reward for accomplishing those goals beyond ending up with the largest returns.

Shipley prefers initially providing some education and then playing simulation games before giving kids real money to invest. She

---

UNINTENDED CONSEQUENCE

Simulations are just that. They do not present all aspects of investing, but are designed to teach a few things. Games are no substitute for other techniques we present in this chapter. Before implementing a sim game, recognize what it will teach and what it may incorrectly simulate. After the game, discuss what you have all learned and what may have been realistic and unrealistic. Discuss what likely outcomes may be of making risky investments in life.

points out, "I'd say it depends on the kids' maturity and interest, and the commitment and involvement the parent is willing to have with the project." She recalls one seventeen-year-old who became very involved in an online investment game. He called the family's investment advisor every other day to ask questions. Shortly after, his parents trusted him to invest $1,000. "The number doesn't matter," says Shipley, "although I wouldn't recommend throwing $100,000 at a fourteen-year-old after two weeks."

Keep in mind that while you want your children to understand financial management and investing, ultimately, you want an expert investing the family's money. "Your kids will not need to become experts and do it on their own. But they can learn a lot, where they have some skin in the game."

Rich worked with his family office executive in 2003 to develop his own family game: Chasing Returns (The Asset Allocation Game). He wanted to teach asset allocation, the consequences of chasing investment returns, and having a long-term view on investing to his three children and several nieces and nephews, ages thirteen to eighteen, without subjecting them to a lot of charts and graphs. The family office executive administered the game in an afternoon over a four-day family get together. She started by describing several managers, who each provide a different class of securities.

Rather than describe the intricacies of asset allocation, she provided each child with data about how each of those managers performed over time. Then each child filled in an asset allocation to these different managers. The office manager ran a simulation of the manager and allocation results for each child. The group of children and the office manager discussed the results after each two-year simulation was run. The game was over after ten rounds: twenty years of data, two years at a time. As a result, the cousins learned the basics of asset allocation in a simple, yet powerful way. They saw how chasing returns in one period may not produce good results in the next period, and how keeping disciplined by sticking to one allocation yielded the best overall gains. (You can view and download the spread sheet and instructions for the Chasing Returns game on our Web site at www.KWandC.com.)

Exhibit 5.1 Online Games About Running a Business, Saving, and Investing

GAME/ WEB ADDRESS AGE RECOMMENDATION	DESCRIPTION
Lemonade Tycoon www.lemonadetycoon.com Available only to members of LearningPlanet.com Cost: $39.95 per year	Players start a virtual business; purchase ingredients with constantly fluctuating prices; decide where in town the lemonade stand will get the most traffic, read the news to learn about trends that may affect sales.
Planet Orange www.Orangekids.com Free For grades four through eight	Players choose a guide to help them explore four continents: Moneyland, Republic of Saving, South Spending, and Investor Islands. At each continent, players must successfully solve fun and silly challenges that help them learn about some aspect of money.
Savings Quest.com www.mysavingsquest.com Free	Tests kids' ability to save for things they want while paying for things they need. Players pick a job, collect a paycheck, and build a budget for six months.
Young investor www.younginvestor.com Free For all age groups K–12	Designed for teacher and the classroom. Provides games and information on investing, saving, budgeting, and earning money.
Investopedia® http://simulator.investopedia.com Free	A stock market game "like a fantasy sports pool for investing"—a simulation game for investing. *Note: If you use this game you may want to find a way to reduce the "winning" the game aspect.*
Stock Trak www.stocktrak.com Variable costs Designed for students: ■ Graduate ■ College ■ High school ■ Middle school	Stock market online investment simulation game. Designed for the classroom. *Note: If you use this game you may want to find a way to underplay "winning" by making unsound, aggressive investment choices, or discussing the risks of employing such investment techniques with real money.*

GenSpring Family Office experts created the Shirtsleeves to Shirtsleeves Game for its clients, but unfortunately it is not available to the general public yet. The game board, in the shape of a dollar sign, moves players from generation one to two and finally to three. Players encounter situations that may add to or detract from their starting wealth of $25 million. The player who ends up with the most cash—or lowest losses—wins. However, each player has a 70 percent chance of going bankrupt! But the purpose, and fun, of the game is the conversations that it evokes.

The possibilities are just about endless for creating family games to have fun, strengthen family bonds, spend time together, and learn important financial skills. Perhaps you can devise for your family a budget or checkbook game, based on your own background and experience. The idea is to get your kids involved in learning and playing together at an early age—in a fun and memorable way!

Expose Kids to the Real World

Once your children have become conversant and confident about basic financial concepts and skills, it's time to get them some real-world experience where they can practice and see the consequences of their decisions before they're on their own and the stakes are much higher. We present several ways you can provide them such experience, such as teaching them how to handle credit responsibly by helping them get a credit card, getting them involved with an investment club, giving them a discrete amount of money to invest for a period of time, involving them in family philanthropy (both donating and volunteering), including them in family meetings, and taking them to work.

■ **Bring the kids to work.** Much can be learned at the place you work, be it a commercial enterprise or a philanthropy—or even if you serve as a volunteer for some nonprofit organization. The experience will not only help your kids understand how a business or non-profit works, but it will also expose them to the different jobs available. You can find plenty of ideas about how to make the experience educational, fun, and engaging at www.kaboose.com, a leading Web site for parents about National Take Our Daughters or Sons to Work Day.

"This is a special opportunity to see where their parents go and what they do when they say goodbye in the morning," says Tiger 21 founder and CEO Michael Sonnenfeldt, who generally works from his home office. "My kids have grown up knowing I'm fifty feet away one or two days a week when I'm not traveling, but they still can't figure out what I do. They think it's talking on the phone. However, there's a presence of words and shouting and smiling and people coming and going. They have a sense of what I'm doing."

Sonnenfeldt also recommends talking at dinner about what you do. "For example, I own a company that manufactures solar-powered street lights. What a great way to talk about the environment, and our responsibility to repair the world through philanthropy and the business."

■ **Credit Cards.** Many financial parenting experts believe giving teens a credit card is not a great idea, that it just teaches them to spend now, pay later. We believe it makes sense to give your kids experience with credit cards while they're still living home, and you can monitor and guide how they use them. However, it's important not to hand them a piece of plastic and let them take off and charge to their heart's desire. It's also advisable to check in regularly to monitor how they're handling their spending and payments.

For instance, when Jayne's son, Ryan, was in high school, she helped him apply for a credit card. She explained that the credit card would serve three purposes: as a convenience so he doesn't have to carry much cash; as a way to begin creating a positive credit rating; and for emergencies (she made clear that pizza is not an emergency!). She made a point of sitting down with him to talk about how to use a credit card responsibly, including saving all receipts and checking them against the monthly statements; being careful to charge only what he could afford to pay off each month; and keeping in mind how much interest he'd be charged if he maintained an outstanding balance month to month and how much he'd have to pay in fees if he paid late.

Imagine her surprise when she learned some months later that Ryan had maxed out the credit card (which only had a $500 limit but would take months to pay off given his hand-to-mouth budget). Not only that, but Ryan shrugged and said, "Well this credit card does not charge interest." How could he harbor that misconception? She suggested he check his statements and lo and behold, he was surprised to see he was paying interest.

It's best to help kids get a card only once they have started working so that they can pay off their own charges. (If you are inclined to pay for their purchases, at least insist that they pay for any interest or late fees themselves.) When the card arrives, parents need to explain how the card works. Each month, at least for the first six months to a year, sit with your child to review the monthly statement and check that the charges, fees, and credits appear correctly.

■ **Investment clubs.** One way to get real-world investment experience with real money, is by creating an investment club that will pool the group's funds. Together, the club members research and vote on which securities to buy. Many such clubs comprise mostly kids—whether siblings, cousins, or friends—with at least one adult member (a parent, grandparent, teacher, family advisor, or mentor) who can place brokerage orders, oversee record-keeping, and attend to taxes. You can find lots of information about how to set up and run an investment club at the National Association of Investors Corporation (www.betterinvesting.org), which has 11,600 investment clubs in the United States.

Teri Lowinger started a moms-and-girls investment club when her daughter entered the fourth grade. Lowinger, who has a CFA and has worked in the finance area, and some of her friends wanted their girls to feel comfortable with the idea of women in business and finance and to expose the girls to math and investing. They also wanted to create a club where moms and girls could do something serious as well as have some social time together. The group was composed of about ten girls and their mothers from four surrounding towns. They met once a month until the girls began high school and became busy with other activities. "At each meeting we designed some type of fun project or quiz. We wanted to bring this complicated subject to the girls in a way that put it in terms kids would understand," Lowinger explains. Together they chose companies that would interest the kids, such as McDonald's, Disney, and the Gap. "We would ask questions like 'how many kids' meals would McDonald's have to sell to obtain its 1999 revenues?'" The kids went on a field trip to McDonald's headquarters arranged by a friend whose husband was an executive there. "The investor relations person met us and took us for a tour. She gave each of us an annual report, which we reviewed at a later monthly meeting." Another technique Lowinger used was to tell all of the girls and their moms to be "on the look out for popular products that we could invest in. When they got a bit older, two of the girls suggested we invest in Coach handbags," a hot product for the affluent girls. Lowinger pointed out that the club was not about making money, although their investments performed well during up years in the market: "It was about learning and the social time together."

■ **Goal-focused investment challenge.** BNY Mellon Family Wealth Services Director Tom Rogerson says that usually when high–net worth families want to teach their kids something about money, they give each one $5,000 or $10,000 to manage and tell them to copy them on the statements. That was not hands-on enough for Rogerson. Instead, he used his family's vacation fund as a vehicle for teaching his four children, then ages eight, eleven, fourteen, and sixteen, how to invest and make decisions together. "Many times the very first decision the children make together regarding some level of wealth in a family is when they're settling their parents' estate. That's not a good time," Rogerson says.

He and his wife came up with a budget for a one-week vacation and put 85 percent of that in an investment account a year and a half before the vacation. "We let our kids invest that money for a year," explains Rogerson. "So if they did well, we went on an A vacation to Disney World. If they did average, we went on a B vacation to a Holiday Inn someplace and visited family. If they did terribly, we went camping." The first time the family did this, his children bought penny stocks in toy companies. "If it was dot-cool, they bought it, and we didn't tell them not to. Most entrepreneurs make the mistake of saying 'No, you shouldn't do that.' Well that teaches them to be very good listeners. But who will they listen to when I'm gone? It would have been counterproductive to this exercise if we stepped in and said no." Predictably, that year the family went camping.

Rogerson emphasizes the importance of having consequences of the kids' decisions for the entire family. The second year, his children were so nervous about winding up in a tent again that they put all the money in a money market account. They neither lost nor made money. So we went to a Holiday Inn someplace and visited family. "My wife and I thought, this isn't working so well. But the third year was worth everything we put into it. That year they started a conversation about the minimum vacation they're willing to take. How much do they set aside for that, and how do they invest the rest to get to Disney World? I thought it was a great conversation. And the older ones were teaching the younger ones. And we were thrilled with that." That year they managed to earn enough to get their Disney vacation. Vacation investing is not the only goal-focused investment you can use to teach your kids about investing and the risks and rewards that come from it.

■ **Real-time money management.** Eventually, kids will have to go beyond simulations and goal-focused investment challenges and experience how to manage and invest larger sums. There is no one correct method. Here are a couple suggestions that you can consider to determine what might fit your philosophy.

Some families use the 25-25-25-25 concept. They give their kids one-quarter of their inheritance at a time to control. They pick an age for the first portion and then spread the rest out over ten to twenty years. If they spend or lose all or most of the first 25 percent, they will have three more attempts to get it right.

Another approach is to start them out with a substantial amount, but not so much that it would change their future lifestyle if they lost it all. Somewhere between eighteen and twenty-one, you may give them this pot of money. First, sit down and have a discussion, deciding together what the money can and cannot be spent on—maybe some percentage of the increase or total value of the corpus. Perhaps the money is for buying a car or a house when the young adult helps it grow to a certain amount.

Your children can sit down with your financial advisor or office executive quarterly and make investment decisions in mutual funds or with money managers, depending on the amount they are investing. The goal here is like that of goal-oriented investing, but now your kids are on their own and developing their own goals. They will get to practice important money-management skills with real consequences before you expose them to the entire fortune they will inherit.

Investing is a complicated and sophisticated art that needs years of education, practice, experience, and mistakes to get it right. Start kids young to provide them the chance to make mistakes, and hope they will learn from it.

■ **Family Philanthropy.** We recommend you start to talk about charitable giving to children as early as age six or seven. The idea is to get them used to thinking of wealth as a responsibility. You can discuss what philanthropic causes the family helps support, and why.

You can also get them started on setting aside a portion of their allowance for their own contributions. At the end of the year, you can ask them where they'd like to donate the money they've amassed, such as the local animal shelter, and arrange to take them there to deliver it personally. As they get older, you can involve them more and more in the process by asking them what kinds of problems in the community or the world they feel they'd like to help improve. If, for example, a relative, teacher, or family friend has been diagnosed with Alzheimer's disease or cancer, they may feel drawn to help people with such medical problems. Would the children prefer the family contribute to organizations that conduct research that might eventually discover a cure or help people currently suffering afford treatments or other services? When a natural disaster such as Hurricane Katrina or an earthquake occurs, the children might want to direct some funds to getting food, toys, and clothes to victims or help rebuild homes that were destroyed.

One side benefit of enlisting your kids in the family's giving decisions is that it can help allay some of the children's fears during a family or world crisis. When they focus on the family's contributions to solutions, they feel empowered and less scared.

■ **Family Foundations.** By the time the kids are eleven or twelve, if you have a family foundation, you can tell them about it, explaining that the family has set aside money that it invests so it will grow, and that each year the foundation writes checks to various charitable organizations. The Foundation Center counts 37,800 family foundations in the U.S. as of 2006,[1] 27 percent of which were established between 2000 and 2006. The largest, the Bill & Melinda Gates Foundation, has more than $30 billion in assets and gives away more than $1.5 billion each year.

There are many benefits to a family foundation. In addition to connecting family members—particularly among different generations—around something meaningful and important, it helps the family focus outwardly instead of inwardly, on making the world a better place, says Bruce Boyd, principal and managing director of Arabella Philanthropic Investment Advisors in Chicago. "It's a great family value to transmit to your children, especially in well-to-do families, where money can sometimes be corrupting. Philanthropy is a way of preventing that from happening."

Another benefit of the family foundation, according to many experts and families who utilize foundations, is that the family can

---

1. The Foundation Center's criteria for what constitutes a family foundation include: "Independent foundations with 'family' or 'families' in their name, a living donor whose surname matches the foundation name, or at least two trustee surnames that match a living or deceased donor's name, along with any independent foundations that self-identify as family foundations on the annual Foundation Center surveys." See http://foundationcenter.org/gainknowledge/research/pdf/keyfacts_fam_2008.pdf.

expose and involve the kids in financial decision making without having to divulge what the family is worth. Many families of high–net worth bring in advisors to explain what an endowment is all about, how money will be invested, as well as the parents' decision-making process and why they want to create this thing called a legacy.

Many advisors whom we interviewed indicated that the family foundation should be not just about "what we fund," but also about "how we fund." The process matters as much as the ends. Claudia Sangster, director of philanthropy, estate, and trust services at Harris myCFO, a division of Harris Private Bank in Chicago, helps many wealthy families create a family mission statement to guide their charitable giving. She launches the process with what she calls the "mailbag exercise." At a family meeting, she dumps 100 direct-mail pieces from a variety of charitable organizations. The only direction she provides is telling them they have one hour to give away $25,000 of real or fake money. "It's fascinating to watch how families do this," says Sangster, who is located in Los Angeles. "They realize how hard it is, if they don't have a mission statement, to guide the process. If parents have tried to impose their ideas, they learn their children have their own passions they want to benefit. It gives parents an 'aha' experience. At the end of exercise the parents can create (or redo) a mission statement and bring their children in on the process."

As with the goal-focused investment challenge (described earlier), creating a family philanthropic mission statement can provide kids with experience and practice making financial decisions together so that they are prepared to work as a cohesive unit after the parents are gone.

For younger-generation family members who have not yet found a passion or direction in life, involvement in a family foundation can be a way to focus on making their lives productive. Involvement in a family foundation or other vehicles for giving (such as donor-advised funds or informal family giving) gives kids business skills, such as how to manage money, budgeting, planning, and evaluating organizations.

Boyd cautions, "There are plenty of dysfunctional family foundations where all the problems of the family get manifested

UNINTENDED CONSEQUENCE

We have seen some families get their kids involved by just coming to the meetings, without giving them any say in where or how money is donated. Then the parents are surprised when their kids reach their twenties and stop coming to meetings and exhibit no interest in family philanthropy. Allowing them some control is more likely to spark their passion for getting involved in giving.

within the foundation. Jealousies and problems can be dealt with in a productive way in the context of the family foundation, but if you let the family slide into its usual way of operating, to the extent that's unhealthy, you miss an opportunity for the family to improve its communication. One needs to be prepared to make the kind of commitment to the process to see it succeed." Sometimes that requires getting outside help from a professional advisor who can help create positive communication processes. We talk more about communication in Chapter 8.

Some family foundations enlist children between ages twelve to fifteen to join a junior board. The junior board, which is not a legal entity, charges the children with working together to decide where to donate a relatively small pot of money, with guidance from a family office or family foundation employee, relative, advisor, or other mentor. Children, who tend to be quite Internet savvy, can research online non-profit groups using criteria their mentor/guide sets up, such as what percent of assets each non-profit grants each year and what percent it spends on overhead and marketing. This junior board is a great place to help the children learn important group decision-making skills. They learn how to work and make decisions together on financial matters.

Depending on the size of your foundation, there are many approaches you can take when your children are between fourteen and eighteen. At large family foundations where full-time staff is employed, teens can serve as interns, performing tasks like they might in any other internship position at a regular company. Smaller foundations might just decide to have them participate in foundation meetings or board meetings as a non-voting member. Foundations of any size that have a large number of family members participating may have teens join the finance committee where they can learn to monitor investments or the grant committee helping to identify worthy grant recipients. Another technique is to give each child an amount of money to donate (the size does not matter) to a cause they have fully researched and to present their decision to the grants committee or board; doing so will give them experience at researching and presenting good grant candidates. Some foundations will split up the family into committees that focus on different philanthropic directions. Teens are asked to pick a committee that is of most interest to them. Other foundations we have seen have a matching fund with the foundation. Participants may even be required to put in a certain amount of their own cash to be matched by the foundation going to a charity of their choice. This puts a bit of their own skin in the game.

There are many ways to involve the kids in the foundation. "By the time they turn nineteen or twenty-one or thirty, they have sat through all of this, they understand their beliefs and values, they understand the hearts of their mom and dad and what they want to represent," notes PNC's Financial Services Group Senior Vice President Bruce Bickel in *BusinessWeek's* January 29, 2007, article, "Philanthropy: Get 'Em Started Early." At that point they can become voting board members or apply for a paid position at the family foundation.

Some families choose to ask some of the nonprofit groups its foundation supports to bring on teens as interns, either as volunteers or in paid positions. For instance, Boyd says his seventeen-year-old son has worked for the past three summers with The Nature Conservancy, the nation's largest environmental organization. Last summer he worked at a wildlife refuge maintaining hiking trails, helping restore an area that was damaged, removing invasive species. In addition to learning some skills, meeting passionate, hard-working people, and having fun, he learned the value of investing sweat equity into a cause he cares about deeply.

Ideally, philanthropy involves more than money. Families that volunteer together—whether once a month or every Thanksgiving serving or preparing food at the local soup kitchen, working at the animal shelter, or taking vacations that involve volunteering in needy communities, such as Habitat for Humanity—send powerful messages about the importance of "walking the talk," share extremely bonding experiences, and learn firsthand about people who are less fortunate. It's harder for kids who experience such profound experiences to develop or maintain a sense of entitlement. And for children who may feel guilty about not having earned the wealth they enjoy, it allows them a way to allay some of their guilt when they devote their time and energy to helping improve the world.

Family business finance expert François de Visscher believes it's important to make sure that he and his sons become actively involved in the causes his family foundation supports. For example, he and his children contribute to Play Pump International, which installs water pumps in Africa and South America at playgrounds. The pumps are brightly painted with a gigantic wheel that looks like a merry-go-round. Normally, girls have to walk miles to get water and cannot attend school. Each pump, which costs $15,000 and provides water for 2,500 people, allows boys and girls to go to school and as they play with the wheel, they pump water. De Visscher did not just grant money to purchase one of those pumps for a village in Africa: this summer he's taking his boys there to help install it and to work in the village.

Now that you've considered the many ideas this chapter has presented, you may be surprised when you return to the self-survey at the beginning to see where your answers may have changed. Consider new ways you can provide your children with financial skills and experience in light of the areas where you have altered your assumptions.

Next, brace yourselves for a lively exploration of helping your children discover their goals and purpose and consider the many ways you and they can measure success.

6

Goals and Purpose

IN ADDITION TO INSTILLING in your children financial values, providing them basic financial literacy, and exposing them to real-life experiences that will help them acquire skills and confidence to deal with wealth responsibly, it's crucial that you help your children discover meaningful goals and a sense of purpose in their lives.

Self-Survey about Goals and Purpose

Below is this chapter's self-survey, which you should fill out before reading further and again after reading the chapter, to find out where your initial assumptions and attitudes may shift after you consider the concepts we cover here.

Self-Survey about Goals and Purpose

1 = Strongly Agree, 2 = Agree, 3 = Neutral, 4 = Disagree, 5 = Strongly Disagree

BEFORE		AFTER
_____	It's a good idea to assure my kids they do not have to worry about money as they search for their career goals.	_____
_____	Self-esteem, pride, and purpose come from tough lessons, hard work, and experience.	_____

_____   One of the advantages of my wealth and   _____
connections is being able to help my kids start
off with a fast-track job or finance them in
a venture.

_____   Working menial jobs is a waste of time for my   _____
kids, who are likely to end up with a professional
career.

_____   Pride, self-esteem, and meaning in life come   _____
from loving parents who tell their kids they are
great and the world should appreciate them.

_____   It's important to protect my children from failure   _____
and to bail them out when they mess up.

_____   I want my children to follow in my professional   _____
footsteps.

The Importance of Goals and Purpose

Having a sense of purpose—including a commitment to something larger than oneself, connecting, and realizing one's passions and interests that go beyond material goods—appears at the top of a list of key attributes of successful leaders in a 2007 Family Office Exchange (FOX) white paper, "Responsibilities of Ownership." But having a sense of purpose goes beyond being a responsible steward of family wealth; it also deeply impacts people's feeling of self-worth, which in turn contributes to their happiness with themselves as well as their lives.

Living a purposeful life—having a reason to get up in the morning, feeling productive and contributing to society in some way—are building blocks of self-esteem, happiness, and success (as we shall discuss in Chapter 7). In this chapter, we will also see how goals and purpose relate to earlier discussions about inter-generational equity (Chapter 1), as the chance that your wealth will extend into future generations depends, to a great extent, on your children's ability to create additional wealth to at least some degree.

How to Find Goals and Purpose

"Like my dad I'll never need to work, and I'm not much of a painter, so I want to ask him what I should do with my life," says Jamie Johnson, fourth-generation heir to the Johnson & Johnson fortune, in his documentary movie *Born Rich.* "He said, 'You might want to get into film, might want to go to graduate school, building a collection of historic documents ... '" Johnson concludes, "There are no courses in college about how to be a hardworking and productive person ... so it was something I'd have to figure out for myself."

The problem for many young people, especially those who are extremely affluent, is that finding their purpose can be painfully elusive. Wealth can, for some, squash ambition, drive, and purpose. Teens and young adults may not see the point of working entry-level jobs that may not pay much when they have access to trust funds that provide a comfortable lifestyle, even though such low-paying jobs could be effective launching pads for future fulfilling jobs. Refusing a low-paying job can narrow their choices as to what will make their lives purposeful. For each of us, finding that purpose is important. Think back to the question we posed in Chapter 1: "What is the money for?" It may be helpful to explore your answers and your child's answers to that question, and to consider how wealth may potentially enhance or stunt your child's ability to find purpose.

Some wealthy children have an unhealthy sense of entitlement that makes it difficult for them to feel engaged or excited about anything. It's not the money itself that dampens drive and fans entitlement, says psychiatrist Kerry Sulkowicz, MD, founder of New York City-based Boswell Group, which advises executives on the psychological aspects of business (he also writes the "Analyze This" column of *BusinessWeek* magazine). "One of best kept secrets about growing up in extremely wealthy families is that while they have enormous resources, the ones who grow up entitled are very emotionally deprived. They are raised by caregivers—which is a set-up for emotional deprivation. They don't receive the kind of nurturing they should get from their parents."

Children who lack sufficient nurturing and attention from their parents can have a harder time feeling good about themselves or believing they are capable of being productive or successful. Sadly, an article titled "The High Price of Affluence" that appeared in *Advances in Child Development* (Academic Press, 2005),[1] reported, "Our results showed that on average, affluent children perceived their parents to be no more available—emotionally or physically— than did youth in poverty." The authors, Columbia Professor Suniya Luthar and researcher Chris Sexton, PhD, senior research associate with United BioSource Corporation's Center for Health Outcomes Research in Bethesda, Maryland, explain, "Somewhat surprisingly, even after considering the emotional quality of parent-child relationships in analyses, parents' physical absence (e.g., at dinner) connoted higher vulnerability not only for distress but also performance at school (e.g., in relation to suburban students' academic grades)."

In fact, the authors point out, "The affluent youth reported more frequent substance use than their inner-city counterparts, with consistently higher use of cigarettes, alcohol, marijuana and illicit drugs. They also reported significantly higher levels of anxiety across several domains, and levels of depressive symptoms were somewhat higher."

Many of us know kids who, from a very young age, just knew they wanted to be a brain surgeon, a musician, or a math teacher. We also have encountered late bloomers who struggled through periods of intense angst and many trials and errors before they experienced that sweet epiphany of knowing how they wanted to spend the rest of their lives. And, unfortunately, we may know children, or even adults, who never discover their passion or passions, some of whom feel tortured by the absence of it and others who seem blithe and just don't give a hoot because they believe they can and will have access to enough money from their trust funds to support themselves lavishly. Few in this latter category are likely to be truly happy.

---

1. Pages 126–162.

The process of figuring out one's purpose involves more than just pinpointing what to do with one's life; it first requires one to answer two questions:

■ **Who am I?** Children must develop an identity beyond their family's wealth and material trappings. They must view their lives in the context of their family, community, and society, and they must sense where they fit in, how they can contribute, and how their lives touch other people's lives in a positive way.

■ **What is important to me?** Purpose is rooted in passion: *What do I love to do, and what am I especially good at?* One doesn't have to be a musical prodigy to find a sense of purpose in music; perhaps a music lover will find fulfillment teaching music, running a guitar shop, or working as a talent scout or talent manager.

Realizing one's passion will likely require some amount of education as well as developing strategies to reach the desired goal or goals, such as some combination of networking, keeping abreast of the latest developments in the field, and a willingness to start at the bottom and work one's way up—that is, a healthy work ethic and a willingness to pay one's dues.

Industrial psychologist Mitch Cohen, partner of Chicago-based Ruda Cohen & Associates, lists many possible elements of what meaningful work represents to his clients and their employees:

■ Having the opportunity to make a difference, to feel that what you're doing is having an impact somewhere in a company or within society.

■ Being rewarded based on performance. People want their efforts to be recognized and appropriately rewarded. Everyone is motivated by different things: some by money, others by getting new responsibilities and challenges; still others covet the "corner office."

■ Having one's ideas and opinions matter. Most people want others, particularly their superiors, to seek out their opinions.

■ Opportunities to get ahead if one does well and works hard.

■ Having a good relationship with the boss. No matter how positive the organization is or how much they love the work itself, employees become disgruntled and quit when they feel their managers do not respect them, do not treat them well, micromanage, are autocratic, or are emotionally volatile.

■ During economic downturns, job security, benefits, and stability of the organization become very important to most people, who want any kind of job that provides a paycheck during difficult times. However, this is likely not too important to high–net worth kids.

■ Work-life balance is absolutely critical, especially to people in their twenties and thirties. That can mean flexibility, keeping work in perspective, and having time with their family.

■ Believing in the company and its products and services. Many people need to feel that what they're doing is important, that the company's mission is a valuable one, and that they're on a winning team.

Notice that money barely appears on this list. Jobs most often represent far more to people than just making a living. A job represents one's purpose and provides meaning to life. It is what gets you up in the morning. Habitat for Humanity founder Millard Fuller found his true purpose in life after becoming a self-made millionaire. It was then that he realized that his purpose and calling in life was to provide housing for those who could not afford it. He gave away his wealth and focused on that purpose. He built what is now a giant organization of paid and unpaid people who share his vision. We are not suggesting that high–net worth people give away all they have, but finding a purpose in life often leads to a good life that cannot be measured by how much money you have. We will talk more about this in Chapter 7.

Working with family businesses and people who have liquidity events has allowed us to see firsthand how purpose can be integrated into what one does on a daily basis. Most families that own a business struggle with whether or not they should try to pass down ownership to their children. Often, this transition can become complicated when the senior generation does not want to leave the business, even after their children have paid their dues and are ready to take the reins. The owner's purpose in life is wrapped up in the business, which is often seen as a big part of the community, offering jobs, donations, and support to non-profit organizations. Their purpose in life is wrapped up in the way they do business, the business's integrity, and quality of the product or service. Unfortunately, this can frustrate members of the younger generation, who expect to have an opportunity to take the helm.

Some family business members reach a crisis when the business sells and they are forced to redefine their purpose. Suddenly, they have liquid assets that may enable them to go anywhere and do anything. Many become frozen by the vast array of opportunities. This is similar to people who win the lottery or suddenly inherit their parents' estate. If they have not defined their purpose in life, they will likely struggle with the money and its meaning. Many embark on lavish spending sprees, thinking it will bring them happiness. Without the grounding of a purpose in life, wealth often has the opposite effect. Helping a forty-, fifty-, or sixty-year-old heir rethink his purpose in life is much more difficult than helping younger kids find purpose. Unlike these adults who may be afraid to reach out for help, your children are likely to benefit greatly from some smart, engaged parenting techniques as they struggle to find a meaningful sense of purpose.

UNINTENDED CONSEQUENCE

In families with strong leaders, such as CEOs of family businesses, parents may display so much enthusiasm for work that their children may view joining the company as the only "successful thing" Mom or Dad would sanction. In far too many cases, kids who would have been successful at architecture or as teachers feel forced into the family business. Their skills and passion did not connect with the business. Whether or not they become effective leaders, they may feel like failures.

It's important to solicit your children's ideas about what excites them, to listen, and to communicate regularly that they are free to pursue work that brings them meaning.

How Parents Can Guide Children to Find Their Purpose

There's a fine line between imposing parents' ideas about what careers they think their children should pursue and offering guidance that will help teens or young adults discover what will be most meaningful to them. But there are many ways parents can be of tremendous help and emotional support.

■ **Share with your children what your own sense of purpose is and how you found it.** "We've found if parents demonstrate a sense of purpose and they are not defined by their money and what they have, it's a lot more compelling for kids," says family business and wealth consultant Leslie Dashew, who is also founder of Scottsdale, Arizona-based Human Side of Enterprise. She says the more effective role models the parents are, the more likely their kids will feel compelled to explore their own sense of purpose. "When parents with wealth have decided to hang out and be trust babies, they wonder why their kids don't have a sense of purpose. It's very difficult to raise kids with sense of purpose if you don't have that."

■ **Think carefully about when and how you communicate to your children about the family's wealth** (which we will cover in greater depth in Chapter 8). It's hard to know whether information about the family's wealth and trust funds will snuff out your teen's drive and motivation to pursue a productive path, and whether withholding that information will result in your children selecting education and careers they may not love because they assume they'll need to earn a lot to replicate the lifestyle your family currently enjoys. After all, one of the truly liberating aspects of wealth can be the luxury of pursuing passions that might not provide lucrative salaries and perks. We will discuss how and when to communicate about family wealth to children in Chapter 8.

■ **Consider *not* buying everything your kids want.** As we mention in Chapter 4, when kids are forced to work and save up for some of the things they desire, they experience a powerful sense of accomplishment and pride. Indulging their every desire and handing everything to them on a silver platter robs them of that pride and the self-esteem it engenders.

■ **Expect your grown kids to support themselves.** Even if your wealth means your children will not need to earn money to support themselves, there is a lot of value, as we've discussed above, to getting up in the morning, putting in a solid day's work, and earning their own keep. If you think your kids don't know that, you may be surprised to learn that more teens expect to work and pay their own bills than their parents expect them to, according to "Growing Up Wealthy: Spoiled and Extravagant or Responsible and Hard Working," PNC's 2007 study of 210 wealthy teens (fourteen to twenty years old) and 272 affluent parents of children under age eighteen. The study found that 20 percent of parents of a child under eighteen expect to support their children into adulthood, while only 10 percent of teens said they would try to live off family money for as long as they could.

Another reason adult children should support themselves is that, as we mentioned in Chapter 1, if each generation does not actively create additional wealth, the family fortune is likely to dissipate in future generations, as family assets are not likely to grow as quickly as the family may grow.

■ **Help your children select summer or after-school jobs.** Industrial psychologist Cohen says, "I like to see younger people take tough jobs early in their career, in factory or construction jobs, to see what hard work is and how other people work hard. You realize what the value of work is and what the value of a dollar is, and that helps them appreciate others a bit more."

When S.I. Newhouse IV, fourth-generation heir to the Condé Nast publishing empire and $20 billion fortune, went off to Trinity College in the fall of 1994, he says in the 2003 movie *Born Rich*, he was out of control and suffering from depression. After failing to do his schoolwork, quitting sports teams, and languishing in his room, his parents agreed to let him take some time off. "They thought it would be a semester, but it ended up being two years," S.I. says in the documentary. "They were the two best years, the most important years of my life. One of my jobs was working in an oil field, working with Cajuns and people who hadn't gone to high school. It was hard at first. Lunchtime they'd be asking me questions, trivia questions, got a kick that I knew all these things, the capital of Chile or something ... I learned that working hard makes me feel good." On May 5, 2007, S.I. purchased the Portland Trail Blazers basketball team for $450 million and became publisher of *The Oregonian*, and the next day sold both properties for $1.95 billion.[2]

A wealthy friend of Rich's gave lots of thought to what kind of job might be good for his teenage son. Because they lived in a privileged area and spent summers in a wealthy lake community, the summer jobs that were most plentiful and that most of his friends tended to choose, such as waiting tables and pumping gas in boats at the dock, would only expose his son to other high–net worth kids. He wanted his son to experience how less privileged people work and live, as a reality check. This father had his son apply for a job in construction, as an electrician's helper. The people who held those jobs, some of whom were only three to five years older than his son, were married and had kids. Yet they were working at the same job he was, getting paid not much more, and had to support a whole family on that salary. He became aware of the difference when he drove up; even though he had a pretty modest vehicle, his was new, while the other kids pulled up in ten-year-old pick-up trucks. He realized that he lived in one of the palatial homes they were helping to build. He heard stories about what it was like living on very little money: both the struggles and the pleasures.

This work experience not only exposed this young man to people outside the wealthy circle in which he was raised; it also profoundly affected his approach to selecting a career path. He realized he

---

2. Helen Jung, "PERS Buys *Oregonian*-Blazers from Newhouse," *The Oregonian*, May 30, 2007, http://www.nottheoregonian.blogspot.com/2007/05/pers-buys-oregonian-blazers-from.html (accessesd October 7, 2009).

wanted his work to be more than just a job. He chose to study economics and business. His work experience became his college entrance essay. After college, he wanted to apply his business degree to a career in which he could improve society. He first joined a company that helped non-profit groups better manage their foundation assets.

Thoughtfully helping your kids find employment at different points in their lives can produce different types of lessons. For instance, between ages fourteen and sixteen, the job might help them learn about the value of hard work. In the later teens or early twenties, they may focus more on testing what they like and don't like in life. For instance, perhaps they'll discover that they enjoy working outside, that they like working with people, or that they want to help disadvantaged people. Exposing your teens to different kinds of work environments can help them discover or hone their goals and purposes.

■ **Encourage them to take risks.** Calculated risks, that is. Here we feel compelled to share with you the essence of a commencement speech Jayne wrote some years ago, even though no school (yet) has invited her to deliver one. The speech focuses on how we think about risk:

> Many people consider it riskier to attempt to take a giant leap than to take a baby step. Say your daughter has earned a bachelor's degree in broadcast journalism with a minor in business and has interned at several radio stations, and also has written for the college newspaper. After graduation, she finds two jobs advertised: one to be an editorial assistant (i.e., a barely glorified go-fer) at a small radio station in a small town in the middle of nowhere; the other an on-air reporter at a mid-size city. Which opportunity seems the riskier one to pursue?
>
> Those who think the second opportunity is riskier are doing themselves a big disservice. Your daughter certainly stands a better chance of getting that first job. If she does not get it, she may therefore feel somewhat disappointed, or even humiliated and defeated. "What," she may think, "I couldn't even get that piddly job?" On the other hand, if she got an offer for that job, it doesn't come with many bragging rights. The downside risk of pursuing a

lateral or incremental step up is fairly steep; the upside potential is a big yawn.

If she dares to go for that second position (and writes a powerful cover letter with a dynamic demo tape), even if it does not result in an offer or even an interview, well, nothing's really lost. No one expected her to get her foot in that door at this point. But if she does get hired there, wow! The downside risk of pursuing this job is nil; the upside potential is almost off the scale.

Of course, the smartest way to go would be to apply for both jobs! The point here, though, is to encourage your children to dream big. Assure them that if those dreams don't immediately bear fruit, the worst that can happen is that they may have gained experience interviewing and met some interesting people in the field who may later think of them for future job openings. You don't want to set up your kids for disappointment by giving them a false expectation of getting every big-leap job they go for, but it can be very empowering even to be considered for such positions.

Jayne has gotten at least two jobs that she was, on paper, not nearly qualified for. But her chutzpah, people skills, and ability to portray seemingly unrelated previous experience as relevant gave her an edge and inspired those bosses to take a chance on her. Those positions happened to be among the most fun and meaningful jobs she's held.

■ **Let them fail.** There may be a sweet smell of success, but people who are not afraid to fail—who experience failure and overcome it—often revel, with a sparkle in their eyes, in their war stories of when they fell on their face and how they survived. Viewing failure as a notch in your belt instead of with shame is extremely important.

For one thing, as Luthar and Sexton point out in "The High Price of Affluence," "High affluence can exacerbate unhappiness partly because it can engender an *inflated sense of one's own control* over life events. ... Americans not only expect perfection in all things but also expect to produce this perfection in themselves. When they fail—which they inevitably must—the ethos of individualism biases them toward attributing the failures to internal and personal factors, rather than to external causes."

Many parents have a hard time letting their children stumble, whether because they over-identify with their children and experience their kids' failures as their own or out of a desire to protect them from disappointment and defeat. But Dr. Sulkowicz points out that failure can be tremendously valuable. "I'm a big believer in failure, regardless of whether you're wealthy," he says. "You can teach children a terrible lesson if every time they stumble you throw money at the problem. It's the wrong lesson, that mommy or daddy will save me."

But there's a big difference between letting your kids fail and helping them fail. For instance, if your young-adult child has entrepreneurial leanings, you may be tempted to fund her venture. It may be better for your child to approach a banker or investors, says Chicago-based psychologist Kenneth Kaye, co-author with his son Nick of *Trust Me: Helping Our Young Adults Financially* (iUniverse, 2009) and author of, *Family Rules* (iUniverse, 2005). "Maybe he wants to start a restaurant. Another child who doesn't have the money has to go out and find investors. He or she has to convince investors that this particular idea—the location, chef, type of restaurant, pricing and all that—will really make money for that investor. They're being forced to do the kind of homework that the one with unlimited financial resources doesn't have to do." Unless one or both parents has experience in evaluating business plans and knows the industry, they will not be able to make an educated assessment of the viability of their child's business idea.

However, Sulkowicz adds that there's nothing wrong with bailing a child out if he's learned something from the failure first. He recommends that parents have a conversation about it. For instance, he says, "Why did you fail law school—because you don't really want to be a lawyer? Or what? I'm trying to emphasize the value of reflecting on an experience rather than just moving onto the next one or calling up the dean of the law school or getting them into another law school. Help your kid figure out what he's more interested in."

What If Purpose Just Doesn't Surface?

It can be frustrating and demoralizing for children (and their parents) when, try as they might, no sense of purpose appears. Your children may have dutifully and diligently searched their souls, schools, society, and the universe and come up empty-handed. Relax. Take a deep breath. Don't lose hope.

For many children, it takes a little longer. In such cases, you can encourage them to get a liberal arts degree that will expose them to many different subjects and fields. They may fall in love with a path they had never considered before. If when they graduate, they still feel no pull in any direction, they may feel frustrated and discouraged. That doesn't mean doing nothing. As the cliché goes, if you don't know where you want to go, any road will get you there. The important thing is to keep moving.

There's a Jewish story that when the Israelites were fleeing the Egyptians and found themselves at the banks of the Red Sea, even after Moses raised his staff, the waters did not part until the first person took that first step. Your young-adult child may need to "test the waters" and experience one (or even several) jobs, before he gets a sense of what he likes and what he doesn't like. He may find enough purpose from working hard, developing high-level skills and feeling productive, regardless of the field. He may never find a career passion, and that's okay, too. Not everyone derives their meaning in life from work. Some of us work so we can pay the bills, and find our deepest joy in raising our children, pursuing outside interests, volunteering, or traveling.

For those who just don't connect to some vocational purpose, it may be wise to choose a job based on the work environment. Encourage your kids to apply for a host of jobs, and, assuming the search results in a few offers, choose the one where the boss, co-workers and/or clients seem positive, nurturing or fun. Once on the job, challenge your child to seek out a mentor who will take your child under her wing, who may see in your child the seeds of some special talent and guide your child on a path that will utilize that talent.

One door will open others; eventually your child may end up feeling deeply fulfilled, even though he may never have envisioned himself on that path or in that role and may never even have known about that type of work.

Truly, the journey can be more important than the destination. "And maybe if you don't find all the answers," notes Jamie Johnson in his movie, *Born Rich*, "it's still important to ask the questions."

Now we invite you to return to the questions in the self-survey near the beginning of this chapter. As in previous chapters, note where your original answers diverge from your initial answers, and consider sharing the quiz and your responses with your spouse and/or advisors. Consider, in light of what you've read and learned in this chapter, how you may want to adjust some of your parenting rules, techniques, and discussions.

Ahead, in the next chapter, we will discuss how, once your child chooses a direction, she may ultimately find success and happiness.

SECTION III

Spiritual/ Emotional Choices

7

Success and Happiness

THE U.S. DECLARATION of Independence guarantees all Americans "life, liberty and the pursuit of happiness." But the pursuit of happiness is elusive business for many people, regardless of their economic status. Just what makes us happy? And under what circumstances can wealth hinder or help our children to find happiness?

Self-Survey about Success and Happiness

Please take a few moments to check your attitudes and assumptions about success and happiness before we dig in to this topic further.

Self-Survey about Success and Happiness

1 = Strongly Agree, 2 = Agree, 3 = Neutral, 4 = Disagree, 5 = Strongly Disagree

BEFORE		AFTER
_____	My kids should grow up with the things I never had.	_____
_____	While money may not buy happiness, I do tend to feel a rush when I purchase a luxury item.	_____

146

_____   When I think about the moments   _____
during the past month when I felt
happy, most such moments
involved material things.

_____   My family would be happy no   _____
matter how much money we
may or may not have.

_____   I believe my children are not   _____
overly entitled.

_____   It's hard to understand why my kids   _____
sometimes seem unhappy or
depressed when they have everything
they could possibly desire.

_____   When my children make mistakes,   _____
I am there to rescue them.

_____   My children understand that they
are very fortunate to grow up in
a privileged environment, and they
have interacted with people in less
comfortable economic and
social surroundings.

_____   I can help my children develop   _____
self-confidence by protecting
them from failure.

_____   I have communicated how I   _____
measure success to my children.

_____   I have asked my children about   _____
their definition of success.

Indeed, the Declaration of Independence did not guarantee the "purchase," but the "pursuit" of happiness. We are all told that money cannot buy happiness, and in fact, research on this subject has not found a strong correlation between wealth and happiness around the world, as long as people can meet their basic needs. A certain level of "creature comforts" and physical needs, such as healthcare, education, and housing, have been found to affect one's sense of well-being.

Exhibit 7.1 shows that rising income does correlate with happiness up to about $50,000 per year. According to the U.S. Census

TEACHABLE MOMENT

Many high–net worth communities that we have encountered have hidden cultures. For instance, one hidden culture emphasizes the importance of keeping a smile on your face, because wealthy people just do not have problems! At the very least, they do not talk about them or let anyone know their true feelings.

This message can make our kids believe there is something wrong with them when they do feel unhappy or speak up about their feelings from time to time. Psychologists warn that bottled up feelings will come out in some other, unproductive way that can lead to dysfunction in relationships and exacerbate the initial unhappiness.

It is important to teach your kids that money cannot buy happiness all of the time. Feeling sad, unhappy, and depressed from time to time is part of life, no matter how rich you are.

Bureau, the Poverty Threshold in 2004 for a family of four was about $19,000. Families with $50,000 can cover basic needs and then some. In developed countries with stable governments, there is a diminishing return to how much wealth brings a sense of well-being. David G. Myers, in his chapter "Will Money Buy Happiness?",[1] calls rising U.S. standards of living and sinking spirits since the 1950s the "American paradox." He explains, "More than ever we have big houses and broken homes, high incomes and low morale, more comfortable cars and more road rage. We excel at making a living and often fail at making a life. We celebrate our prosperity but yearn for a purpose." Studies in other developed countries have reached similar conclusions.

Recent research in the growing field of "positive psychology," pioneered by University of Illinois psychologist Ed Diener, has found that wealth can, in fact, hinder happiness. In fact, rich materialists tend to be less happy than people who care less about acquiring goods and spending.

---

1. In *Positive Psychology: Exploring the Best in People*, ed. Shane J. Lopez, 37–56 (New York, Greenwood, 2008).

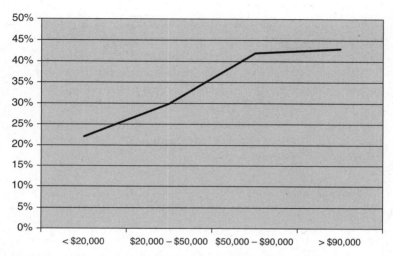

Exhibit 7.1 Percent of People "Very Happy" by Income

Source: David G. Myers (davidmyers.org), based on data from National Opinion Research Center General Social Survey, 2005.

Happiness among members of the ultra-wealthy, whose basic needs and desires are more than well met, obviously varies widely. In 1985 Diener and his colleagues surveyed the *Forbes* 100 wealthiest Americans and found they were only slightly happier than the average person. About 80 percent of the forty-nine people who responded agreed that "money can increase or decrease happiness, depending on how it is used."[2]

Columbia University Professor Suniya Luthar and Chris Sexton, PhD, senior research associate at United BioSource Corporation's Center for Health Outcomes Research, explain that one reason wealth may not correlate with happiness is, "Aside from potentially damaging illusions of control, another reason for the enhanced vulnerability of the rich lies in the *addictive potential* of wealth, wherein rapid habituation to accumulated riches leads to an endless escalation

---

2. Ed Diener, Jeff Horowitz, and Robert Emmons, "Happiness of the Very Wealthy," *Social Indicators Research* 16 (1985), 263–274.

of expectations. ... Thus, winning a lottery can result in intense joy, but this elation tends to be short lived and in order to be revived, will require further increases in personal fortunes."[3]

We have worked with family businesses in which the younger generation members were looking forward to inheriting their parents' estate so they would be able to do whatever they wanted with the family fortune and the family business. They realized, after Mom and Dad died, that the extra money did not improve their happiness for very long.

Transitory versus Sustained Happiness

While we may know on an intellectual level that money cannot buy happiness, many of us can't help note the "high" we feel when we purchase a new expensive toy. However, as mentioned above, we may not realize that this high is short-lived, and that to achieve a similar high, the next "fix" will need to be bigger, better, and more expensive.

It's important to distinguish between transitory emotional bursts of joy or a psychological high—which some people may experience

UNINTENDED CONSEQUENCES

A lawyer we encountered at a seminar on trusts talked about a client who had a troubled son who was not motivated and flunked out of college freshman year. The father attempted to soothe his son's bad feelings by buying him a Ferrari. As Dr. Kerry Sulkowicz points out, this Ferrari at best will have a temporary happiness effect. The true cause of this teen's unhappiness will not be solved by this gift. Understanding why he failed college and finding out his true source of unhappiness would be far more productive than receiving an expensive gift.

Many wealthy people buy things to allay unhappiness and to avoid the uncomfortable task of talking about and understanding why we or someone we love is unhappy.

---

3. S.S. Luthar and Chris Sexton, "The High Price of Affluence," in *Advances in Child Development* 32 (2005): 145.

after purchasing a new car, yacht, jewelry, clothes, or even a dream home—and a more enduring state of underlying happiness.

BusinessWeek "Analyze This" columnist Dr. Kerry Sulkowicz, MD, founder of New York City-based Boswell Group, which advises executives on psychological aspects of business, says what determines people's happiness "depends how they're made up. People need to feel cared for, understood, stimulated or engaged by what they're doing in their lives," he notes. Reflecting on his own experience of happiness during his life and career, which brought him from fairly humble roots to enjoy significant financial success, he says, "Ever since I was a kid I wanted a sports car. It got to the point when I was around 40 that I actually could afford one and I didn't buy one. I couldn't justify it. There's no justification for it of course. Finally, I thought, I'm fooling myself because I'll never come up with a rational justification, besides it'll be fun. So I finally did buy myself a sports car and it's been a lot of fun. But did it make me happy? I think I was happy before. If I'd been unhappy before and then gotten the car, I would've been deeply disappointed."

In other words, while we may enjoy our material indulgences, they are not the core source of happiness. They're just the icing on the cake. If we have not achieved that underlying default state of happiness—the cake—what good is the icing, really?

Traits of Happy People

If wealth does not bring happiness, what does? A series of studies of four groups of college students in the United States and South Korea by University of Missouri-Columbia psychologist Kennon M. Sheldon, PhD and his co-authors found that attaining popularity, influence, money, or luxury are at the bottom of the list of psychological needs. The top of their list includes autonomy, competence, closeness with others, and self-esteem, according to their research.[4]

---

4. Kennon M. Sheldon, Andrew J. Elliot, Youngmee Kim, and Tim Kasser, "What Is Satisfying About Satisfying Events? Testing 10 Candidate Psychological Needs," *Journal of Personality and Social Psychology* 80, no. 2 (July/August 2001), 325–339.

University of Pennsylvania psychologist Martin E. P. Seligman, author of the book, *Authentic Happiness: Using the New Positive Psychology to Realize Your Potential for Lasting Fulfillment* (New York: Free Press, 2004), focuses his interventions not on trying to fix weaknesses, as traditional psychological interventions do, but on incorporating strengths such as humor, originality, and generosity into everyday interactions with people.

Seligman's research, reported in the July/August 2008 issue of *The American Psychologist*, has demonstrated that regardless of one's financial, physical, or other circumstances, it is possible to feel more satisfied, be more engaged with life, find more meaning, have higher hopes, and probably even laugh and smile more.[5] His Web site, www.authentichappiness.sas.upenn.edu, offers several questionnaires for measuring your overall happiness, depression symptoms, current happiness, and enduring happiness.

The Positive Psychology Center (PPC) (www.ppc.sas.upenn.edu) defines happiness as "a state of well being or pleasurable experience, but this notion of happiness is only a small part of positive psychology. Positive psychology is the scientific study of the strengths and virtues that enable individuals (and communities) to thrive."

External, surface characteristics such as popularity, physical beauty or wealth do not appear to impact one's subjective well-being. R. Eckersley, author of "Is Modern Western Culture a Health Hazard?"[6] has found that not even health has a long-term impact on happiness, as many studies find that several months after one is diagnosed with serious diseases such as AIDS or ALS or after suffering loss of sight or use of one's legs, people tend to revert to whatever level of happiness they felt prior to their loss of physical health.

Many of us derive fulfillment from our work, where we may have an opportunity to exercise creative ideas and activities, curiosity (about

---

5. Martin E.P. Seligman, Tracy A. Steen, Nansook Park, and Christopher Peterson, "Positive Psychology Progress: Empirical Validation of Interventions," *The American Psychologist* 60, no. 5 (July/August 2008), 410–421. http://www.authentichappiness. sas.upenn.edu/images/apaarticle.pdf.
6. R. Eckersley, "Is Modern Western Culture a Health Hazard," *International Journal of Epidemiology* 252–258.

2002), Karen Reivich and Andrew Shatté point out, "Everyone needs resilience. More than fifty years of scientific research have powerfully demonstrated that resilience is the key to success at work and satisfaction in life. ... It is the basic ingredient to happiness and success." As we described in the previous chapter, letting kids fail so they can learn from their mistakes also helps them develop life and work skills and figure out their purpose. Failure is also the best way—if not the only way—to develop resilience. Reivich and Shatté point out that how one chooses to think about life's events when adversity happens is critical. Successful and happy resilient people "understand that failures are not an end point. They do not feel shame when they don't succeed. Instead, resilient people are able to derive meaning from failure, and they use this knowledge to climb higher than they otherwise would."[7] It's not that resilient people don't feel anxiety or question their decisions and actions. They do. But their thinking style keeps those feelings in check.

No amount of money can short-circuit the process of developing resilience. The sooner you help your children see failure and hardship as a useful tool, the better. We all try to avoid unpleasant things in life. No one wants to be unhappy or constantly stare at failure. However, we cannot totally control our lives, let alone our children's lives. Hurricanes hit, illnesses develop, stock markets crash, and sometimes we make bad choices and things just don't go our way. As clergyman Charles Swindoll has pointed out, life is 10 percent what happens to you and 90 percent how you react to it.

Therefore, how we choose to react to life's ups and downs can improve or hinder happiness and future success. Teaching our kids productive thinking styles to react to these situations can make a huge difference. As Reivich and Shatté point out, "Non-resilient thinking styles can lead us to cling to inaccurate beliefs about the world and to inappropriate problem-solving strategies that burn through emotional energy and valuable resilience resources."[8]

---

7. Karen Reivich and Andrew Shatté. *The Resilience Factor: 7 Keys to Finding Your Inner Strength and Overcoming Life's Obstacles* (New York: Broadway Books, 2002), 3–4.
8. Ibid., 5.

They also note, "Resilience transforms. It transforms hardship into challenge, failure into success, and helplessness into power. Resilience turns victims into survivors and allows survivors to thrive. Resilient people are loathe to allow even major setbacks to push them from their life course."[9]

Parents who use their money to try to create perfect environments—bubbles—where their children can hide from problems may actually be setting up their kids for a life of failure. Experiencing difficulties and learning effective ways to deal with them are important life skills that cannot be imparted except through experience.

While money will not necessarily make you happy, you can be happy with money. And while wealthy people can't buy immortality, they can leave a legacy built around healthy values and exposure to the many facets and faces of the outside world.

Can Wealth Help You Find Happiness?

There is a major difference between buying happiness by buying a palatial home, sports cars, designer clothes, and so on, and using wealth wisely to help find happiness. This question of "finding happiness" brings us back to the first chapter of the book. How much can you or do you want to leave behind, and what is its purpose?

If one of your intergenerational goals is to make your kids happy with the money you leave behind, this is a great time to reevaluate, in light of the information this chapter offers, whether or not your spending, investing, estate planning, communication, and parenting activities are likely to enhance or hinder your children's ability to

- find work they enjoy
- care less about conspicuous consumption
- manage their expectations and entitlement
- feel and act altruistically
- find their own identity
- feel cared for and understood

---

9. Ibid., 5.

- be autonomous and independent
- possess self-esteem and competence
- develop close relationships and the capacity for love
- feel financially secure

Before we move ahead to the next chapter, please go back to the beginning of the chapter and re-answer the self-survey questions, noting which questions you have answered differently. You can discuss these topics with your spouse, advisors, and children and explore areas of your work, life, and family that you may want to adjust to reflect any new revelations you have experienced.

In the next chapter we will explore how we communicate to our families about wealth.

8

Communication

MONEY MAY TALK, but few with money like to talk about it. Many wealthy people are even uncomfortable discussing wealth with family members. Keep in mind that even if you believe it is in bad taste to discuss money, you are communicating your beliefs, values, and attitudes about it pretty much all the time.

While many wealthy people believe that their legacy is their wealth, the attitudes and values we pass along with that money comprise the larger legacy, yet it is often not discussed.

When is it appropriate to discuss with children what, when, and how they will inherit? Should parents try to dictate how their children will spend, save, invest, and donate the money they'll inherit? How can they help their children develop a positive identity that is not defined by money? We will explore these questions in this chapter, as well as different communication styles and how one type of communicator can communicate effectively with other types of communicators.

Self-Survey about Communication

Let's first weigh in with our attitudes and assumptions related to communicating about wealth with our children in the self-survey below. As in previous chapters, please write your answers now in the column to the left; after reading the chapter, you can survey yourself again and write the answers in the right-hand column to see how your perceptions and attitudes may have changed.

Self-Survey about Communication

1 = Strongly Agree, 2 = Agree, 3 = Neutral, 4 = Disagree, 5 = Strongly Disagree

BEFORE   AFTER

_____   My kids are prepared to make financial decisions   _____
           together after I am gone.

_____   I feel comfortable about what age to tell my kids   _____
           about the family's trusts and wealth.

_____   Money is a private matter, so discussing it as a   _____
           family group is a bad idea.

_____   I believe my kids understand and buy into my   _____
           ideas about what money is for and its legacy.

_____   I should reveal our family's trust structure,   _____
           inheritance value and my expectations about "what
           the money is for" in one integrated discussion as
           the way to introduce them to the family money.

_____   I'm comfortable with the messages my children get   _____
           from observing the way I handle and spend money.

_____   I understand how my communication style may   _____
           sometimes get in the way of effectively discussing
           sensitive issues with my children.

The Instinct to Avoid Talking about Money

Research indicates that fewer wealthy people are loathe to discuss money with their family today than previous generations were.

A Harris Interactive® study, commissioned by PNC Wealth Management in 2006 titled "Growing Up Wealthy: Spoiled and Extravagant or Responsible and Hard Working?" surveyed 210 wealthy teens (ages fourteen to twenty) and 272 affluent parents of children under age eighteen. Most of the teen respondents said they had discussed family wealth with their parents, and 39 percent said their parents had a serious discussion with them on the subject before eighth grade. But only 28 percent of parents said they had discussed the meaning of the family's wealth with their children, and 11 percent said their family avoids the topic of family wealth altogether.

Most wealth experts and psychologists we have interviewed believe that people who do not directly and clearly verbalize to their children their beliefs about money and their intentions risk having their children growing up with potentially harmful misconceptions and expectations. In fact, many studies have traced the failure to sustain wealth across generations to a lack of communication and trust. If you are uncomfortable talking openly to your children about wealth, this chapter will suggest how to discuss the topic in a way that feels more palatable.

As Charles Lowenhaupt, CEO of St. Louis-based wealth-management firm Lowenhaupt Global Advisors, cautioned in Chapter 2, wealth secrets don't work because children may assume you have much more or much less than you have. "The starting question whenever you're talking about family and money, is what is the wealth for?" he says. "Until that question is under discussion there can be no reasonable conversation and there can be no unambiguous communication."

Communicating effectively involves knowing the what, who, when, how, and why of communicaton. The interplay between the message (the what), how it is communicated, when it is communicated, and why we are communicating it makes a huge difference in how your children will hear and understand your messages.

What Should We Communicate?

Children derive their financial values and their expectations about what kind of lifestyle they want and will be able to maintain into adulthood from what parents tell them as well as from what they observe about how and how much their parents spend.

■ **Non-verbal, inadvertent messages.** Some of the messages we send that come from our actions are not messages we intend to give our children.

Consider what messages you believe your children may have already received based on the examples you set:

- Do they see you indulging every whim?
- Do they watch you research the quality of big-ticket items and the best deals at local stores and online?
- Are they aware of your philanthropic gifts and involvement in charitable events?
- If you work, would your children sense you enjoy work and find it meaningful, or might they conclude that you feel stuck in a job out of obligation to the family business, or perhaps that you are motivated and measure your self-worth by earning money?

If you believe that the messages your actions send your children about money, spending, and values are less than ideal, you may want to identify and adjust the areas where you set the worst example. Susan Goldenberg, a partner at Chicago law firm Neal, Gerber & Eisenberg LLP, explains, "People live in a locale for a lot of different reasons, partly because they want their kids to experience certain things and grow up in a certain way. It's not just about what you tell your kids about money, it's about where and how you live. Even if you can afford to take kids to school in a Rolls Royce, do you choose to do that?"

Of course, not every high-priced expenditure you make is an indulgence; perhaps you have perfectly good reasons for many of your purchasing and lifestyle decisions. For example, you may send your child to a particular exclusive school that can deal with certain learning difficulties or special academic talents that a public or less-expensive private school cannot accomodate. In addition, keep in mind that parents need not personify every good habit or value they want their children to maintain. But they can still help their children by discussing honestly and openly some of the apparent incongruities between the ideals they aspire to and their own struggles to reach those ideals.

- **Verbal, intentional messages.** It's also important to identify information about the family's wealth and financial values that would benefit the children. **Exhibit 8.1** lists just some of the issues you might want to broach with your kids.

By being direct with your kids in the messages you want to communicate, you can clear up some of the misconceptions you may inadvertently be sending. You should also discuss the messages communicated by the surrounding environment. Are there messages you want to discuss with your children that they are hearing from their friends, cousins, and other people with whom your children interact in their high–net worth environment? We will consider unintended messages of the high–net worth environment in further detail in Chapter 9.

Who Should Tell Your Kids?

Ideally, you and your spouse (if you have one) should try to control as much as you can the important messages you send your children about wealth and values. In some cases, your trusted advisors might help you deliver the messages. In other cases, a sibling or family member can also be helpful, especially during the rebellious teen years, when kids may be more open to hearing out a family friend, an uncle, or trusted advisor more than to listening to you. For example, if you try to suggest that your teen get a job or become involved in a philanthropic endeavor, your child is likely to do the opposite. If Uncle Bruce delivers the same message, your kid may take this cool uncle's advice. Don't be offended; Uncle Bruce's kids probably will take your advice over his. Use this to your advantage in family meetings and other communication opportunities. Keep in mind that you need to be the one who crafts and controls the messages to the extent you can. In most cases, you and your spouse or partner should be the ones to deliver the information and discuss the values about your family's wealth. No matter how uncomfortable you may feel about discussing money, your kids are bound to get earfuls of information from friends, other family members, and even the media. Much of that information is bound to be incorrect, and your children will have no context for absorbing the information and will be unprepared to handle the taunting from others who call them spoiled brats or worse.

Exhibit 8.1   Money Messages

- What is money for?
- How much will my children inherit, and when?
- Where did that money come from? A family business? From Mom or Dad's side? How many generations back does it go?
- What are some examples (in families of multi-generational wealth) of relatives who handled the wealth responsibly and those who did not—and what were the consequences of their actions?
- What do you (and should you—or not) feel entitled to concerning the family wealth?
- What actions and values do you, as a parent, not model that your kids should value and why?
- How has money helped and hindered you (the parents) in your own life? What mistakes have you made, and lessons have you learned?
- What misconceptions about money did you harbor as a child?
- What is the structure of trusts in which the children are beneficiaries, and what contingencies are attached to those trusts?
- What is the family's approach to philanthropy, and what role might the children play at different stages of their life?
- Should you try to dictate how your children will spend, save, invest, and donate the money they will inherit?
- How can your family develop a positive identity that is not defined by money?
- Will your children be able to afford to live the same lifestyle with their inheritance?
- Will your children have to work to afford the same level of comfort they currently enjoy?
- Under what circumstances would you "bail" out your children from problems and failures, and under what circumstances will the children have to solve their own problems and learn in their own way?
- How do you spot and avoid gold-diggers among "friends," family, lovers, and colleagues?
- Do you expect your children's future spouse to sign a prenup? If so, have you told them so? When would be the best time to raise the subject?
- How do you help your children understand how to resist requests from every friend and acquaintance who might approach your child to invest in some harebrained business venture?
- Do you expect your children not to discuss the family's financial status with friends, or even with a potential future spouse?

In his documentary movie, *Born Rich*, Johnson & Johnson heir Jamie Johnson admits that he didn't know he was rich growing up in the country. He says he thought "everyone had carriages and horses and stuff like that." His father never talked about inherited wealth. When he was in the fourth grade, during a trip to the school library, one of his classmates found Jamie's father's name on the *Forbes* 400 list of wealthiest people in America. "The kid read the article aloud to the whole class," recalls Johnson. "Everyone, including my teacher, ran over to check it all out for themselves. It was strange, all my friends and me finding out at the same time how rich my family was. I felt like I was learning a secret I wasn't supposed to know."

One of Johnson's friends, Vanderbilt/Whitney heir Josiah Hornblower, says in the movie that his father "brought us up, always telling us we were poor. We never were given too many presents, and I didn't know anything about the Vanderbilts or the Whitneys. ... I remember when I was a little kid, my mom let me spend the day with my uncle. And he took me to Grand Central Station and he said, 'This is yours.' ... He'd just take me all around New York and be like, 'Yes, we own this.' It was the dumbest thing in the world to do to a kid."

As attorney Susan Goldenberg pointed out in Chapter 2, parents need to control the process of disseminating the information. Not relatives, classmates or even the advisors. "Parents should be there every step of the way," she says.

When: The Perfect Time

Sorry to get your hopes up, but there *is* no perfect time. And, like many aspects of parenting, communicating about family wealth and values is not a one-shot deal. Ideally, you have been initiating age-appropriate discussions regularly, as issues and your children's questions arise.

■ **Small, frequent discussions** provide a context for the big picture—by progressively telling their children in small doses information about how much the family is worth, how much your children are likely to inherit, and the timing structure and restrictions/

contingencies attached to trusts in their name. Making any message understandable to the child at any given age is only part of the process. It's important to connect your values with your day-to-day living and communication with your children. Once you've laid that groundwork, your children will have an easier time understanding that information without it jolting them, as it jolted Jamie Johnson and Josiah Hornblower. That will give you more leeway in the timing that big discussion, in terms of the child's age and maturity.

■   **The pros and cons of waiting.** Cambridge Associates' Managing Director Doug Macauley believes it may be better to err on the side of telling kids about family wealth a little too early.

Henry Hutcheson, a partner with ReGENERATION Partners in Raleigh, North Carolina, is not so sure. "There's an ongoing debate that says do you hide the fact that you have wealth from your kids and try to instill traditional values into them? Or say hey, this is something you need to know about and you'll have to be responsible about? The former seems to be the more successful than the latter," he says. He feels it may be best to not disclose "the true degree of wealth and get them grounded in traditional values in a world where they're not assuming there's wealth," although he acknowledges that may be easier to do with a family that has $10 million of net worth than a family with $100 million, if the lifestyle is extremely opulent.

Many parents choose to tell their children about the family wealth when they're about to get married because they want to encourage their children to have a prenup. This should not be the first the child learns about her future inheritance.

But Jeff Brodsky, director of Midwest Area Personal Financial Services for Ernst & Young, has noticed a trend over the years in which parents are much more focused on sharing information. "In the old days, they were more hesitant. Now there's an awareness of sharing information, in the right amount," he says.

At least one study, GenSpring Family Office's "Women & Wealth," agrees. The 2007 study (of 115 women with at least $1 million in net worth or who are potential inheritors of significant wealth) found that growing up, the majority of women respondents from upper-class households were not told about their inheritance or their parents' estate plan. However, a majority of the women agree that they have communicated to their children specifically about their inheritance (64 percent) and their estate plan (62 percent).

"You can't dump a lot of money in someone's pocket or trust without giving them some education along the way," says Brodsky. "Clients are more focused on trying to educate children about the benefits and responsibilities of wealth. It varies how much education gets shared. In some cases they don't give [children] the book with the numbers in it. The purpose is not so much the amount, as the concepts." He says laying out the whole estate plan, including how much wealth the children will receive, typically happens when the children are well into their thirties. But "I see the education process starting at much younger ages, when they are teenagers in some cases."

Each child will mature at a different rate. Specific information about inheritances and trust funds may impede some children's motivation or their search for purpose (as we discuss in Chapter 6). Others may find the information liberating, especially if they had worried about making a tradeoff between pursuing their passion in an area not likely to provide substantial earnings and their desire to live a comfortable lifestyle. It's helpful, Brodsky says, to begin educating family members at least by the time they're in the mid-twenties and up, "on the basic concept of trust planning, the reasons for trusts, and prenuptial agreements."

■ **Finding the right time.** One couple we know, with children ages twenty-one and twenty-four, realized that because each child is different, they had to handle how and when they communicate information about their wealth differently for each one.

When the older son, Robbie, was about to go to college, his father says, "I asked him if he felt ready to be told some specifics about the family wealth, and he said no. He felt it might negatively affect his motivation to study and figure out what he wants to do in life." He ended up with a degree in business and worked for an investment management firm after graduation.

A few years later, when his younger child, Deidre, was preparing
to go to college, she was confused about what she wanted to study
and what kind of career she might like. She is extremely artistic,
but she was concerned that pursuing music or art might not
produce enough income to produce a comfortable lifestyle. She
saw her brother heading toward a financial career where he could
earn a lot of money and started thinking her career choices would
limit her financially. "My wife and I decided it was time to tell her
some of what she can expect financially in the future, without getting
into specific numbers or trust features," says her father. "We told
her that she needs to figure out what her passion in life is and
go for it, that she should not worry about whether she'll be able
to support herself because our family is lucky; we have enough
money that we have been able to set aside sufficient funds to
supplement whatever she will eventually earn. We encouraged her
not to base what to do in life on living a certain lifestyle because
she would wind up unhappy." After her first couple years in college,
she realized that if she had to do art for a living it would no longer
be fun. She picked her major, hotel and restaurant management,
one of the better programs at her school, and plans to go on
to graduate school for interior/architectural design. She wants to
design restaurants and hotels. So she found a way to combine her
creativity in a business context.

Prenuptial agreements can be a very difficult conversation that
some parents put off until it is too late. "In a perfect world you try to
impart the importance of having a prenup before the child has a significant other, so it's not interpreted as 'you don't like my boyfriend
or girlfriend,'" points out Jeff Brodsky. "It's never an easy subject
when it comes time to implement, but having the discussion when
there's no significant other is important." In fact, late high school
or early college may be a good time to broach the subject. While
people are marrying later, they might meet their future spouse in
high school or college.

Durham, New Hampshire, psychologist Dr. Kenneth Sole says
the "right" time to raise the topic of wealth with kids is likely "sooner
than whatever you're planning. Often the 'when' gets connected

to the 'how.' For many adults, having that sort of conversation is of profound significance and there is probably the tendency to delay: until the youngster is sufficiently mature; until the moment is absolutely right; or until my own comfort as an adult reaches a point where I'm ready. The problem is as we delay, in our mind the conversation becomes bigger and bigger and takes on overwhelming proportion."

He explains that, from a psychological point of view, wealth management is no different than self management. If children begin to learn how to manage any aspect of their behavior only when they become adults, it's far too late. "If a young adult hasn't started thinking about those issues, feeling what it means to be connected to those questions when they're three, four, or five years old, we've got trouble," he says.

Still, better late than never. If you have not had "the talk" with your nineteen-year-old, better to start now than when she turns twenty-five or thirty.

How to Broach the Topic

"The way to get families to be able to communicate takes practice," says Jill Shipley, GenSpring Family Offices director of next generation education. She helps her clients develop structured, multi-generation family meetings, at which GenSpring presents many discussion activities and projects, including the creation of a family mission statement to help members unite under an explicit set of family goals and values. "This process has been used for years with businesses," she says. "We ask individual members to answer 125 questions, resulting in a personal values report that outlines a list of eight to fourteen core personal values." Then GenSpring helps them identify where their family values overlap and facilitates a discussion to get members to share their thoughts about why these values are important, where they come from, and to share some stories. "This is one of the most bonding experiences," she explains. "From that they write their mission. It grounds the family."

Discussions about wealth should involve not just your own family's circumstances but also your perspectives and values about money. Sole believes, "If a person disconnects issues of wealth from issues of other values in their life, the conversation is likely to fall apart. If, on the other hand, a person's value system is well integrated, connected to other aspects of their life experience, and if they learn the good values early, the specifics relating to their wealth are just one more set of expressions of the values that are already well integrated."

■ **Factoring in communication styles.** Institute for Private Investors (IPI) member Jeffrey Horvitz illustrates how easy it is to misinterpret what someone intends to communicate, especially between family members, which can be emotionally charged. "You're not sure when you tell a child something, what they heard or how they interpret this. My father used to say if I got a B+, 'Why didn't you get an A?' You can take that as encouragement, meaning 'my father thinks so highly of me, he thinks I could get As.' Or as, 'Nothing I can do will ever please him, nothing I do is enough, so I shouldn't even try.'"

Corporations, teams, non-profits, family businesses, and just about all types of organizations are well served by implementing some type of personal profile testing of its members. All of us process information differently. Some people like great detail; others make decisions quickly with seemingly little information: "Ready fire aim." Understanding how people listen, talk, and make decisions, and how they react to each other can be useful in any group setting, including and especially the family.

Exhibit 8.2 describes some of the most common assessment tools and programs recommended by Executive Coaching Connections,

---

UNINTENDED CONSEQUENCES

Personality profiling systems can be a great way to learn the vocabulary to understand different communications styles. However, be careful not to pigeonhole yourself or your children in any one communication style. People do not always stick to any given style or respond the same way to other people's styles.

Exhibit 8.2   Communication and Personality Profiling Systems

Myers-Briggs Type Indicator® (MBTI)
www.myersbriggs.org

The MBTI is a personality inventory based on the psychological types described by C.G. Jung. We all see the world and make decisions based on the basic differences in the ways we prefer to use our perception and judgment. MBTI categorizes how people differ correspondingly in interests, reactions, values, motivations, and skills; identifying these helps describe how people differ in what they perceive and in how they reach conclusions and decisions. To be most effective, MBTI requires a professional consultant to administer the questionnaire and analyze results.

DISC Personal Profile System
www.discprofile.com

DISC is a personality profile system developed in the 1920s by psychologist William Moulton Marston. DISC is behaviorally focused. It identifies each person's personality preferences: Dominant, Influential, Steady, Cautious. By understanding everyone's preferences in non-judgmental language, people can explore how to better relate to each other. This tool has the least business feel and can be applied to all aspects of life's negotiations with others. DISC provides an online questionnaire and to be most effective requires a professional consultant to administer it and interpret results.

Team Management Profile (TMP)
www.tms.co.nz/webpages/products/tmp.htm

TMP's results focus on each person's unique approach to decision making and team building. The report can help identify critical success factors and potential development needs for each individual and the team. TMP provides an online questionnaire, but like the other systems above is most effective when administered by a professional consultant who can also analyze results.

LLC based in Wilmette, Illinois; Ruda Cohen & Associates based in Chicago, and Changepace, also based in Chicago.

If you decide to test family members' personality and communication styles, you can all benefit by learning how to customize the way you communicate to individuals in your family. Many communication breakdowns result not from disagreements about the substance of the issue but because of differing communication styles. For instance, if you are a touchy-feely person and are trying to discuss the value of charitable giving to a child who is analytical, instead of focusing only on how emotionally rewarding the experience may be, you would be wise to stick to pragmatic, fact-based points, such as how learning about how the family foundation invests and makes grant decisions will provide experience they will need to manage their own money in the future. If you tend to be autocratic and want your child, who questions everything you say, to participate in a new cousins' investment club, instead of telling her she must do so, you would be wise to find compelling reasons that are likely to lead that child to buy into the idea.

Psychologist Sole adds, "It's important for adults to appreciate the uniqueness of the situation in which the need for communication arises. Too often we tend to focus on the content rather than trying to learn more about the process. There are moments to negotiate; then there are moments to scream and grab a kid by collar and get the kid safe." In other words, regardless of your or your child's communication style, some circumstances warrant playing the "because I'm the parent and I say so" card.

■ **Optimizing group interaction.** As we discussed in Chapter 5, your children's ability to communicate and work together effectively will prepare them to make important decisions when they are adults,

---

TEACHABLE MOMENTS

Time is an interesting component of communication. We all have a different tolerance of how much time we can give to difficult or complicated conversations. It may help to simply ask your child, is now a good time to talk? Setting time limits for a conversation can also be helpful.

Consider also whether your family enjoys the formal nature of a meeting or if a conversation works better over breaking bread. Finding out what process works the best for each situation will lead to more successful communication.

which will affect their future financial wealth. Like just about every other topic we discuss in this book, this is a process best begun early. And you don't need to start by assuming the role of teacher. You may find your children respond better when you solicit their input, says Sole. For instance, you can bring up at the dinner table that you're looking to contribute some money to an educational institution and say, "Because you're students, I'd really value your input." "That casts the problem as providing Mom and Dad info. That's meaningful. The next year you might say, 'We want to make another contribution, but this time we'd like the three of you to provide us with your input collectively. Put you heads together, talk about what would be the most important things you'd like to convey to us to inform the contribution. The third year you might turn it over to the youngsters by saying, 'The three of you did a spectacular job the past two years, so Dad and I would like you to make the contribution decision, and we'd like you to do it together.'"

Claudia Sangster, director of philanthropy, estate, and trust services at Harris myCFO, describes a client family in which the third-generation children don't work or play well with others. While trying to help them work together on a family mission statement for a donor advised fund, they were all doing their own thing instead of talking it through together. One daughter had so much friction between her and the rest of the family that she decided not to participate. Sangster says, "The family is not forcing her to participate in the family meetings. They were spending so much time and energy to try to keep her happy, as they had been doing for decades, they finally, said 'You don't have to participate; it's voluntary. We love you, we want you to be there, but it's up to you.'"

Many families insist that there be no empty chairs and that everyone must engage in the family foundation, family council, or family forum. "If you try to force them, it can blow up in your face," says Sangster. While conflict training, mediation, personality tests, or other solutions might help, it's not always possible or even productive to force reluctant relatives to participate. While it's very important to attempt to be inclusive, when doing so prevents the rest of the family from moving ahead in a positive way, it may be best to let brother Barry or cousin Cathy storm out of the room. Just keep the door open; maybe one day they will return, ready to work productively with the rest of the family.

The goal of communicating effectively with your children—about wealth or any other issue—is to enhance their ability ultimately to take over the family wealth, notes Sole. This requires many discussions throughout the years.

Please return now to the beginning of this chapter to take another stab at answering the self-survey questions, noting where you have adjusted your thinking about the issues this chapter has addressed.

The next chapter will delve into how to navigate the sometimes rough terrain of the high–net worth environment.

9

Navigating the High–Net Worth Environment

T HE HIGH–NET WORTH environment creates hidden messages.
Some of the messages can have a positive effect on our children,
and some communicate just the opposite of what we want to impart.
In Chapter 8 we mostly dealt with the verbal, intentional messages: the
who, when, what, where, and how we communicate. In this chapter,
we will investigate the unintended, non-verbal messages of the high–
net worth environment. We will ask you to evaluate how your value
system lines up or contrasts with your choices and your environment.

You may drive a modest car, and you may not drip in diamonds
or nibble on caviar, truffles, or sip from $4,000 bottles of cham-
pagne while the private jet shuttles you to San Tropez. But if you
live in a neighborhood where that sort of lifestyle is the norm, it has
a profound effect on you and your children.

If you dare, this chapter will help you take an inventory of your
lifestyle and the broader high–net worth environment in which you
live, work, and play. We hope you will examine the often unspoken
messages your children may glean from what they observe at home
and the world around them, in school, the community, summer
camp, and on family vacations. By taking an inventory of your consumption choices, you will be able to understand what your lifestyle
may say about what you value and the degree to which it enhances
your ability to pass those values to your children.

Self-Survey about Your High–Net Worth Environment

Before we move ahead please take a few moments once again to fill in the following self-survey about your current attitudes and assumptions surrounding your high–net worth environment.

· Self-Survey about Your High–Net Worth Environment

1 = Strongly Agree, 2 = Agree, 3 = Neutral, 4 = Disagree, 5 = Strongly Disagree

BEFORE		AFTER
_____	The neighborhood and community in which I live exposes my children to people, culture, and values that will make them successful and happy.	_____
_____	The majority of media messages and culture we experience helps me teach my kids the value of money and wealth.	_____
_____	My values, actions, and lifestyle are aligned.	_____
_____	Buying expensive houses, cars, jewelry, vacations, etc., all have the same meaning and purpose—they allow us to enjoy the money we have.	_____
_____	Economic downturns, such as the one that began in 2008, put pressure on truly wealthy people to reduce conspicuous consumption, but when times get better, we can go back to spending.	_____
_____	The high–net worth environment does not affect my buying or spending habits.	_____

Media and Money

Our society is fascinated, if not obsessed, with how "the other half"—your half—lives. This is not a new fascination. Carnegie,

consultant Kenneth Kaye points out, "I hate to generalize, but with old money, at least one of the parents has been through this before as a child in growing up. They've been to the private schools, seen things they thought their parents did right and wrong. They have views about it. And it's very striking in families I've worked with who've had sudden, self-made wealth, it's not that they're not intelligent about it, but they haven't had that experience themselves. So it's overwhelming to the person who made the money."

James E. Hughes Jr., a sixth-generation counselor of law and author of *Family Wealth—Keeping It in the Family* (Bloomberg Press, 2004) and *Family: The Compact Among Generations* (Bloomberg Press, 2007), points out, "Really old money—the New England definition that you live on the income of your income—those families continue quietly, unobtrusively and every generation produces a couple of people of great service to society." They have been able to dynamically preserve the family wealth for multiple generations "by hard work and conscientious thinking by those most able to take on those responsibilities. It's not random at all."

On the other hand, Nancy Donovan and her husband are both first-generation wealth creators from their careers in finance. They live in one of the wealthiest suburbs of Chicago and send their children to an exclusive private school. She and her children have noticed that many of the children of multi-generation wealth in their community exhibit a huge sense of entitlement. They have come to expect always to "go on a great vacation, have a great new car. My parents were very middle class and felt the only thing they owed their children was a great education. My husband and I both went to work and did exceptionally well in our jobs. So it's different how we talk to our kids about wealth. We try to explain and associate how the material things we have are related to the work we've been doing."

Donovan believes her children don't take things for granted because she and her husband have been very explicit about setting an example that they both work hard. She explains, "When my kids see that, they understand what it takes to support a family. Whereas a lot of the kids that they deal with, their parents haven't had to work." She's even noticed a difference between how some of the "old money" families approach team sport involvement. "There tends to be less of a competitive environment when you have groups of entitled children. They are used to having things taken care of for them, having parents make sure that they're in the right place at the right time, on the right team. There are many kids that are passionate about their sports, but their sense of their having to reach the highest level of achievement is not necessarily there." If the coach benches the child, these parents—especially those who may have donated the new locker room or soccer field—are more likely to call him and demand putting their son or daughter in the game more often.

One way Donovan has avoided the impact these issues of fairness these parents' behavior might have on her sons, now sixteen and twenty-one, has been to sign them up for community-based sports leagues instead of those at their school. An added benefit of this is that her children have friends who come from families from all different economic backgrounds. "We've tried to expose our kids to the other side and show that there are different ways you can grow up."

Keeping Up with the Neighbors

The media alone are not responsible for our desires to buy more goods. Many people get caught up with trying to keep up with their friends and neighbors. If you choose to live in a high–net worth community, your neighbor is bound to have a full range of extravagant toys, from expensive cars to exquisite landscaping. It is difficult to live in such a neighborhood and not feel the desire, or even pressure, to keep up with the latest home theater equipment or to install a new kitchen with the latest in cabinets and gadgets. The game of keeping up with the neighbors can subtly influence your value system and skew your sense of what is important, especially when it comes to lifecycle parties and events.

Different people are bound to have a different definition of excess. Many families that participated in the *My Super Sweet 16* TV program either did not think their parties were over the top or felt that their kids deserved an over-the-top party. Similar excesses abound with bar/bat mitzvah parties, graduation parties, proms, quinceañeras, debutante parties, and other special occasions like milestone birthday celebrations, which can cost into the millions of dollars.

Some families may feel obligated to purchase a palatial house and maintain whatever outward appearances they believe the community expects of a family of their wealth and position. But keeping up can be a moving target, as the neighbors attempt to one-up the standards set by friends' and neighbors' previous parties, home renovations, and yachts. Parents can decide how lavishly they spend based on what they can afford or on what message they want to send to their kids about what they value.

If having a blow-out party fits your value system, then have a great time planning, executing, and hosting the party. If it is not part of your value system, then you may want to think about whether or not the environment in which you live allows you to feel comfortable being who you want to be. There in no judgment implied here in terms of what you choose. The point is that your choices should emanate from your thoughtful assessment of the consequences of your decisions. There are many ways to plan a lavish party around some of the family's deep values. For instance, some families have opted to spend hundreds of thousands of dollars on a lifecycle party, but asked invited guests to donate money to a charity in lieu of bringing a gift. Others have used the party as a way to help express the family values to their children by having them research a charity or world problem that will serve as the party's theme. The money, time, and attention will focus on learning and expressing their values and donating money to a cause rather than just on the indulgence of the party or trying to keep up with or out-do the neighbors.

Don't forget the importance of devoting time and energy—not just money—to major lifecycle moments as well as to family rituals or traditions that focus on the meaning of having reached a milestone. Even if you still throw the lavish party, setting aside time for the family to celebrate in other ways, such as writing the event in a generations-old family bible that lists the hand-written dates and events of ancestors or passing down a family heirloom, can offset some of the material excesses with more down-to-earth, meaningful, and perhaps even spiritual values.

Transcending External and Internal Economic Shocks

Charlotte Beyer, founder of the Institute for Private Investors (IPI), recalls that in late 2008, a man asked his daughter what she wanted for her eighteenth birthday. She said what she most wanted was a purse, price tag $1,700. When her father hit the roof, she responded, "You would have given that to me last year!" He answered, "Well, we're in a new world." Beyer notes, "Many families are observing how sadly easy it is to move from a sense of privilege to a feeling of entitlement."

Before the financial fiasco that began in late 2008, many wealthy families did not think twice about their spending and lifestyle choices. Some who come from inherited money justified their charmed lives, reasoning, "my parents or grandparents worked hard to provide their offspring a good lifestyle." People who have earned their money felt that this is the American dream and spending the money was the reward for all of the hard work. Many in both camps happen to be extremely generous philanthropists, giving away tens or hundreds of millions of dollars to worthy causes each year. They—and you—have a right to enjoy what the portfolio provides.

The economic situation in late 2008 and 2009 found many wealthy families unable to maintain their previous lifestyle. Could their children adjust to a less exclusive, or even public, school? Even if it did not come to that, for the first time, many ultra-rich families cannot escape the possibility that they might have to make some major lifestyle adjustments. Worse, many have insisted on living in denial, not even admitting to their spouse that the family's funds have taken a dramatic hit. Some have borrowed heavily to maintain their lifestyle; others are facing choices such as selling their vacation homes or cutting back on their charitable giving. They may feel keenly embarrassed, even humiliated, not to mention shaken and frightened.

Many who could maintain the same spending level as before the crisis have started to question whether they should continue their conspicuous consumption while so many people across the socio-economic spectrum are suffering financially.

Nancy Donovan has noticed how many of her friends changed their spending habits. "This is the first time in my thirty years I've seen such an impact, where some won't take a vacation or won't buy another car. It's incredible. We've seen a lot of people lose their wealth. In 1989, when we were just coming up on Wall Street, people had lost jobs, but there was not this huge destruction of wealth where it's literally disappeared in Ponzi schemes as well as the stock market." She has been open with her children about the need to be especially careful in this kind of economic crisis. "I like to say we manage our life efficiently, and we're not outrageous in our spending, but I look at things and say we don't need that."

The idea is not to make you or your children feel guilty about your wealth, about enjoying some of its benefits, or worry about the family's future stability and security. It's about understanding the impact your wealth imposes on your family. It's about preparing yourself and your family to enjoy life with or without your family's wealth and current trappings. It could take something far less imposing than a worldwide financial crisis to change your lifestyle. A heavy investment in a fund like Bernie Madoff's or a medical tragedy could suck the bank account clean. Are you and your family prepared emotionally to stick together and bounce back emotionally? Could your marriage survive a sudden shift in your financial circumstances? Those who can honestly answer "yes" to these questions likely consciously choose to factor their values into their life and lifestyle decisions.

Fritzi Hallock, who works for her family office and is a member of IPI, is among those who can answer "yes." She and her husband decided very early to live in a way that, "if all my family's money went away we could continue to live. That money pays for upgrades, like private school. They could go to public school, because there's a good one in our neighborhood. So we're not trapped into the money."

Discretionary Wealth

Donovan also noticed that this financial shakedown has brought down many people who lived a wealthy lifestyle using leverage, who could not sustain their high-overhead lifestyle. She points out, "Everyone wants to look like they have $50 million and just have $10 million. There will be a lot of children used to having a lot of things and won't have that going forward because they don't have the asset base to support it. In an economic environment like this, that leverage will disappear and that will hurt a lot of families."

One way to prevent that from happening is to pay attention to "discretionary wealth." In *Investment Management for Taxable Private Investors* (Charolottesville, Virginia: The Research Foundation of CFA Institute, 2006) Jarrod Wilcox, Jeffrey E. Horvitz, and Dan diBartolomeo define discretionary wealth as "what is left over after implied and tangible financial assets have been added and after implied and tangible financial liabilities have been subtracted. In this context, 'discretionary' implies 'what the investor would not like to give up but the loss of which would not be considered disastrous. ... As the investor goes from youth to maturity to middle age to retirement to old age, the ratio of discretionary wealth to total assets will determine appropriate levels of investment aggressiveness." Discretionary wealth should also factor into one's spend rate. The authors explain, "What happens if discretionary wealth falls to zero or even becomes negative? People in this situation have to readjust their thinking—even if it is painful—about what they must earn or can spend." [1]

Families spending on credit, without assets or earnings to cover their purchases or lifestyle overhead, will have the toughest time adjusting and bouncing back if their discretionary wealth disappears.

It essentially boils down to living within one's means. To do that, one needs to tally the limits of one's means. Many wealthy families have come to think of their wealth as an infinite resource. They would be wise to rethink that idea, to discuss the reality with their children, and to adjust their spending to reflect this reality.

---

1. Page 16.

Staying Safe and Secure

Security is often a hidden reason behind many affluent families' spending decisions. Chicago-based psychologist and family business expert Kenneth Kaye points out, "If your name is [Smith or Jones] and you come from a family with a couple hundred million dollars, you can live in a community without most people knowing [you're wealthy] if that's your goal. If your name is Rockefeller, you cannot. People assume that you're a billionaire. That's a bigger issue than how much money is actually in the bank. If you don't have the visibility, you have choices all along the way about how ostentatiously or not you want to live."

If your name, face, or wealth is well known, safety may become a crucial issue, affecting where and how your family travels. Flying on a private jet may provide the greatest security. Kaye points out, "That really can affect children of my billionaire clients. If they never or rarely fly commercial, they're treated lavishly—way beyond first class. Their own chauffeur drives them to their own hangar, and everyone who sees them go and arrive looks at them as though they're royalty. That puts them in a world that it's hard to put in perspective without extra attention, including a discussion about why we do this—for security, for example."

This extends beyond air travel. If your name or your lavish lifestyle makes it obvious that you are wealthy, you may need to live in a gated community or a home with security guards, or have a chauffer who doubles as a body guard, because you and family members become a visible target for things such as kidnapping. Kaye also warns, however, that "families that are less visible may not require such extra attention, but their parents can do harm by exaggerating their wealth."

Additionally, families that feel the need to hire body guards, install high-tech security systems into their homes, and take other safety precautions may find it difficult to trust outsiders, may feel nervous walking about in the outside world, and may harbor fears about break-ins or abductions. It's important to bring these fears into the open and perhaps call in the help of a psychologist to work through these scary feelings and learn how to trust people.

The safest children are those who can spot a dangerous person or situation, and react swiftly and effectively. One wealthy parents' son went to a private school in a wealth suburb of Chicago, about twenty minutes from their home. On occasion, neither parent could pick up their son after school, so they showed him how to find his way to the nearest train station on foot and how to take it home. Many school parents initially expressed concern, asking, "How can you let your twelve-year-old boy take the train home by himself?" This train did not pass through any bad neighborhoods and the majority of passengers were business commuters. The student had a cell phone and was learning valuable skills: to be self-sufficient, how to be self-aware and safe in public.

Children who never get the chance to experience the world beyond the safe bubble their parents try to build around them become essentially imprisoned within that environment. They will likely live, work, and travel in high–net worth circles that exclude them from potentially interesting people, places, and experiences.

Taking Inventory of Your Lifestyle and Values

Why do we make the choices we make? How do our choices affect our children's attitudes, values, and their ability to navigate and feel comfortable in other environments? Whatever degree of opulent or modest lifestyle you choose, it's important to think through how your lifestyle aligns and where it may conflict with your values.

Those without substantial wealth may think a few million dollars would solve all of their problems. Those who have the millions, or billions, know that money can distort their values and create unintended consequences. **Exhibit 9.1** illustrates how the hypothetical Jones family's values interact with the material world around them. This chart raises the question we first posed in Chapter 1: "What is the money for?" It explores how the Jones family views the purpose (according to their values) of some of their big-ticket purchases and some of the effects (unintended consequences) those expenditures may have on their children, or even themselves.

Exhibit 9.1 Inventory of the Hypothetical Jones Family's Lifestyle

EXPENDITURE	OPULENCE LEVEL M-Q-L*	PURPOSE/ DESIRED VALUES	UNINTENDED CONSEQUENCES
Home	L: 14-room mansion in exclusive neighborhood L: Summer home on lake	■ Impresses others ■ Entertains family/ friends ■ Provides security ■ Provides a place where the Joneses can host extended family and friends	■ Isolates us from neighborhood/ community ■ Keeps Joneses from getting to know their neighbors ■ Sets family up as a target for robbery, kidnapping, etc.
Cars	Q: Low-end BMW Q: Classic Mercedes convertible L: chauffer-driven Hummer	■ Is reliable ■ Is safe ■ Provides moderate brag value ■ Is fun ■ Is reliable ■ Is safe	■ Does not allow the family much opportunity to drive their own cars
Education	L: Exclusive private school	■ Provides academic excellence ■ Improves odds of getting into the best colleges ■ Provides safety	■ Creates pressure to keep up with peer purchases ■ Has limited diversity

*M = Modest; Q = High Quality; L = Luxury

Exhibit 9.1 Inventory of the Hypothetical Jones Family's
Lifestyle (*Continued*)

EXPENDITURE	OPULENCE LEVEL M-Q-L*	PURPOSE/ DESIRED VALUES	UNINTENDED CONSEQUENCES
Vacations	L: First class all the way L: Their other homes	■ Allows a getaway from the rat race ■ Provides the only place where the kids can run freely and spend quality time with their parents	■ Keeps the children from really seeing the places they visit—they just see the private accommodations where they stay ■ Communicates a sense of great wealth and some isolation
Travel	L: Private jet; chauffeur / limo	■ Provides safety ■ Provides convenience	■ Further isolates the Joneses from the broader world ■ Prevents children from gaining experience traveling commercially if the need to do so suddenly arises
Clothes	L: New designer wardrobe each season	■ Fulfills parents' work needs	■ Teaches the kids that luxury is part of their lifestyle. ■ Creates in kids an insatiable appetite for constant and conspicuous consumption

*M = Modest; Q = High Quality; L = Luxury

(*Continued*)

Exhibit 9.1 Inventory of the Hypothetical Jones Family's Lifestyle (*Continued*)

EXPENDITURE	OPULENCE LEVEL M-Q-L*	PURPOSE/ DESIRED VALUES	UNINTENDED CONSEQUENCES
Jewelry	L: $30,000 watch; 2-carat diamond ring; some inherited pieces	■ Fulfills parents' work needs ■ Forms part of a collection in the family for years. ■ Reminds them of the family heritage	■ Blurs where opulence ends and family values begin
Electronics	L: Home theater etc.	■ Provides entertainment in the home, as the Joneses only get out for public events and stay home for other forms of entertainment	■ Results in the kids spending most of their time watching TV, movies, or playing videogames
Art	L: Mostly paintings and some sculpture	■ Allows Joneses to fulfill their passion for collecting art and to enjoy it at home and at work	■ Results in restrictions on the children's movements in the house so that they don't damage some of the art or expensive furnishings. ■ Requires security cameras in every room that make the kids feel like their every move is scrutinized and they have no privacy

*M = Modest; Q = High Quality; L = Luxury

The Joneses live in a large home in an exclusive enclave on the outskirts of their city, opulently decorated. The walls display a vast collection of fine art, some by up-and-coming painters, plus several originals by masters such as Matisse, Van Gogh, and Picasso. Mrs. Jones, CFO at a *Fortune* 100 corporation, is in the news at least once a week. She is well known in her city's corporate, philanthropic, and arts communities. Working for a public company, her salary and net worth are easy to find on the Internet. Mr. Jones is the curator of the city's main museum of modern art. They both travel at least two or three days most weeks and employ a domestic staff that includes a part-time cook for important occasions, a chauffer, and a live-in nanny/housekeeper for their two elementary-school children who attend the most exclusive private school in their city. Once or twice a month, they entertain business colleagues and clients with parties and large dinners.

Casual acquaintances may assume the Joneses flaunt their conspicuous wealth. They do meticulously maintain their home and spend lavishly on a complete new designer wardrobe each season. However, given the amount and level of entertaining they do as part of their professions, and their prized art collection, they would argue that the size, location, and décor of their home and other trappings are necessary for work as well as security. Even sending their children to their particular school is necessary, as it offers a high level of security for students, many of whom face the real threat of kidnapping given the wealth, and in some cases, the fame of their family. However, the parents did choose a school that provides scholarships for academically and artistically gifted students of lesser means to provide a diverse environment.

Whether you view the Joneses' lifestyle as pretentious or pragmatic, there are many unintended consequences to their choices. For instance, because their home is set way back from their street and is gated, the family knows their neighbors but has few opportunities to interact with them. They do not carpool with their children's friends' families, as the chauffer (who doubles as a security guard) drives them to and from school and activities. Parents and children alike have therefore not forged close relationships with others in their community. They find it difficult to trust people because they have never been in a position to help or ask for help from any of their acquaintances. They find it hard to know if those who make social overtures want to establish a genuine friendship, want to network, or have ulterior motives.

Everything the family needs, a hired person provides. Their children have never made their bed, cleaned up their toys, or even poured cereal into a bowl. They are easily bored, surrounded by every toy they ever desired, with few casual, unstructured "play dates." Their time is highly scheduled around organized activities geared to develop skills and expose them to the arts and culture. Most nights their parents are either traveling or return home too late to sit down to dinner with them, or tuck them in. Even during their lavish vacations to exotic resorts around the globe, they spend most of their time with their nanny, while their parents play tennis or sip cocktails with business associates.

The Joneses' large summer lake home, which sleeps eighteen people, may seem like a luxury "chest beater" of a house that screams, "look at me I am rich!" However, it is large enough to accommodate a family get-together several times a year. This is nice, but because it is more modest than their primary home, it does not require the same level of security, and the Joneses don't have to remind their kids to not run around for fear of breaking a priceless vase.

In Chapter 11 we will discuss some options for putting values more in line with your lifestyle and the messages you want to send to your children. In the meantime, **Exhibit 9.2** lets you take your own inventory of your wealth, the purpose of your purchases, and their effect on your family. You may want to have each member of the family fill out a copy and then have everyone share answers; or you can fill it out together and discuss your answers as you go along.

As you fill in the chart, think of conspicuous consumption as showing off by buying things that will lose most of their value over time. Can you truly justify the items on your list as necessary? Are they an investment? A hobby? No matter what the combination of purposes behind your purchases, what unintended consequences affect you and your children? Notice there is an extra column in

Exhibit 9.2 Inventory of Your Lifestyle

EXPENDITURE	OPULENCE LEVEL M-Q-L*	PURPOSE	UNINTENDED CONSEQUENCES	POST MELT-DOWN

*M = Modest; Q = High Quality; L = Luxury

Exhibit 9.2. Before the economic meltdown, you may have considered some purchases as needs, not wants. Since that financial shock, you may see some of your purchases differently. And the consequences may have shifted, as well. Maintaining a luxurious lifestyle when the country is growing and prospering may feel fine. Some people may, for the first time, feel the need to pull back at least a little, if only to communicate to their children that it's possible to enjoy life without all their creature comforts and to demonstrate empathy and sensitivity to less fortunate people in their community who lost their jobs or homes. Or not.

Even if you do not possess enough fame or fortune to relate to all the issues we have ascribed to the hypothetical Jones family, taking inventory of your lifestyle can produce interesting discussions with your spouse and children, especially about values and whether or not any areas of your lifestyle conflict with those values.

Connections and Disconnections between Wealth and Lifestyle

As we mentioned in the section on discretionary wealth earlier in this chapter, some parents maintain a lavish lifestyle even though they are not nearly as wealthy as people in their neighborhood, school, or social circle. Their children may get the impression that the family has great wealth and that they will be able to inherit enough to afford the same lifestyle. But the parents may wind up spending their net worth down to zero. They may be living off of credit. Parents do their children tremendous harm if they do not help their children understand the consequences of the parents' choices, do not check their children's assumptions about future inheritances, and do not prepare them to support themselves at their desired lifestyle.

In another family, the parents may have significant wealth but prefer to live modestly. Greenwich, Connecticut-based family business finance expert François de Visscher believes, "You can't deny the wealth. The wealth is there. In Europe, many families that are very wealthy live like homeless people because they don't want to show the wealth." He knows, because his family's business is based in Brussels, where de Visscher was born. "I've told my kids, we're fortunate. It may not be there tomorrow, but while we have it wealth creates opportunities, as well as huge responsibilities *vis à vis* people who don't have what you have, and how you conduct yourselves in life." Even though his sons attend private school, he chose a school in Stanford that has students with diverse backgrounds.

It may seem counterintuitive, but Kaye, whose consulting practice specializes in high–net worth family businesses, says when one parent grew up with wealth and the other was raised in a more middle-class environment, they may, together, find a balanced way to raise their children with a healthy perspective about their wealth. He recalls one such family in which the wife came from a middle-class family. She had been an employee in one of the businesses her husband owns. "She worked hard to be the appropriate chatelaine of their many homes and ranches, but constantly tries to get their children back to reality," says Kaye. She recognizes there are things the children can't do because of security (such as walk to school—they must be driven by the chauffer). But she and her husband want to give their children a normal childhood. "That might not have been the case had she not had a normal childhood herself," points out Kaye.

One of Kaye's client families maintains perspective by holding onto a rustic piece of property that has been in the family for generations. The extended family leaves their hectic city lives to take annual retreats there, roughing it with no electricity, although there is a generator that runs a water pump. "This is old money," notes Kaye. "Having learned the value of unostentatious living, they are passing that on to their next two generations so they can have a significant part of their lives that's not wrapped up in their wealth." Families that have a great love of land, even if they do not take such rustic retreats, tend to value conservation and stewardship. "It's grounding in a way that yachts and private jets are not," says Kaye.

As you return to the beginning of this chapter to re-take the self-survey, you may be surprised to find your answers have changed from before you read these pages. You may feel confused or even frustrated that perhaps you are not living according to your values, which could negatively impact your children. You may worry that your children may not be able to adjust in less fortunate circumstances, and may be unprepared to make decisions as adults who will not only keep the family fortune intact, but the family itself intact.

If that is the case, you will find the next two chapters especially helpful. In Chapter 10, we present ways to strengthen your family bonds. Cohesive, close families are best able to stick together through life's ups and downs, and to preserve the family's legacy of values as well as wealth. In Chapter 11, we pull together the more technical financial focus of the first section of this book and show how you can integrate the choices those chapters present with the intellectual, emotional, and spiritual choices outlined in the later sections.

SECTION IV

Integrating
Your Choices

10

The Family Glue

B Y NOW WE HAVE covered many key variables that determine the extent to which your wealth can help or hinder your children's success, happiness, and preparedness to manage the wealth for which they may one day be responsible. The last element to our equation is family glue. If it is weak, no matter how financially educated and experienced your children may be, without the ability to work closely together to manage the family wealth, it will likely dissipate in a generation or two.

As Claudia Sangster, director of philanthropy, estate, and trust services at Harris myCFO, points out, "If the family members can't work together, after the parents die, all bets are off. That's when all things fly to the surface. So if you haven't dealt with strengthening family ties before then, the family can explode."

Even a perfectly airtight estate plan (if there were such a thing) will not ensure that your wealth will wind its way down to your children and grandchildren, or that they will work together to manage future family assets rather than squabble over who gets what and when. Sometimes, as we've seen throughout this book, money impedes healthy relationships and causes discord. It's therefore imperative that you devote significant time, attention and thought to how you can strengthen your family's cohesiveness. The degree to which you and your children are able to communicate, connect, work, and play together will help immunize all of you from some of the most insidious unintended consequences that wealth can impose.

Self-Survey about Family Glue

Before we delve into what it takes to strengthen that family glue, please take one last self-survey to assess what attitudes and assumptions you're bringing to this discussion.

Self-Survey about Family Glue

1 = Strongly Agree, 2 = Agree, 3 = Neutral, 4 = Disagree, 5 = Strongly Disagree

BEFORE		AFTER
_____	Each member of my family can articulate the values that we share.	_____
_____	My children feel empowered to express their beliefs and feelings to the rest of the family.	_____
_____	My children and I feel comfortable that our ideas and feelings will be heard and accepted by each other.	_____
_____	Our family is familiar with our history and traditions and has integrated those traditions with new rituals that we have created in this generation.	_____
_____	Individually and as a family unit we value continuing education and learning, and we support each others' efforts to learn and grow.	_____
_____	As a family we make time to participate in group activities that maintain and deepen our bonds.	_____
_____	For the most part, family members have healthy boundaries and respect for each other's privacy and individual choices and beliefs.	_____

_____ There is a wealth of trust between
family members: no matter how
tense a family relationship may
become at any point, we know we
have each other's best interests
at heart and will be there for
each other. _____

The Ingredients of Family Glue

What keeps families connected and able to enjoy their common history without feeling that their individual personalities, dreams, quirks, and opinions get lost or disregarded?

David Bork, one of the founding members of the Aspen Family Business Group (AFBG), researched 250 of his client cases twenty years ago to uncover what best practices kept those who were close knit together. What emerged was a list of ten qualities shared by family businesses that have lasted for more than two generations. This list applies to families whether or not they own and run a business together and whatever degree of wealth they may have amassed, says AFBG partner Leslie Dashew, who is also founder of Human Side of Enterprise, a Scottsdale, Arizona-based family business consultancy. She says her own work with families of wealth and the consulting practices of her other five partners at AFBG have validated these ten qualities. However, she cautions that this list is descriptive, not prescriptive. There's no guarantee that you can just read this, begin incorporating these qualities into your family, and will suddenly feel magically close and work and play together nicely.

Let's take a close look at some of these qualities and how your family can develop tools to instill these qualities in your family.

■ **Shared values**—in particular, around people, work, and money. If in a family of wealth some members say it's nice to live off the fat of the land, others say we need to give most of it away, and others say no matter what we need to work hard, they will have a hard time making decisions together. Likewise, you can expect some conflict if some family business shareholders believe employees are a dime a dozen, while others value employees and want to provide them with generous benefits and training opportunities. "It doesn't mean family members have to share all values, but they should share core values," says Dashew. When values conflict, family businesses with several siblings or cousins as shareholders often encounter difficulties. For example, when one family group highly values generational longevity, honesty, and human respect, and another family group values how the business funds their lifestyle, there is going to be a clash in decision making. The cultural values of a family are important. When some family members focus solely on financial return, they may not recognize other important rewards operating the business brings to the family. This is bound to create conflict in decision making for the family.

"We do a lot of exercises around individual and shared values to help develop a shared vision and sense of how to do things so they have those parameters to guide them in making decisions together," says Dashew.

The forty mostly inactive family shareholders of Rich Morris' former family company, Fel-Pro, *did* have strong, shared values, especially about treating all employees extremely well. The company was listed as No. 4 on *Fortune* magazine's 1998 list of the "100 Best Companies to Work for in America." Even shareholders who never worked at the company took so much pride in their identity as members of such an esteemed company that they understood dividends came after reinvesting in the company so it would continue to grow, thrive, and afford to provide generous employee benefits. In fact, after the company sold in 1998, some branches of the family felt an enormous loss, even as they acquired significant financial gains from the sale. For many family shareholders, their family glue was much easier to maintain when there was a company uniting them. Once the substantial wealth was distributed to family members, it became easy to fall into the trap of entitlement. Without Fel-Pro providing their legacy, what united them around those values was now gone.

Business owners and managers invest considerable amounts of time and money teaching employees to work as a team and developing a values, vision and mission statement—yet they rarely if ever do so with their families. But developing team skills and articulating shared values can be as effective and valuable at home as at the office.

Indeed, while Fel-Pro had a values, vision and mission statement, the owning families did not. The family can, without too much effort, reinvent their shared values and create a family mission statement. They just need to have a conversation about what the money is for and how much of it should go to non-profits as well as about what they, as a family and as individuals, should be doing for society.

For any family, the process as well as the mission and values statements themselves can strengthen a family's bonds. You can start by brainstorming a list of words that describe your family's values. What do we, as a family, want to pass down to future generations? What do we want to leave behind personally? What do we want the family to be known for?

Every ten to twenty years, the family should revisit its values, vision, and mission statements to factor in how the family, its operating business (if it has one), its wealth, and the world have changed, and to welcome the next generation's input about any revisions that will keep it relevant and meaningful to current and future family members. In the end, says Harris myCFO's Sangster, who helps wealthy client families articulate shared values and develop mission statements, "Values have to be caught, not taught. If parents delegate some responsibility to their kids, they will generally rise to the occasion."

The family's shared values guide how it invests shared assets and how it decides on family foundation grant-making. "Identifying the family's shared values and using the values to articulate their mission statements creates the connective tissue between the generations, an important legacy builder that helps the family stay together over time," says Sangster.

■ **Shared power.** While parents would be negligent if they gave their children *carte blanche* with all or most family or parenting decisions, it's important to help children develop and to provide space for them to exercise a certain amount of power in age-appropriate areas.

Dashew explains, "Power should be shared between spouses, among generations and between siblings. It doesn't mean equal power, but sharing it so all decisions are not concentrated in one person, so there's a sense of psychological ownership of decisions. That means in-laws are included, and the younger generation is not waiting until the folks die to make decisions."

■ **Traditions that define how our family is different than other families.** Many traditions, says Dashew, center around food.

During the Passover holiday, Jewish families around the world retell the ancient story of Exodus, eating food symbolic of that story and singing songs that have been sung for countless generations. "It helps people feel what is special about their family, what their shared history is," says Dashew.

However, she adds, it's also important, as you add in-laws and generations, to fold everyone in and connect them to the core family. Families accomplish this by embracing new traditions, rituals, and stories that younger generation members create and that new members of the family bring with them. "They need some sense that this is my family, not just your family," says Dashew. Allowing linkage between the old and the new helps people express their values and remain connected.

Not all family traditions are worth preserving. If there had been a tradition of emotional or physical abuse, for example, the family should work hard to break that pattern. However, many parents can identify positive rituals and stories from their own childhood, some that may date back two or more generations that they want to hand down to future generations.

One family may have several musically talented members who gather around the piano after family dinners to sing show tunes, or play chamber music. Some families may enjoy simple pleasures, such as a family outing each fall to pick apples and then returning to one relative's home to cook apple pancakes together for dinner. Another family may enjoy cooking traditional foods from the "old country" during certain holidays. Some may include homemade gifts as part of their winter-holiday celebrations.

Traditions can comfort and hold families together during crises. For instance, Dashew's family emulates the Native American tradition of the talking stick, which each person takes a turn holding while they contribute their thoughts to a discussion or their stories during a family gathering or meal.

James E. Hughes Jr., author of *Family Wealth—Keeping It in the Family* (Bloomberg Press, 2004) and *Family: The Compact Among Generations* (Bloomberg Press, 2007), finds value in another Native American tradition called seventh-generation thinking. At the beginning of gathering, the elder recites, "Let us hope that the seven generations of our family from today will honor the care, wisdom and diligence which we bring to the decisions we will make today, as we honor those seven generations ago who made it possible for us to be here today." Hughes explains, "then the elder names the names of those who are meaningful in the lineage. Those faces appear to all the people sitting there, even if they've been dead, like Hiawatha, for 400 years. All the intellectual capital is immediately present in the decision-making process." Every decision the elders make is also informed by factoring in all the ways that decision may affect not just the next generation, but the next seven generations.

■ **Willingness to learn and grow.** In Chapters 4 and 5 we presented many ways parents can help their children acquire the necessary financial acumen and experience they'll need to manage the family wealth when they come of age. In addition to providing those opportunities and helping guide and fund your children through their higher education, learning should be an ongoing and shared activity for members of every generation. That can mean taking lessons in a new sport, learning a new language, musical instrument or craft, or creating a family investment club. Not everyone will enjoy the same avocations, but you can encourage your children, parents, cousins, nieces, and nephews to develop affinity groups that teach each other skills in which one relative may be proficient or to find an outside class to take together.

Dashew points out that "families that stay positively connected don't say you have to always do things the way we've done things in the past, but are responsive to changes in the environment and the world. To maintain our success in business or wealth, we need new ways of doing things, we must be committed to growing."

Learning together can be especially bonding. Families that go to seminars together, that bring in consultants, and that pass along inspiring or fun books to each other don't just acquire information but also create shared experiences that guide them in their shared decision making. "It creates a shared context for the family's growth and capability as a family," adds Dashew.

A great example is the 380 members of the seven-generation Laird Norton family. Every June they hold a four-day retreat that includes the Laird Norton University, where family volunteers share professional skills, personal interests, or hobbies in small group presentations; a facilitated, informal family forum where family members can ask questions and discuss family or company concerns; a half-day community-service project; and a camp offering children a curriculum of activities and field trips focusing on the family's history.

■ **Activities for maintenance of relationships.** Dashew thinks of family activities as part of a relationship bank. "If you give each other calls, cards, e-mails, stay in touch, you're continuing to maintain the relationship and you're putting 'money' in the bank. Each time you do that you add support to the relationship. So when a problem arises, if you have reserves in the bank, you're not going into deficit spending and hurting the relationship. When tough times come, members remember when they did this for me and we had that experience. Relationships are like engines in a car. If you don't lubricate them, more friction happens and you destroy parts of the engine."

Charles Jahn, a third-generation family member of Chicago Metallic, a ceiling-suspension manufacturer, remembers fondly vacations he spent with cousins at the family summer home. "We worked together one summer on an abandoned car and got it working. There was camaraderie, a joy in doing things together that clearly is the foundation for what enabled us to go through a difficult maturing process," he says. "Sharing family experiences and values is the key to forming the glue that will keep families together. At the end of the day, we can set aside our differences and be together socially. I remember shareholder meetings with intense arguments. Yet twenty minutes later we could be sharing a drink together and talking about something else going on completely outside the business." One source of glue that holds all the family together to this day clearly comes from their continuing to share the family vacation home. "There's no junkered car now, but I see the younger generation out there playing together, doing their own things," says Jahn.

Fritzi Hallock, who works in her family office and is a member of the Institute for Private Investors (IPI), relates how her extended and nuclear family maintained their glue with weekly get-togethers and outings when she was young. "When we grew up, we had dinner every Friday night at my father's mother's house and every Wednesday night at my mother's father's house with all the cousins. Also, one weekend day a week was always family day with my two brothers and parents. It was mandatory. Whether we went to the zoo or a restaurant, whatever we did, my parents, two younger brothers (four and eight years younger than me) and I were always together one day a week. We laugh about how we hated family day, but I gotta tell you, it was really key. We had to get along. We learned how to be together all day." She and her husband continue the tradition with regular (although not quite weekly) outings with their children. They avoid five-star vacations in favor of low-key places that allow them to bond deeply. For instance, she says, "One of the vacations I know they'll remember is when we played racquetball and had a family ping pong tournament, at a hotel off season, where we ate the best pizza we ever had."

■ **Genuine caring.** You can feel the warmth and caring in families that stay positively connected, says Dashew. "This is something you cannot be prescriptive about. It's tough to fake. If you don't genuinely care, even if you have shared assets, it's tough to continue the family connection over multiple generations."

Ira Bryck, director of the University of Massachusetts Family Business Center, believes it is possible for some family members who do not genuinely care about each other to fake it if they keep in mind the consequences, to the family, its wealth or its business, of letting the family fall apart. He recalls, "One family brought in teams of mediators to have discussions between two or three warring branches of the family. There was no bigger Hatfiled-McCoy division, but they knew that there's a big price tag to not getting along, so they make an effort and stay at the mediation table. If the goal is worth achieving they will continue to sit there."

Families that are suffering from division and conflict may benefit from some tips for couples offered by Dr. John Gottman, co-founder of the Gottman Institute, director of the Relationship Research Institute and emeritus professor of psychology at the University of Washington. The Gottman Institute Web site, www.gottman.com/marriage/self_help, says, "In a happy marriage, while discussing problems, couples make at least five times as many positive statements to and about each other and their relationship as negative ones."

Even in loving families, many people assume their family members know how much they care about each other. But it's important to articulate and demonstrate that caring overtly and regularly. In addition, just spending quality time together, sharing adventures, stories and discussions about school and work can strengthen the bonds of love within the family. As we mentioned in previous chapters, regularly having dinner together is one of the key predictors of whether or not kids will engage in an array of at-risk behaviors.

■ **Mutual respect.** Trust underlies almost all family glue, says Dashew. "It refers to respecting each others' right to be here because you're a co-owner or a family member, but I may not respect you individually. More importantly, close families respect that each person has the ability to contribute something."

It's important for parents to model the kind of respect they want their children to display in dealing with each other and with the outside world—as well as with their parents. No matter what your parenting philosophy or approach may be, demanding that your children respect you (or anyone else) is bound to backfire. When we show our children we respect them and that we treat employees (domestic or at work) and other people we encounter with respect, our children genuinely emulate that behavior. And when families generally exhibit respect in the way they talk and act, they are more likely to feel close to each other.

■ **Assist and support one another.** Even when the occasional argument or "falling out" may occur, healthy and functional families step up to the plate when the need arises. Despite any unresolved jealousies, animosities or rivalries that may exist, they know they have the other's back covered. Dashew says it's especially crucial to be there for each other, during times of loss, shame and difficulties— even if a family member is going through a divorce and that's just not done in your family, or they are going to jail, or an alcohol or drug treatment program. "It's easier to support each other when there's a flood or a loss," says Dashew. "I had two clients who were respectable people in the community who spent time in jail because of a tax issue. There were those who ran, who didn't want to assist and support that person versus those who said, 'I don't approve but I'm there for you' during difficult times."

■ **Well-defined interpersonal boundaries.** While healthy, connected families bail each other out when the going gets rough, they maintain enough distance so that they are not imposing their personal (as opposed to shared family) values or expectations on each other. They allow each other some privacy and don't invade other people's space. One example is avoiding "triangulation," where two warring individuals draw a third person into a battle, demanding that third person take a side.

Dashew says allowing some private space is particularly critical in a family business, because they operate in so many areas with overlapping roles and responsibilities that it's difficult to maintain healthy boundaries between family members.

One factor that can cause weak boundaries is when one or more family member tends to be overly reactive to any criticism, such as "if you get anxious and upset when there's the slightest conflict, if you take things personally rather than letting it bounce off your back, if you can't take feedback without being destroyed by it," points out Dashew. "Families of wealth or who work together have so many decisions and issues to work through together, they need to not take things as personally."

It's also important to respect people's privacy. "Sometimes families that have shared assets need transparency—but what I do with my money, how I budget, how I manifest my values in my money, what I'm doing privately with my spouse or my kids should be private," says Dashew. "Everyone doesn't have to know everything. It's difficult to have separateness, particularly in smaller towns where everyone shops at the same mall and goes to same school. It's important to honor separate information and time, to be mindful of what's shared and what's not, and that having some private information is not withholding. It helps to have explicit expectations about those things."

■ **Trust.** Trust is absolutely essential. "I find the greatest sense of betrayal in families comes with a sense of distrust. Of all people, they should be helping me and they're not. Families that have this trust are way, way ahead of those that don't. It's so difficult to rebuild that trust if it's not there," says Dashew.

In addition to the ten qualities of tight-knit families described above, Dashew suggests another important ingredient: communication (to which we devoted all of Chapter 8).

Strengthening Your Family Glue

It bears repeating that the qualities outlined above are descriptive, not prescriptive. There's no guarantee that even if you could incorporate these qualities into your family, that your relationships would magically become loving and close if they are not. However, your family might find it useful to figure out what glue already binds you, and which qualities are weak or lacking.

■ **Identifying strengths and weaknesses in your family glue.** The four qualities you may find easiest and least threatening to develop are shared values, traditions, family activities, and learning together. At your next family gathering, you can present family members with copies of **Exhibit 10.1** and spend an hour or two working together to brainstorm ways you can improve in each area.

Many of the other qualities that tight-knit families tend to display may require the help of a consultant or psychologist to facilitate meetings or discussions that may help the family acquire or strengthen those qualities.

Exhibit 10.1   Strengthening Your Family Glue

QUALITIES	EXERCISE	RESULTS

Shared values	■ Individually write down the top 3–10 values that are most important, each on a separate sheet of paper.
	 ■ Hang each sheet from each person on the wall.
	 ■ As a group arrange the values into categories.
	 ■ Have everyone vote on all of the value categories that *everyone* in the group shares.
	   a) Eliminate the categories the family does not share.
	   b) This list will be a starting ground for finding glue that will hold the family together.
		List the common values on which you all agree:

Traditions that define our family	Have a playful discussion to uncover traditions that the family enjoys and wants to maintain. If the family cannot think of any, are they interested in trying to develop and adopt one or two traditions?	*List current or new traditions:*

Exhibit 10.1   Strengthening Your Family Glue *(Continued)*

QUALITIES	EXERCISE	RESULTS
Activities for maintenance of relationships	■ Have family members write down any day trips, outings, or activities they have found fun and meaningful in the past. ■ Compare lists and vote on annual, quarterly, or monthly activities you can enjoy together.	*List planned activities:*
Willingness to learn and grow	■ Have each person write down any skills—athletic, artistic, musical, business, financial, language, or spiritual—they would like to acquire or improve. ■ Compare everyone's lists and develop affinity groups of those who share a desire to learn a particular skill; then find courses or workshops you can attend together.	*List who will take each course and workshop together:*

■ **Getting formal with family governance.** Many families create rules and governance systems, such as family councils, family forums, or family meetings, to keep the family glue strong. Some involve a formal structure and professional advisors or mediators; others are more informal ways for the family to get together. They may involve some combination of an agenda to discuss family issues (financial or other), learning, and structured or unstructured playtime.

Charles Jahn says his family wisely created a family council in 2002 for thirty-five shareholders in three generations of their family business "to hang in there through difficult financial times in business, with perseverance and willingness to invest time, effort and financially towards this entity." Mostly, he says, it's about the next generation.

What do family shareholders want out of that time together? Is it issues that are related to finance, or purely personal, sharing what's going on in their lives? "Underneath that is this understanding that in order to cooperate together and get on the same page you have to have this desire to hang out together," Jahn explains.

Bryck adds, "It's important to have codes of conduct, rules and governance structures. But people who need it most will not succeed nearly as easily as people who have the inborn goodwill, the 'I have his back, he has my back.' They won't need all the formal governance and policy because it will come naturally. Ironically, those are the people least resistant to putting things like that in place because they want to protect what's in place in case future generations may not feel that way. People who can only rely on rules and governance structures have a hard time abiding by them because they feel constrained."

When All Else Fails

Sometimes it's impossible to avoid separating from the family or its business. As we mentioned in Chapter 8, letting people walk out or storm out or just secede from whichever family activities may incite divisiveness will enable the majority of members to continue to interact more peacefully and productively.

Certainly, grounds for separating from a relative or branch of the family include physical, emotional, or substance abuse. In such circumstances, the family can offer to help that individual get professional help or find a treatment program as a condition of remaining part of the family's social get-togethers and formal governance groups.

However, it's important to keep the door open. Sometimes, an individual (or his or her children or grandchildren) may mellow or mature enough to want to return to the fold. Welcoming them back can help heal old wounds, as long as they are willing to behave and work together respectfully.

Now that you have considered how families maintain and strengthen their glue, to sustain them through thick and thin, please retake the self-survey at the beginning of this chapter. If you have changed any of your answers, consider that a red flag for topics you can discuss and work on with your family.

In our next and last chapter, we will attempt the ambitious task of helping you stitch together all the ideas, opinions, suggestions, tips, and techniques this book has offered. You will find tools for identifying where and how to start, which we hope you will find useful.

11

Pulling It Together

IN THE PREVIOUS ten chapters, we have attempted to consider wealth from several perspectives to help you think critically about your day-to-day choices and the long-term impact those choices impose on you and your family. We are aware that it's possible to feel overloaded and overwhelmed with information and suggestions that appear in the preceding pages. This book intends to inspire and guide wealthy families to reflect on how to adjust some of their spending, investing, estate, and parenting decisions.

You may feel that it is too late; your kids are already grown. "Start early is the ideal," Durham, New Hampshire, psychologist Dr. Kenneth Sole recommends. However, "if you have a nineteen-year-old, you can't roll back the clock—but we can start today rather than when the kid is twenty. Whatever forces in your life, as a parent, have caused you to delay thus far could cause you to delay even further. And we need to work against that tendency—so the sooner the better rather than not at all."

You may feel paralyzed. Where should you begin? How can you commit yourself to change what may feel like a comfortable lifestyle? How can you integrate some or all of the areas we explore to find the areas that might be most in need of fixing? And how might changing one aspect of your life affect other areas?

These are all valid concerns, which we hope this chapter will help you sort through.

Getting on Track

Embedded in this book are the tools to help you identify issues and concerns: We have taken the tools—checklists, inventories, and self-surveys—from the previous ten chapters and assembled them into Appendixes 1 through 7. We have put these tools in one easy-to-access section to help you see how your answers in each appendix relate to each other. You will also find the intergenerational calculator from Chapter 1 on our Web site (www.KWandC. com) along with some other useful calculators and updates from readers like you who share with us their ideas about *Kids, Wealth, and Consequences*. Now that you've read through the book, you can use these tools to map out areas of your life you may feel require some changes. Here are some specific suggestions that may help you integrate these tools into a comprehensive financial parenting plan.

■ **Checklist of financial skills.** Appendix 1 provides a checklist of financial skills and potential educational ideas, first introduced in Chapter 5, to help your children learn these important skills.

Make several copies of this checklist. Start with you and your spouse; identify what you both feel qualified to teach and what might be best for others to teach. Pass another copy of this checklist to advisors and relatives who know your kids and ask them to indicate what they believe your children need to learn. Ask your kids to tell you what they want to learn and what they think they already know. This is a simple way to start taking action and to map your direction, as the checklist has built into it some educational suggestions.

■ **Money messages.** Appendix 2 replicates Exhibit 8.1 in Chapter 8, which lists messages that are important to bring up with your children. We suggest you devote time to sit down with your children to discuss the messages appropriate for their age, either informally over dinner or, for the more complex or emotionally charged messages, at a family meeting or family retreat facilitated by a family office manager, investment advisor, or even a psychologist to address any technical questions that your children ask.

■ **Lifestyle inventory.** Appendix 3, the lifestyle inventory discussed in Chapter 9 helps you identify the purpose of each element of your lifestyle as well as the unintended consequences that may follow.

Your answers to this survey may motivate you to question aspects of your high–net worth environment that may conflict with your deepest personal and shared family values. Even those aspects of your lifestyle that do not conflict with those values may come with some disadvantages, which we call unintended consequences. A discussion with your family about this inventory can focus on the purpose you each assign each element of your lifestyle and the darker, unintended side of those choices. This discussion is bound to help you brainstorm things you may want to adjust or reconsider. This can help you form a list of discussions you may want to have with your kids. The more they understand your lifestyle choices and, perhaps, the changes that may come from reading this book, the more they will understand your value system. One positive consequence is that it can help you strengthen your family glue.

■ **Values inventory.** In Chapter 10 we asked you to list the values you want to impart, which will help you define the legacy your money will provide future generations. Appendix 4 lets each family member older than, say, age thirteen, capture the values surrounding wealth they believe the family should stand for. You can discuss how those values align with the elements of your family's lifestyle (listed in Appendix 3) and how you can individually and as a family make adjustments where values may conflict with your lifestyle.

■ **Self-surveys.** Each chapter begins with a self-survey for you to take before and again after you read each chapter, to highlight where your thinking has changed and may lead to new choices; Appendix 5 pulls together all ten of these surveys.

This is an easy, yet provocative way to help you identify areas you may consider adjusting. This would be a great time to make a list of any questions you answered differently before and after you read each chapter. Those assumptions may have informed many of your previous parenting, investing, spending, or other decisions. How might different assumptions affect those decisions going forward?

Another approach is to ask your spouse or your children to take any of these self-surveys (feel free to copy and distribute Appendix 5 to family members). Compare your answers. Discuss why you each answered the way you did. How might the issues your discussion raises affect your family's lifestyle choices? How do your answers align with or conflict with your family's shared values? These discussions can be fun and enlightening for all. They often bring out misconceptions about what each of us may be thinking and lead all family members to clarify, or perhaps, rethink, their assumptions and beliefs.

■ **Unintended consequences.** Not all of the unintended consequences that appear, by chapter, in Appendix 6, may apply to your circumstances. Check off any that do. Add to this list any unintended consequences you identified in the lifestyle survey (Appendix 3) or additional ones that may have come to mind as you read this book. Again, this can be fertile material for discussions with your spouse and children. What questions arise about your parenting approach, spending choices, and lifestyle in general? Often, unintended consequences result from choices you make. They likely affect perceptions your kids may have and impact other parts of your life. Understanding how your choices and actions intertwine can help you to avoid these consequences from having disruptive affects.

■ **Teachable moments.** Which items on the list of teachable moments in Appendix 7 feel most useful and relevant to your family's situation? Check those off and consider ways you and your spouse may take advantage of those teachable moments on a regular basis or as opportunities arise. Look for your own teachable moments and integrate them all into your plans for educating your children that you identified in your checklist of financial skills—Appendix 1.

Integrating All the Pieces

We suggest you make a list from each of the seven appendices of changes you'd like to make, in the "action items" column in **Exhibit 11.1**. Some of the changes may seem to fit under more than one category of choices. That's okay; just plunk them into one area for now. Notice whether or not most of your list of changes tend to cluster within one or a few categories. If that's the case, you may only have to work on a few changes to your lifestyle or center on a few educational needs.

You may want to take a close look at the last column, where you can list how each item in the "action items" column may conflict with your personal or shared family values (Appendix 4). The idea is not to put yourself down or make you feel like a hypocrite for not fully living your values. No one is perfect in that department! But this is an opportunity, with your family's future wealth and happiness and your own legacy at stake, to identify ways you can try to chart the most successful course for your family's future. It may be helpful to discuss with your spouse and kids how your values may not always be able to match up with your actions, and how you can remedy that together. Reviewing this action plan every several months will help keep you on track.

Intergenerational Equity, Revisited

How might your action plan affect your future intergenerational equity—which we defined in Chapter 1 as how your spend rate (as a percent of your net worth), investment returns, taxes, inflation, and other factors may impact your children's future ability to replicate your current lifestyle? We have introduced a spreadsheet (and a calculator) at our Web site www.KWandC.com to help you predict what your wealth will be in the future, based on best-guess assumptions about average inflation, investment returns, tax rates, and spending levels. In any one year, any of these assumptions may be way off. People do not spend at a steady rate, the market swings up and down, inflation gyrates, and tax rates change with each administration. Our model is based on long-term thinking. If you are interested in creating

Exhibit 11.1 Action Plan

CHOICES		ACTION ITEMS	VALUES IN CONFLICT
Financial	**Intergenerational equity** Have you identified how much you want to leave behind and whether your current lifestyle choices will accomplish that?		
	Trusts Will the current structure of your trust accommodate your children's needs and accomplish what you intend?		
	Investing ■ Have you diversified your assets and your advisors and managers to best manage future risks? ■ Do your portfolio and managers align with your intergenerational needs and are the right assets in the correct trusts?		
Intellectual	**Financial literacy** Are you providing your children a solid basis of knowledge about saving, spending, banking and personal finance?		
	Skills and experience Are you exposing your children to the world of wealth so they can develop skills and confidence to manage their future wealth?		
	Goals and purpose Do your children feel passionate about anything?		

(Continued)

Exhibit 11.1   Action Plan (*Continued*)

CHOICES		ACTION ITEMS	VALUES IN CONFLICT
Emotional/Spiritual	**Success and happiness** Have you discussed with your children different ways to measure success?		
	Communication ■ Do you have ongoing discussions with your children about wealth and what it means? ■ Are your children involved in learning how to make decisions and communicating together?		
	High–net worth environment ■ Have you exposed your children to the world outside your wealthy environment? ■ What can you do to offset any negative effects of the environment you live in?		
	Family glue ■ Has your family identified values it shares and enjoy making time to spend together? ■ Has your family written a mission statement to review every so often?		

intergenerational wealth and a meaningful legacy, then year-to-year fluctuations in these variables will be less important because statistically, over the long-term, all of these numbers will likely revert to a mean—some average number over time. In your effort to create intergenerational wealth, it is important to lay out your long-term assumptions about these numbers and stick to a plan without becoming distracted or discouraged by wild economic changes.

The question then becomes how to monitor your progress. You certainly do not want to wait until your grandchildren are forty to find out your assumptions were incorrect. There may also be economic shocks like we saw in 2008 that may lead you to make extraordinary changes in your investing or spending; or unexpected opportunities to which you may want to respond. Let's take a look at data your financial advisors are likely providing and other data you may want to add to whatever investment tracking system you currently use.

Financial advisors primarily focus on portfolio management. In many cases, that is the only area you let them control under your guidance. So naturally they will show you performance numbers, such as those in **Exhibits 11.2** and **11.3**.

Exhibit 11.2 shows four typical investors, each with a different set of investment goals, objectives, and risk profiles. Your financial advisor will typically show you the total return of your portfolio each year, plus a geometric average for a certain time period. He is also likely to show you individual managers' performance in much the same way.

In addition, your investment advisor may show you how a dollar invested with him over time has grown cumulatively. Exhibit 11.3 shows this for our four typical investors over a five-year bull market and during the six years that included the 2008 stock market meltdown.

This exhibit portrays a typical way to evaluate portfolio and management advisors. The measurement methods seem to indicate that Investors 2, 3 and 4 did fairly well during both time periods, especially compared against the benchmark S&P 500 (Portfolio 2's returns "hugged" the S&P 500 performance). No one blew the ball out of the park, but all of these investors, even the most aggressive, wanted to sleep well at night and know they would not lose their entire portfolio. The most aggressive portfolio (Investor 3) looks like she had the best strategy for 2003–2007. In 2003–2008 she still held the number-two spot in cumulative return, while the most conservative portfolio (Investor 1) took over the best return strategy. However, these numbers do

Exhibit 11.2 Investment Strategies and Performance

	INVESTOR 1 CONSERVATIVE STRATEGY: 100% MUNI BONDS	INVESTOR 2 MIXED STRATEGY YIELDING AN S&P 500 RETURN	INVESTOR 3 MODERATELY AGGRESSIVE STRATEGY	INVESTOR 4 MIXED STRATEGY – MORE CONSERVATIVE
Return 2008	–1%	–38%	–42%	–38%
Return 2007	3%	6%	8%	5%
Return 2006	4%	16%	18%	13%
Return 2005	4%	5%	6%	4%
Return 2004	4%	11%	13%	10%
Return 2003	5%	29%	31%	28%
6-Year Geometric Average (12/31/02–12/31/08)	3.34%	2.19%	2.50%	1.25%
5-Year Geometric Average (12/31/02–12/31/07)	4.23%	12.93%	14.87%	11.68%

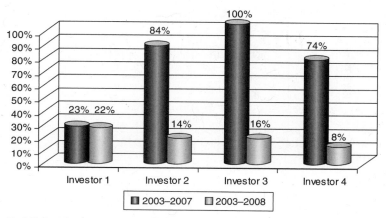

Exhibit 11.3   Portfolio Returns

not factor in how spending and taxes impact these portfolios' performance.

Exhibits 11.4 and **11.5** factor in the spend rate. The first three investors had a spend rate of 4 percent and Investor 4 spent at a rate of 1 percent. Investor 4 (Bob from Chapter 1) eked out a 1 percent return 2003–2008—the only investor of the four in positive territory. Investor 3 suffered a double whammy: her portfolio declined in 2008 at a larger rate due to its more risky and aggressive nature, plus her 4 percent spend rate resulted in the second worst cumulative return, down 10 percentage points.

We are not done yet. We now have to reduce the portfolio value by taxes. The tax efficiency of a portfolio can be difficult to measure. For **Exhibit 11.6**, let's assume that taxes were minimal during this time period, with mostly unrealized capital gains in stock, real estate, and private equity. Therefore, we figure only a 15 percent average tax (or about $1 million 2003-2008) for each Portfolio 2 through 4. Portfolio 1 had virtually no tax, as it consisted of 100 percent muni-bonds. As a result, between 2003 and 2008 Portfolio 1 returned the same return (–4 percent) it produced in the pre-tax example. After accounting for investment performance, spending and taxes, Portfolio 1 has actually performed the best of our four portfolios

Exhibit 11.4   Effects of Spending on Portfolio Performance

PORTFOLIO REDUCED BY SPEND RATE	INVESTOR 1	INVESTOR 2	INVESTOR 3	INVESTOR 4
Spend rate	4%	4%	4%	1%
Cumulative return 2003–2008	−4%	−11%	−10%	1%
Cumulative return 2003–2007	1%	53%	67%	66%

in this six-year example, mostly due to the after-tax performance. Portfolios 2 and 3 were in negative territory by about −22 percent and −21 percent, respectively, and are the worst of the four investors due to a combination of spending and taxes. Portfolio 4 still took a −10 percent hit, but it performed about twice as well as Portfolios 2 and 3. This set of portfolios suggests that taxes and spending can affect your portfolio value as much as or more than your investment choices! The positive returns shown in Exhibit 11.3 were eaten up by spending and taxes 2003–2008.

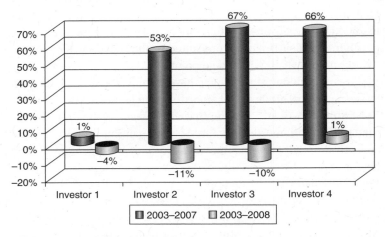

Exhibit 11.5   Portfolio Reduced by Spend Rate

start conversations in a different way." He says he asked his audience, "Promise me that for the next hour every single time I use the word 'wealth' you will think of the three people you love the most. Bring their faces into your consciousness, quietly." He found that by asking people to do that one thing, "the word 'wealth' would become the warmest, most valuable thing in the English language."

You may find, as you consider how you approach your wealth and how you make future spending, investing, and parenting decisions, that if you follow Hughes' suggestion and think of the people you love the most, you will be more likely to make healthy decisions that lead to your wealth enhancing the future generation's ability to make responsible choices and live productive, happy lives.

■ **Think long term.** You have to have a long-term view. For instance, if you choose to buy yourself a Bugatti, what are the ramifications in the future for your family? In the short term, you and your family may enjoy seeing heads turn as you round the corner. In the medium term, you'll have a cool $2 million or so less to grow in your portfolio. In the long term, your children will receive certain messages from such an extravagant purchase, especially if that purchase occurs during a worldwide economic crisis when so many people are suffering. Even if you've also been extremely generous in your philanthropic giving, will your progeny mostly remember you for all the material excesses with which you surrounded yourself and your family? If you're thinking about legacy, you need to think about several generations, not just your generation or the next.

And so much of this book boils down to legacy. You may have ascertained at this point that wealth can provide the resources and the freedom to resolve just about every issue this book discusses. However, instead of providing all of those advantages, wealth often gets in the way and turns out, in fact, to be the problem itself.

Susan Remmer Ryzewic who works with her family office, has found that "one of the biggest challenges of parents in a high-net worth environment is there are so many wonderful opportunities to do things that you want your kids to do or take advantage of, it can end up undermining their ability to commit to regular jobs or even to sports teams." It's difficult to consider the long-term ramifications of this, but there are many. "High-net worth families are much more likely to be traveling or have commitments or opportunities in different places, so they don't allow their children to have 'typical' summer jobs that help them develop work and life-skills experiences. Parents often don't want to have to be committed to being home because there are other things we want to be doing." She admits, "I have not been very successful at dealing with this."

However, Ryzewic has learned how important it is to consider the long-term consequences of using one's wealth or connections to bail children out of mistakes. "All parents want their kids to learn the lessons of life, but we never want them to have to experience pain or disappointment. The most effective thing is to detach and have your kids be responsible for themselves and learn lessons through suffering the natural consequences of their actions. My parents always had to work when they were growing up. They felt it was much more important that we have meaningful experiences than having a low-paying job. I've carried that over to my kids as to what they are doing summers. I've come to realize the value of old-fashioned hard work where they learn about the value of a dollar, how hard it is to make money, the responsibility of having to show up and having someone in charge of them who they have to deal with when they oversleep."

■ **Liberate your legacy from your wealth.** When legacy is integrally connected to wealth, it's easy to confuse the two and, in the process, create all sorts of distorted messages and behaviors. In family businesses, the younger generation often feels pressure to preserve the founder's legacy, which the family often defines as the business and the wealth it created, or to continue to support the wing of the local hospital or university that bears the family name. The family's wealth, visibility, and respect in the community all come from members of a previous generation, which gets handed down as the focal point of the family legacy. When later generations take this baton, which they had nothing to do with creating, it can feel like a weighty obligation that may not feel relevant or meaningful, and they may find it almost impossible to live up to. There may not be space for younger generation members to assert their own dreams. In fact, the shadow of previous generations' accomplishments may obscure their own drive and intimidate them, paralyze them or make them feel useless.

Parents can help prevent the wealth-infused legacy from stymieing the younger generation from exploring and expressing their own creative ideas and dreams. Future inheritors may feel their family's wealth makes it unnecessary for them to build new wealth. Parents cannot afford to be subtle; they must disabuse their children of this notion. They would be wise to instill in their children the expectation that they be productive, develop skills, and feel free to venture into any commercial or non-profit endeavors that interest them.

You may be familiar with the "Generations" ads for the Patek Philippe watches that sell for $10,000 or more, in which a father has just given his teenage son his first Patek Philippe, with the slogan, "Begin your own traditions." The ad reads: "You never actually own a Patek Philippe. You merely look after it for the next generation." The intended message seems to be that this emblem of wealth represents the start of this child's legacy, which he will hand down to his children, and later to his grandchildren. But aside from the fact that this watch may last a couple hundred years longer than a plain old Timex (which may keep time just as well), is this truly a legacy to get choked up about, as the ad seems to imply? Does this watch reflect the parents' most meaningful accomplishments and values in life, or just their ability to create, inherit, or steward family wealth? Does this watch represent the possibilities for their children to harness their own dreams; to live productive, independent lives; to bounce back from adversity; or to be able to find meaning and happiness in life whether or not they wind up in the lap of luxury?

If every family member in every generation considers herself the first producer of something—be it a company, wealth, or whatever passions she pursues—she may feel less paralyzed by the family's wealth and more compelled to be productive. Ideally, your children will grow up and apply the meaning and lessons of your actions and advice to their own directions and dreams. Dr. Kerry Sulkowicz, MD, founder of New York City-based Boswell Group, which advises executives on psychological aspects of business, describes a client, the CEO of a *Fortune* 500 company, whose wife is a college professor. They have a son and daughter, both grown. "One works in large company having a good time doing that, the other devotes all his time to a nonprofit he founded right after college, not making a nickel. He doesn't need to. Both are rather well adjusted, and very productive members of society because their parents raised them with a sense of responsibility, and both their sons were well nurtured," says Sulkowicz, who also writes the "Analyze This" column for *BusinessWeek*. The message was not to become a millionaire like Mom and Dad. The message was to be productive. They each took a different path to that end.

It's not that there's no place for honoring and transmitting previous generations' accomplishments, rituals, values, or heirlooms. But each generation should be encouraged to contribute its own accomplishments, to develop new rituals, and to express new values that reflect the changing world and their own individuality.

Parents who redefine their legacy can help their children redefine themselves as first producers. Instead of thinking of wealth or the family business as the legacy, parents can broaden their concept of legacy as its ability to harness its resources—financial, intellectual, emotional, and spiritual—to enable future generations to discover and fulfill their own legacies.

It is our deepest hope that this book helps you get closer to this goal. More than handing you answers, we hope we have raised provocative, meaningful questions and provided you with resources and new ways to approach finding answers that fit your own values and family circumstances.

If the volume of information and recommendations feels overwhelming, we will leave you with these last few suggestions: Choose one or two areas to focus your energy and changes. Well–thought out baby steps will likely produce longer-lasting and more meaningful results than overly ambitious changes. If you do nothing else, consider talking to your spouse and children about some of the issues that resonate for you, and keep the dialogue going! Consider unintended consequences of your future spending, investing, parenting, and other choices you make.

Feel free to share your experiences of what works and what doesn't, and any thoughts any section of this book may have triggered, on our Web site: www.KWandC.com. Good luck!

Appendix 1

Checklist of Financial Skills Assessment

Skill *levels*:

B   Basic Skills are often overlooked by high–net worth parents. These are skills that you hopefully possess and can teach to your kids. They are best taught informally in discussion surrounding an event or situation.

I   Intermediate Skills are the next step in teaching the nuts and bolts or blocking and tackling of a basic skill. They are more sophisticated skills that are necessary for understanding the complex investment world.

A   Advanced skills are most often needed by high–net worth adults or those that plan on making investing their career or serious hobby.

Every child will not have the same interest in learning about finance. We believe that every child should learn most of the skills described below, whether they have a natural interest or not. These are the skills children will need to manage their wealth and daily finances successfully.

On the other hand, those kids who have a great interest in learning financial skills will be motivated to learn the basics, as well as more technical skills—what learning experts call nice-to-know skills. We have marked these learning experiences with a **T** (for technical). They can be introduced to children as they seem interested and able to grasp that level of information. They should not be forced on kids who do not have interest, although you can encourage them to learn as much as they want.

°Items marked with an asterisk are described in detail in Chapter 5.

TOPIC	OUTCOME: THE CHILDREN WILL BE ABLE TO...	TECHNIQUES[1]	SKILL LEVEL
Banking	... describe what a banking institution provides such as: ■ deposits ■ compound interest ■ lending ■ access to cash — an ATM, withdrawals.	■ Take your children to the bank with you. ■ Have your banker line up a loan officer and others to discuss banking concepts.	B
	... describe the difference between a savings and checking account. ... write a check. ... balance a checkbook and reconcile monthly statements. ... use a savings account. ... access online banking to check balances, transfer funds, etc.	■ Have your children help you fill out deposit and withdrawal forms. ■ Let them help you balance a checking account one month. ■ Help them open a checking and savings account so they can save up for things they'd like to buy. ■ Show them how to reconcile their statements online or off-line.	I

| Credit and Debit Cards | … identify on a statement the amount owed, interest, and credit limits.
… describe the consequences of charging more than they can afford to pay off at the end of the month.
… describe the consequences of making only the minimum monthly payment over time.
… explain how to save and check receipts against monthly statements.
… describe when it is appropriate to use debt and when it is not. | ■ Help them apply for a credit or debit card while they're living home so that they can practice using it responsibly; oversee their management of the credit card, including payment of monthly bills on time.
■ Discuss when you believe it's appropriate to take on debt and when it's not. | — |
| | … explain what a FICO score is.
… describe what is needed to obtain a loan.
… explain loan securitization. | ■ Have your children meet with a loan officer and go over the loan process | — |

(Continued)

237

TOPIC	OUTCOME: THE CHILDREN WILL BE ABLE TO...	TECHNIQUES	SKILL LEVEL
Budgeting	... describe what discretionary and nondiscretionary expenses mean for the family and the child. ... describe the financial outcomes of spending more than you make and having to pay interest versus saving and buying on when you have the money. ... describe the importance of including saving and charitable giving in a budget.	See the list of Internet tools on this subject in **Exhibit 5.1*** ■ See teachable Moments on page 117. ■ Challenge your child to save up for something she wants; for a big-ticket item, consider a matching grant.	B
	... set up a budget for a household vacation or some complex situation. ... describe different likely lifestyles they may be able to achieve based on different job choices, and itemize budgets for those lifestyles/job choices. ... explain how possible future trust income may supplement income from whatever jobs they choose.	■ Just as Bill Cosby did on an episode of his TV show with his "son" Theo, have your teen figure out what he might be able to earn on his own and what he might be able to afford (and not afford) living on his own. ■ Put the children in charge of the meal budget during a family vacation. ■ Have children play simulation games—see **Exhibit 5.1**.*	I

238

Investing		
... describe the following concepts: interest, compound interest, stocks, and bonds. ... describe at least two reasons why stock prices go up or down. ... describe why it is important to invest in lots of different types of asset classes.	■ Select several companies that make products or provide services your kids enjoy, such as Nike versus Reebok, and track how those stocks have performed in the past and continue to perform. ■ Have children explore simulations.*	B
... describe at least six different types of asset classes that can be used in asset allocation. ... describe how asset allocation and diversification may reduces risk. ... describe the pros and cons to sticking to an investment strategy or allocation. ... describe the potential danger in chasing the best returns.	■ Have children play simulation games such as Morris Family Chasing Returns: the Asset Allocation Game).* ■ Encourage children to join or create an investment club.* ■ Have children sit in on the quarterly or yearly family foundation's review of the investment managers and asset allocation.* ■ Ask children to read the business section of the newspaper and listen to some business programs. ■ Encourage teens or young adults to explore more advanced simulation—see Exhibit 5.1.* ■ Have children partici-pate in a goal-focused investment challenge.*	I

(Continued)

239

TOPIC	OUTCOME: THE CHILDREN WILL BE ABLE TO...	TECHNIQUES	SKILL LEVEL
	... describe parents' personal investment goals and risk tolerance.	■ Use the 25-25-25-25 approach.*	A
	... describe the issues you need to explore when choosing an investment advisor.	■ Give your kids small amounts (appropriate for their age and ability) to invest.*	
	... read the family's (or advisors') performance reports and accurately describe what each section indicates.	■ As a family, join a group of high-net worth individuals such as the Institute for Private Investor (IPI) or the Family Office Exchange (FOX) for training, advice, and camaraderie.	
	... briefly describe the process and due diligence needed in choosing an investment manager.	■ See the list of Internet tools on this subject in Exhibit 5.1.*	
	... briefly describe the process for developing asset allocation for your portfolio.	■ Talk with your children about your investment experiences.	
	... describe the difference of a mutual fund and an individually managed account.	■ Have your family office or investment advisor develop, run or bring in financial education classes.	

240

	A
	T
... describe volatility and how the VIX index describes volatility. ... describe how stock market capitulation (bottoms and tops of market cycles) is derived. ... define the following terms correctly: price-earnings ratios, dividends, return on investment, and other terms one needs to know when investing. ... define terms such as alpha, beta, etc., as they relate to investing. ... describe terms used in option trading: options, puts, etc. ... in detail describe the process for developing asset allocation for one's portfolio. ... describe, in detail the differences in potential tax implications to the portfolio of at least four asset classes and investment styles.	■ Encourage children to join/develop a family foundation finance committee.* ■ If the children are interested, give them a portion of the money to invest as if they were the money manager. Make sure to measure their results against the appropriate index.* ■ Have children help you invest the family money. ■ Study annual reports and other investment materials. ■ Have your adult child join a high–net worth investment group such as Tiger 21,IPI, or FOX.

(Continued)

241

TOPIC	OUTCOME: THE CHILDREN WILL BE ABLE TO...	TECHNIQUES	SKILL LEVEL
Trusts	... identify how the trusts are structured including ownership, trustees, successor trustee, and tax implications. ... identify the trust managers and assets. ... identify any areas of the trust that must be dealt with to avoid negative tax implications. ... work with trustees to choose investments, asset allocations, and distributions (as long as it does not violate trust law, etc.).	■ Set up meetings between emotionally mature children and your trustees, legal counsel, and/or family office professionals to discuss trust structure, ownership successor trustees, and tax issues.	I
	... read and describe the fine points of the trust documents. ... work with lawyers to design the best trust structure for the family.	■ Have children meet with an estate-planning lawyer who can go over the terms of the trust in detail.	A T

Charitable Giving		B		I
	... explain why giving is important to the family. ... identify at least one charitable organization that is important to them. ... arrange to help out or visit this organization.	■ Discuss with your children your views on charitable giving. ■ Encourage children to volunteer for a cause that they are passionate about; they can start at any age. ■ Bring children with you when you volunteer. ■ Invite someone from the organizations you support to an informal dinner to discuss their organization with your kids. ■ Arrange visits to meet the recipients of the money.		
	... make a list of causes that are important to them and to the family. ... explain how the family selects non-profit groups to support. ... explain what the word "endowment" means and how the family foundation does or does not run like an endowment. ... explain the process that the family uses to agree upon a donation.			■ Provide each child with $1,000 to donate to non-profits that meet agreed-upon criteria.* rich: what kind of junior board? ■ Have the children form a junior board of your foundation with some decision-making responsibility for them.* ■ Develop family foundation committees that focus on different non-profit causes. Have the kids join the committee that interests them.* ■ Become actively involved in what you support—just don't give money, give time.*

(Continued)

243

TOPIC	OUTCOME: THE CHILDREN WILL BE ABLE TO...	TECHNIQUES	SKILL LEVEL
	... explain the leadership role of running a family foundation. ... explain the financial responsibility of the board and finance committee in terms of continuing to have the funds available for the foundation's purpose and goals.	■ Have the children join the family foundation's board. ■ Join a donors' forum. ■ Find an educational opportunity to learn how to run a family foundation.* ■ Provide an internship at the foundation.*	A T
Business Skills	... describe the basic laws of supply and demand. ... describe the flow (channels) a typical product goes through from manufacture to retail sale.	■ Take advantage of spontaneous opportunities while shopping, over dinner, or while watching TV, to discuss basic economic and business principles.* ■ Have children explore basic simulations games.* ■ Talk about your business experience with your children	B
	... describe the basic functions of any business: manufacturing, marketing, sales, accounting, HR.	■ Have children explore simulations. ■ Encourage children to take a summer and/or after-school job.	I
	... read a balance sheet and income statement.	■ Have students take courses in business subjects such as accounting, marketing, and management.	I T

Appendix 2

Money Messages

- What is money for?

- How much will my children inherit, and when?

- Where did that money come from? A family business? From Mom or Dad's side? How many generations back does it go?

- What are some examples (in families of multi-generational wealth) of relatives who handled the wealth responsibly and those who did not—and what were the consequences of their actions?

- What do you (and should you—or not) feel entitled to concerning the family wealth?

- What actions and values do you, as a parent, not model that your kids should value and why?

- How has money helped and hindered you (the parents) in your own life? What mistakes have you made, and lessons have you learned?

- What misconceptions about money did you harbor as a child?

- What is the structure of trusts in which the children are beneficiaries, and what contingencies are attached to those trusts?

- What is the family's approach to philanthropy, and what role might the children play at different stages of their life?

- Should you try to dictate how your children will spend, save, invest, and donate the money they will inherit?

■ How can your family develop a positive identity that is not defined by money?

■ Will your children be able to afford to live the same lifestyle with their inheritance?

■ Will your children have to work to afford the same level of comfort they currently enjoy?

■ Under what circumstances would you "bail" out your children from problems and failures, and under what circumstances will the children have to solve their own problems and learn in their own way?

■ How do you spot and avoid gold-diggers among "friends," family, lovers, and colleagues?

■ Do you expect your children's future spouse to sign a prenup? If so, have you told them so? When would be the best time to raise the subject?

■ How do you help your children understand how to resist requests from every friend and acquaintance who might approach your child to invest in some harebrained business venture?

■ Do you expect your children not to discuss the family's financial status with friends, or even with a potential future spouse?

Appendix 3

Inventory of Your Lifestyle

EXPENDITURE	OPULENCE LEVEL M-Q-L*	PURPOSE	UNINTENDED CONSEQUENCES	POST MELT-DOWN

*M = Modest; Q = High Quality; L = Luxury

Appendix 4

Strengthening Your Family Glue

QUALITIES	EXERCISE	RESULTS
Shared values	■ Individually write down the top 3–10 values that are most important, each on a separate sheet of paper. ■ Hang each sheet from each person on the wall. ■ As a group arrange the values into categories. ■ Have everyone vote on all of the value categories that *everyone* in the group shares. a) Eliminate the categories the family does not share. b) This list will be a starting ground for finding glue that will hold the family together.	*List the common values on which you all agree:*

QUALITIES	EXERCISE	RESULTS
Traditions that define our family	Have a playful discussion to uncover traditions that the family enjoys and wants to maintain. If the family cannot think of any, are they interested in trying to develop and adopt one or two traditions?	*List current or new traditions:*
Activities for maintenance of relationships	■ Have family members write down any day trips, outings, or activities they have found fun and meaningful in the past. ■ Compare lists and vote on annual, quarterly, or monthly activities you can enjoy together.	*List planned activities:*
Willingness to learn and grow	■ Have each person write down any skills—athletic, artistic, musical, business, financial, language, or spiritual—they would like to acquire or improve. ■ Compare everyone's lists and develop affinity groups of those who share a desire to learn a particular skill; then find courses or workshops you can attend together.	*List who will take each course and workshop together:*

Portfolio Management

_____ I believe good asset allocation should include a wide variety of stocks, bonds, international, and alternative investments.

_____ Although I know asset allocation is a good idea, I think it's best to invest in what I understand and in what I'm confident will give me the best return.

_____ The least risky way to invest is to hire people I know as investment advisors.

_____ It's important to do due diligence on managers and investment advisors and take emotions and feelings of friendship out of the equation.

_____ It's best to structure each trust with its own separate asset allocation.

_____ It's prudent to look at all trusts and assets as one family asset allocation.

_____ Asset-allocation needs ought to be structured to support the family's consumption (living) expenses/distributions in a down market.

Financial Literacy

_____ Allowance is not necessary for high–net worth children.

_____ I don't need to bother encouraging my children to get after-school or summer jobs.

_____ It's not necessary to force kids to live within a budget when the family does not have to do so.

_____ There's no purpose to encouraging my children to save because they will inherit enough money to cover their needs.

_____ My children do not need to learn about investing because professional advisors will be managing their trusts and other family funds.

_____ I believe it's important for my children to create their own wealth, regardless of how much I may be able to and choose to leave them.

_____ My children are savvy about and responsible with money.

_____ My children would be financially and emotionally prepared to survive even in the unlikely event that the family fortune were lost.

_____ I believe I set a pretty good example for my kids when it comes to modeling positive financial values.

Skills and Experience

_____ My children understand the basics of money management.

_____ My child has learned most of what she needs to know about finance from a program she attended.

A _____ B _____ Children learn the most about personal finance from:
A: School
B: Parents

_____ My children will not need to learn about finance, as they will hire trusted advisors to invest for them.

_____ Financial experts such as my advisors or family office professionals can best assess my children's financial educational needs.

_____ Getting the kids together to discuss finance and investing is a good way for them to learn those subjects.

_____ I need to be involved in teaching and modeling to my kids the basic as well as the more advanced points of finance.

_____ If my kids do not show an interest in finance, they will not be able to learn what they need to handle their own financial affairs

_____ Kids do not belong in the family foundation as active participants, although they can attend meetings to listen and learn.

Goals and Purpose

_____ It's a good idea to assure my kids they do not have to worry about money as they search for their career goals.

_____ Self-esteem, pride, and purpose come from tough lessons, hard work, and experience.

_____ One of the advantages of my wealth and connections is being able to help my kids start off with a fast-track job or finance them in a venture.

_____ Working menial jobs is a waste of time for my kids, who are likely to end up with a professional career.

_____ Pride, self-esteem, and meaning in life come from loving parents who tell their kids they are great and the world should appreciate them.

_____ It's important to protect my children from failure and to bail them out when they mess up.

_____ I want my children to follow in my professional footsteps.

Success and Happiness

_____ My kids should grow up with the things I never had.

_____ While money may not buy happiness, I do tend to feel a rush when I purchase a luxury item.

_____ When I think about the moments during the past month when I felt happy, most such moments involved material things.

_____ My family would be happy no matter how much money we may or may not have.

_____ I believe my children are not overly entitled.

_____ It's hard to understand why my kids sometimes seem unhappy or depressed when they have everything they could possibly desire.

_____ When my children make mistakes, I am there to rescue them.

_____ My children understand that they are very fortunate to grow up in a privileged environment, and they have interacted with people in less comfortable economic and social surroundings.

_____ I can help my children develop self-confidence by protecting them from failure.

_____ I have communicated how I measure success to my children.

_____ I have asked my children about their definition of success.

Communication

_____ My kids are prepared to make financial decisions together after I am gone.

_____ I feel comfortable about what age to tell my kids about the family's trusts and wealth.

_____ Money is a private matter, so discussing it as a family group is a bad idea.

_____ I believe my kids understand and buy into my ideas about what money is for and its legacy.

_____ I should reveal our family's trust structure, inheritance value, and my expectations about "what the money is for" in one integrated discussion as the way to introduce them to the family money.

_____ I'm comfortable with the messages my children get from observing the way I handle and spend money.

_____ I understand how my communication style may sometimes get in the way of effectively discussing sensitive issues with my children.

Your High–Net Worth Environment

_____ The neighborhood and community in which I live exposes my children to people, culture, and values that will make them successful and happy.

_____ The majority of media messages and culture we experience helps me teach my kids the value of money and wealth.

_____ My values, actions, and lifestyle are aligned.

_____ Buying expensive houses, cars, jewelry, vacations, etc., all have the same meaning and purpose—they allow us to enjoy the money we have.

_____ Economic downturns, such as the one that began in 2008, put pressure on truly wealthy people to reduce conspicuous consumption, but when times get better we can go back to spending.

_____ The high–net worth environment does not affect my buying or spending habits.

Family Glue

_____ Each member of my family can articulate the values that we share.

_____ My children feel empowered to express their beliefs and feelings to the rest of the family.

_____ My children and I feel comfortable that our ideas and feelings will be heard and accepted by each other.

_____ Our family is familiar with our history and traditions and has integrated those traditions with new rituals that we have created in this generation.

_____ Individually and as a family unit we value continuing education and learning, and we support each others' efforts to learn and grow.

_____ As a family we make time to participate in group activities that maintain and deepen our bonds.

_____ For the most part, family members have healthy boundaries and respect for each other's privacy and individual choices and beliefs.

_____ There is a wealth of trust between family members: no matter how tense a family relationship may become at any point, we know we have each other's best interests at heart and will be there for each other.

Appendix 6

Unintended Consequences

■ The lifestyle you choose to live will create certain expectations in your children as to what lifestyle they will maintain. Communication with your children about this, even when they are mature enough, may be uncomfortable or unpalatable, but it is one of the best gifts you can give them, regardless of how much or how little they may ultimately inherit.

■ One family office director was concerned for one client's children. The family always flew on their private jet. At the parents' current spend rate, it was clear there wasn't going to be any money left for the kids to maintain that lifestyle, and they would be ill-equipped to deal with the emotional baggage and basic skills when they eventually have to fly commercially. Growing up with a wealthy lifestyle can leave offspring clueless about how to handle a different lifestyle.

■ There is a tradeoff between writing too specific a trust that allows the trustee to control the beneficiaries and make them feel impotent and writing a trust that permits so much discretion that potentially irresponsible beneficiaries could use trust assets to support risky behavior, such as gambling or alcohol or drug abuse.

■ If a trustee were to look at your family's assets as one big allocation and then locate the assets, this may not be considered

.responsible from a fiduciary perspective. Depending on who the beneficiaries are, the laws surrounding the trust, the state in which you live, and the lawyer you consult, this asset location approach may not be suitable.

■ Splitting up managers can create extra costs, even if you can invest enough with each manager to meet their minimums. That's because it costs more to follow twenty managers than to follow ten.

■ Giving your kids an allowance to spend money however they want instead of tying it to some financial responsibility, to pay for some needs, not just wants, may backfire in terms of teaching them how a budget works. When children only need to choose between, say, a pair of $500 jeans one month and going to five rock concerts, they are not learning how to make trade-offs between wants and needs. If there is no pain, there will likely be no gain.

■ Simulations are just that. They do not present all aspects of investing, but are designed to teach a few things. Games are no substitute for other techniques we present in this chapter. Before implementing a sim game, recognize what it will teach and what it may incorrectly simulate. After the game, discuss what you have all learned and what may have been realistic and unrealistic. Discuss what likely outcomes may be of making risky investments in life.

■ We have seen some families get their kids involved by just coming to the meetings, without giving them any say in where or how money is donated. Then the parents are surprised when their kids reach their twenties and stop coming to meetings and exhibit no interest in family philanthropy. Allowing them some control is more likely to spark their passion for getting involved in giving.

■ In families with strong leaders, such as CEOs of family businesses, parents may display so much enthusiasm for work that their children may view joining the company as the only "successful thing" Mom or Dad would sanction. In far too many cases, kids who would have been successful at architecture or as teachers feel forced into the family business. Their skills and passion did not connect with the business. Whether or not they become effective leaders, they may feel like failures. It's important to solicit your children's ideas about what excites them, to listen, and to communicate regularly that they are free to pursue work that brings them meaning.

■ A lawyer we encountered at a seminar on trusts talked about a client who had a troubled son who was not motivated and flunked out of college freshman year. The father attempted to soothe his son's bad feelings by buying him a Ferrari. As Dr. Kerry Sulkowicz points out, this Ferrari at best will have a temporary happiness effect. The true cause of this teen's unhappiness will not be solved by this gift. Understanding why he failed college and finding out his true source of unhappiness would be far more productive than receiving an expensive gift.

■ Many wealthy people buy things to allay unhappiness and to avoid the uncomfortable task of talking about and understanding why we or someone we love is unhappy.

■ In 2008 and 2009, when the stock market crashed, even many wealthy people who had focused their lives more on altruism than consumerism found themselves in an unexpected wealth trap. As their portfolios fell by 50 percent or more along with other investors, they could no longer give as generously as they had in the past, creating a tremendous blow to their sense of purpose and happiness. For some this also caused tremendous embarrassment.

■ Personality profiling systems can be a great way to learn the vocabulary to understand different communications styles. However, be careful not to pigeonhole yourself or your children in any one communication style. People do not always stick to any given style or respond the same way to other people's styles.

Appendix 7

Teachable Moments

■ If your kids are old enough, which could mean when they know who they are and what they want to be—probably sometime in their twenties—you might want to include them in this discussion about what money is for.

■ Will saving money in a one-year certificate of deposit (CD) provide the same buying power, after inflation, when it comes due? Try an experiment with your kid. Find something she wants to buy and have her put the money in a one-year CD. See if she can afford it after a year. Is there money left over to reinvest?

■ How did you make your money? Is most of your wealth from your own earnings, investing acumen, entrepreneurial expertise, luck, or inheritance? What stories—with lessons learned along the way—can you impart to your children about your successes and failures along the way? Do you expect your children to make their own way even if eventually they will inherit significant money?

■ The time to bring up the topic of prenuptial agreements is before your child becomes involved in a serious relationship so he or she does not believe you dislike or distrust the romantic partner. It's best to discuss prenups with your children as soon as when they're in their early teens. You might want to wait for the subject of money or wealth or someone's recent marriage or divorce to come up to mention that, in families with some degree of wealth, it's necessary to tell an intended spouse that it's the family's custom to have a prenup.

■   Ask beneficiaries to put in writing their understanding of what the trust money is to be used for. They should list what needs of theirs they think it will and will not fulfill. This way, parents can correct any misconceptions before the trust goes into effect, minimizing potential future conflicts between beneficiaries and trustees.

■   Imparting financial literacy and values to children is not a one-time event, say Sara Hamilton, founder and CEO of Family Office Exchange (FOX), and Joline Godfrey, founder and CEO of Independent Means Inc. (a provider of financial education products and programs) in their 2007 white paper, "Responsibilities of Ownership":

> Distinguished from the conventional "water hose approach" to education, in which a young person, on coming of age, is sent to the trust officer to receive instruction, the drip, drip, drip method utilizes a carefully designed education plan employing family members, nannies, mentors, advisors and family office staff members in the education of children.

This "drip, drip, drip" method includes:

— family talk (in a plane, car or over dinner);
— family traditions (such as retreats, meetings, foundations, gifts, and benefits);
— family mentoring (by aunts, uncles, professionals and friends); and
— education programs (financial camps, tip sheets, newsletters, e-mails, activities, products, nanny training, family coaching).

■   The best way to teach kids to be frugal, is to model frugal behavior. Many wealthy parents may not be willing to rein in their own spending. However, giving children less allowance than their peers receive challenges them to choose doing without some things their friends have or earn money to pay for things they want.

■ We sometimes like to turn on some of the financial talk radio shows while we're on the road with our kids, to hear issues and problems people raise. It's an opportunity to discuss the answers radio experts offer, such as Clark Howard, Ken and Daria Dolan, Bob Brinker, or Dave Ramsey.

■ Many high–net worth communities that we have encountered have hidden cultures. For instance, one hidden culture emphasizes the importance of keeping a smile on your face, because wealthy people just do not have problems! At the very least, they do not talk about them or let anyone know their true feelings.

This message can make our kids believe there is something wrong with them when they do feel unhappy or speak up about their feelings from time to time. Psychologists warn that bottled up feelings will come out in some other, unproductive way that can lead to dysfunction in relationships and exacerbate the initial unhappiness.

It is important to teach your kids that money cannot buy happiness all of the time. Feeling sad, unhappy, and depressed from time to time is part of life, no matter how rich you are.

■ Time is an interesting component of communication. We all have a different tolerance of how much time we can give to difficult or complicated conversations. It may help to simply ask your child, is now a good time to talk? Setting time limits for a conversation can also be helpful.

Consider also whether your family enjoys the formal nature of a meeting or if a conversation works better over breaking bread. Finding out what process works the best for each situation will lead to more successful communication.

Index

About the Authors

Richard A. Morris is principal of Resource for Ownership Intelligence (ROI) Consulting, which helps family business owners grow and pass their business to subsequent generations. He is also an adjunct professor at Lake Forest Graduate School of Management. Previously, he spent many years working for the family business, Fel-Pro Inc. Morris has written articles for print media and is often quoted in the press. He received his MBA from Northwestern University.

Jayne Pearl has been a financial journalist for about thirty years, focusing mostly on family business and financial parenting. In addition to hundreds of articles, she is the author of *Kids and Money: Giving Them the Savvy to Succeed Financially* (Bloomberg Press, 1999) and the co-author of *Keep or Sell Your Business: How to Make the Decision Every Private Company Faces* (Dearborn Trade, 2000). She has appeared in numerous media outlets, including PBS, CNN, the *Christian Science Monitor*, CNBC's Power Lunch, NPR, Reuters, PRI, *Forbes, Money, Parents, Parenting, Working Mother, US News & World Report*, and Bankrate.com. Pearl was a senior editor at *Family Business* magazine and editor of a syndicated daily business public radio show.

About Bloomberg

Bloomberg L.P., founded in 1981, is a global information services, news, and media company. Headquartered in New York, the company has sales and news operations worldwide.

Serving customers on six continents, Bloomberg, through its wholly-owned subsidiary Bloomberg Finance L.P., holds a unique position within the financial services industry by providing an unparalleled range of features in a single package known as the Bloomberg Professional® service. By addressing the demand for investment performance and efficiency through an exceptional combination of information, analytic, electronic trading, and straight-through-processing tools, Bloomberg has built a worldwide customer base of corporations, issuers, financial intermediaries, and institutional investors.

Bloomberg News, founded in 1990, provides stories and columns on business, general news, politics, and sports to leading newspapers and magazines throughout the world. Bloomberg Television, a 24-hour business and financial news network, is produced and distributed globally in seven languages. Bloomberg Radio is an international radio network anchored by flagship station Bloomberg 1130 (WBBR-AM) in New York.

In addition to the Bloomberg Press line of books, Bloomberg publishes *Bloomberg Markets* magazine. To learn more about Bloomberg, call a sales representative at:

London:	+44-20-7330-7500
New York:	+1-212-318-2000
Tokyo:	+81-3-3201-8900